Against Sex

Against Sex

Identities of Sexual Restraint in Early America

Kara M. French

The University of North Carolina Press CHAPEL HILL

*This book was published with the assistance of the
Authors Fund of the University of North Carolina Press.*

The University of North Carolina Press has been a member of the
Green Press Initiative since 2003.

Library of Congress Cataloging-in-Publication Data
Names: French, Kara M., author.
Title: Against sex : identities of sexual restraint in early America /
    Kara M. French.
Other titles: Gender & American culture.
Description: Chapel Hill : The University of North Carolina Press, [2021] |
    Series: Gender and American culture | Includes bibliographical
    references and index.
Identifiers: LCCN 2020051251 | ISBN 9781469662138 (cloth) |
    ISBN 9781469662145 (paperback) | ISBN 9781469662152 (ebook)
Subjects: LCSH: Shakers—United States—History—19th century. |
    Catholic Church—United States—History—19th century. |
    Sex customs—United States—History—19th century. | Sexual ethics—
    United States—History—19th century. | Sexual abstinence—
    Religious aspects. | Grahamites.
Classification: LCC HQ18.U5 F73 2021 | DDC 613.9—dc23
LC record available at https://lccn.loc.gov/2020051251

Cover illustration: Shakers at Lebanon, 1830, courtesy of the American
Antiquarian Society; pale old yellow paper background © iStock.com/Paladin12.

Portions of chapter 1 were previously printed in a different form as "Prejudice
for Profit: Escaped Nun Stories and American Catholic Print Culture," *Journal
of the Early Republic* 39, no. 3 (Fall 2019); it is © 2019 Society for Historians of the
Early American Republic, all rights reserved.

Portions of chapter 4 were previously printed in a different form as "You Can Be
a Catholic If You Want: Protestant Social Capital and Catholic Education in the
Antebellum Era," *U.S. Catholic Historian* 35, no. 3 (Summer 2017); it is © 2017
The Catholic University of America Press.

For my family

Contents

Figures

Acknowledgments

Many years ago, Mary Kelley taught me to always read the acknowledgments first—so here they are printed for your convenience at the front of the book. As a reader, the acknowledgments are a useful way to locate the author's influences and training. As an author myself, now, they represent so much more—a way to thank the many people and institutions that have supported me throughout this process and without whom this project would not have been possible.

The first thanks must of course go to Mary Kelley, who believed in the potential of this research from the very beginning. I am very grateful for the numerous times Mary read drafts, suggested readings, and asked meaningful questions. *Against Sex* would not exist without her support, both personal and professional, over the course of my career. Her philosophy of generous mentorship is one I can only hope to emulate with my own students.

I am also very grateful for education I received at the University of Michigan. The initial seeds of this research were nurtured in seminars taken with Sue Juster, Jay Cook, and Elizabeth Wingrove. The provocative intellectual discussions sparked in those classes remain among my favorite memories of Michigan. I consider myself fortunate to have been blessed with not only the wonderful mentorship provided by the faculty at Michigan but also the camaraderie of my fellow graduate students at Michigan, where I was fortunate to find a group of young scholars passionate about gender and cultural history. Many thanks to Will Mackintosh, Allison Abra, Dan Livesay, Susanna Linsley, Colleen Woods, Marie Stango, Ronit Stahl, Elspeth Martini, Amanda Hendrix-Komoto, Sara Lampert, Emma Amador, Christine Walker, Aston Gonzalez, and Cookie Woolner for many thought-provoking discussions over the years. Your friendship meant so much then, and it means even more now as we continue to grow as professionals.

This project was made possible by generous financial support provided by the University of Michigan and other research institutions. Fellowships from the Winterthur Museum and Library, the American Antiquarian Society, and the New England Regional Fellowship Consortium allowed me to discover rich archival collections. Research support from Rackham Graduate School and the Department of Women's Studies at Michigan also funded archival research at the Library of Congress, the New York State Archives, the Catholic University of America, the Cushwa Center at the University of Notre Dame, De Paul University, and Hancock Shaker Village. I am grateful for the assistance provided by the librarians, archivists, and support staff at these institutions, especially Paul Erickson, Jeanne Solensky, and Rosemary Krill.

Against Sex has benefited from the insight of many throughout the years. I am very thankful to have been able to present my work to scholars at Penn State's Emerging Perspectives on Race and Gender Workshop, the 2014 Rome Seminar sponsored by the Cushwa Center at Notre Dame, and the 2017 NEH Seminar on the International Women's Year. My research has also benefited from audiences and commenters at meetings of the Society for Historians of the Early American Republic, the National Women's Studies Association, the Organization of American Historians, and the Conference on the History of Women Religious. My deepest thanks to my fellow participants in the 2017 Omohundro Institute Scholars' Workshop; your feedback and cheerleading came at a key juncture and helped me make the final push toward publication. I particularly wish to thank Kathleen Cummings, Karin Wulf, Carolyn Eastman, Lucia McMahon, Ann Fabian, Nadine Zimmerli, Thomas Rzeznik, Catherine O'Donnell, Lindsay Keiter, Emily Conroy-Krutz, Kelly Brennan, Jennifer Putzi, Claire McKinney, Leisa Meyer, Cathy Kelley, Martha Jones, and Nick Syrett for offering their support throughout this process. Many thanks to my editor, Mark Simpson-Vos, and the editorial team at the University of North Carolina Press for their continued faith in this work. Thank you also to the anonymous reviewers of UNC Press and the *Journal of the Early Republic* for their time and comments, which helped strengthen the arguments and evidence presented here.

I have been very fortunate for the ways Salisbury University has supported my work as both a teacher and a scholar. The Salisbury University Foundation and the Fulton School of Liberal Arts and its dean, Maarten Pereboom, provided crucial research funding as well as research leave which allowed me to complete the manuscript. Creston Long and Emily Story have been excellent department chairs, and I am thankful for the ways they championed my work as a junior faculty member. I have been lucky to find in Dean Kotlowski a research mentor and colleague who provides warmth, humor, and encouragement. Thank you also to Céline Carayon, Kristen Walton, April Logan, Diane Illig, Joe Venosa, Manav Ratti, Corrine Pubill, and Colleen Clark for making Salisbury feel like home. Artura Jackson, Emily

Depasse, Alec Staley, Molly Dyer, and the rest of my Gender and Sexuality Studies Program students are a continual source of inspiration and delight.

Finally, I would like to take the opportunity to thank my friends and family for always encouraging my pursuit of an academic career. The many members of the Castillo and French families have provided a joyful break from teaching and research during visits to Wisconsin and upstate New York. I am grateful for the ways my parents, Jeff and Carol French, supported my decision to become a historian, and I am fortunate to have a brother, Darrin French, who shares my love of history and performance culture. My grandparents, Bertha and Harold Hallenbeck, unfortunately did not live to see this book in print. Their memories of life in the Great Depression and war years were among the first histories I ever heard and sparked a lifelong fascination with the past. I am grateful in a way I can never repay for the many ways they nurtured and believed in me. Meg Ronsani-Bressette has been a constant source of encouragement since first grade, and I could not ask for a better best friend.

Victoria and Eva, you have made me happier than I could have ever imagined, and I am blessed beyond words to call you my family.

Introduction

On a Monday morning in late August 1810, a group of over 500 armed men surrounded the fledgling Shaker settlement on the banks of Turtle Creek in southwestern Ohio. The Ohioans called themselves "an expedition," a self-anointed mission charged with determining whether reports of the sect enslaving women and abusing children were true. To the Shakers, ardent pacifists, these men "equipped in uniform, and in military order," armed with guns, staves, hatchets, poles, and sticks, were no less than an unruly mob. "Old gray-headed men, boys, and others, who exhibited a very mean & moblike appearance" and "women, of the baser sort, who were in fellowship with the riot" had turned out that day in hopes of witnessing "the destruction of the Shakers."[1]

Foremost among the expedition's demands were the requests of three grandfathers that their grandchildren who had been placed within the community by one or more Shaker parents be returned to their custody. They also issued an ultimatum: the Shakers must completely stop their preaching, their religious practice, and their entire way of life "or depart out of the country by the first Monday in December next." The Shakers boldly refused the militia leaders on all counts. In the case of the children, they permitted family members to visit them at the Shaker settlement as they had always done, but deferred the question of their custody to the civil courts. Frustrated with the Shakers' noncompliance, Reverend Wallace asked the pacifist leaders if they were prepared to "withstand a thousand men," to which the Shakers offered no reply. Dissatisfied, the militia pressed that another committee be allowed to visit the Shaker settlement and question the women and children who lived there, to discover whether any were being abused or held against their will. The Shakers agreed on "conditions of [the militia men] behaving civilly." After the interviews failed to produce a single abused woman or child, the committee departed "well satisfied" and the mob dispersed, the would-be massacre averted.[2]

Two months prior to the Turtle Creek riot, Colonel James Smith, a Continental army veteran and leading citizen, published an incendiary pamphlet attacking and discrediting the Shakers. Smith and his allies threatened the sect would "extirpate Christianity, destroy marriage and also our present

1

free government, and finally depopulate America." Also, that they had "trea-sonous dealings" with Tecumseh and the Shawnee and had plotted with them to attack white settlements. Some accused the Shakers of being Brit-ish spies or secret Catholics. The most scandalous charge of all was that the Shakers' devotion to celibacy was a mere ruse and that secretly the sect's men and women fornicated with each other. Testifying from his own short-lived experience as a Shaker convert, James Smith related that Shaker men were promised "if they bore the cross and abstained from women for some time, they would become so holy that it would be no sin for them to have carnal knowledge of their own holy women." Responding to the unasked question of where all the offspring of the Shaker elders and their women might be, Smith concluded that the sect must be committing infanticide: "If they beget children, they put them out of the way, or by some means prevent propagation; because this would be an injury to their money-making plan." The colonel assured his readers that despite their humble appear-ances "the leading Shakers live in luxury in wine and women as far as their plan of secrecy will admit of."[3] The Shakers' celibacy had destroyed Smith's family, and he desired their destruction in return.

Nearly a quarter of a century later during the sweltering summer of 1834, a gang of working-class men—brickmakers, sailors, apprentices, and firemen—surrounded the Ursuline convent in Charlestown, Massachusetts. The crowd, acting on rumor that Mary St. John Harrison, a prospective nun, was being "secreted or abducted" to Canada against her will, threatened to burn the convent to the ground unless she was released. When Harrison did not come forward, they set fire to the convent and school with "twelve Nuns and *fifty-seven female* scholars inside."[4] Newspapers from Maine to Maryland reported on how the rioters stole the Mount Benedict ciborium, smashed the sisters' expensive musical instruments, and converted the per-sonal library of Boston's Bishop Fenwick into fuel for a bonfire. As a final act of desecration, the mob "burst open the tomb, and ransacked the coffins" of dead nuns, searching for the bodies of Sister Harrison and the Ursulines' young Protestant pupils, rumored to have been murdered behind convent walls.[5]

Analogous to Colonel James Smith's pamphleteering that provoked a mob attack against the Ohio Shakers, tales of illicit sex and abused women rose from the ashes of the Charlestown riot. Just as the Charlestown rioters were being brought to trial in 1835, ex-novice Rebecca Reed's autobiography, *Six Months in a Convent*, detailed a life of horrors. According to Reed, the sisters of Mount Benedict heaped slavish devotion on their Mother Superior and were subjected to bizarre and cruel penances. The convent was a place of unmentionable sexual deviance, where confession with the bishop led to "various improper questions" regarding the novices' sexuality and where Superior Mary St. George Moffat was inclined to "caress" the sisters who were her "great favorites."[6]

Reed's pamphlet may have persuaded Bostonians that it was no crime to set fire to a corrupt institution like a convent. The gang of convent rioters offered no alibi at their trial. Only one man was ever convicted, and even he was released within a year. The Ursulines never received restitution for their damaged property, nor were they ever able to rebuild the grand edifice that once stood high upon Mt. Benedict. In the 1870s, one could visit the ruins of the convent and view the burn marks still visible on the crumbling stone walls.[7]

Three years later, the city of Boston would witness another riot when Dr. Sylvester Graham attempted to deliver his "Lecture to Mothers" on sexual restraint. A crowd of 200 to 300 gathered at Boston's Amory Hall and plastered the area with "inflammatory placards" to prevent Graham discussing "the Science of Human Life" with an all-female audience — "no spinsters or male monsters (except Mr. Graham) were admitted." When the ladies in attendance attempted to speak in Graham's defense, they were shouted down by male rioters imitating the noises of animals: "barking, mewings, howlings, yellings, crowing, hissings and groaning." As the situation escalated out of control, the city marshal forced Graham to cancel his lecture for the day, acting on orders from the mayor himself.[8]

The "anti-Graham riot" in 1837 was actually the second occasion Dr. Graham's "Lecture to Mothers" was shut down by an angry mob — the first was in Portland, Maine, in 1834. Newspapers reported that Graham's "lecture, his language, and his conduct in its delivery, was of a nature too immodestly indelicate for the ear or eye of modest woman." The "Lecture to Mothers" was so controversial that not a single extant copy of it survives. Historians believe it encouraged women to control and prevent "the solitary vice" not only in their sons but also in themselves and to practice greater sexual restraint within marriage. In preaching chastity and crusading against masturbation, Graham ironically acknowledged female desire. His lecture gave greater weight to a wife's desire to determine sexual relations within marriage and created a space for middle-class women to have sexual agency in their families and in society at large.[9]

There were certainly other factors that helped turn neighbor against neighbor in these three circumstances, whether that was the Shakers' unusual communal property arrangements or "treasonous dealings" with Native Americans, or working-class resentment against a wealthy convent or a perceived elite like Sylvester Graham.[10] Antipathy toward extremes of sexual abstinence, however, emerges as a provocative theme in these events, one that might be harder to discern when they are studied in isolation. It cannot be denied that in the 1810s and 1830s, discussions of celibacy and sexual self-control seemingly provoked "sex panics" about people who were *not* having sex. These riots represent neither the beginning nor the end of debates on sexual restraint. They are best understood as flash points in a larger story. This book investigates sexual restraint to better understand the sexual dimensions of American identity between the American Revolution and the Civil War. *Against Sex: Identities of Sexual Restraint in Early America* highlights three prominent groups who were advocates of sexual restraint in early nineteenth-century America: Shakers, Catholic priests and nuns, and followers of sexual reformer Sylvester Graham. In the decades between the American Revolution and the Civil War, mobs attacked Shaker villages, burned Catholic convents, and rioted against Graham's lectures. Advocates for celibacy and chastity also faced hostility in the form of armed violence, prejudicial lawsuits and legislation, and print attacks from editors and pamphleteers. For some Americans, extreme sexual abstinence was nearly, if not as, disturbing as sexual excess. The question is why. By promoting sexual restraint, Shakers, priests and nuns, and reformers denaturalized the assumed naturalness of sex within marriage. They also challenged marriage's exalted and central place in the cultural imagination of Americans. By refusing to adhere to normative definitions of marriage, advocates for sexual restraint openly challenged the white male privilege enshrined within the legal principle of coverture. Coverture gave a husband not only dominion over his wife's property and labor but also control over her sexual being.

Who were these sex-critical dissidents? To students of nineteenth-century America, Shaker brothers and sisters are perhaps the most obvious to come to mind. The Shakers, or United Society of Believers in Christ's Second Appearing, had been founded by Ann Lee in 1774. Lee, a blacksmith's wife from Manchester, England, was the anointed leader, or "Mother," of the "Shaking Quakers," a sect known for their prophecy, ecstatic worship, and celibacy. Though Lee herself had once been married and had borne four children who died in infancy, over the course of her life she became convinced that sexual intercourse was "the root and foundation cause of all human depravity."[11] The local Manchester authorities found both the medium and the message of the Shakers disruptive. To maintain public order, they imprisoned Ann Lee in a madhouse. A year after her release, Lee received a revelation that the Shakers' doctrine would flourish across the sea when planted in American soil.

Ann Lee and the founding Shakers arrived in New York City to find the colonies on the brink of revolution. For two years, the band toiled in the city as servants and laborers in near poverty before journeying upriver to found a community of their own. The first Shaker settlement at Watervliet, seven miles outside of Albany, was "an obscure place in the wilderness, remote from the public eye."[12] For four years, Lee and her band practiced their controversial religious doctrines in peace and relative obscurity. In late 1779, a spiritual revival occurred in the nearby town of New Lebanon, New York. Finding in the revival a type of ecstatic spirituality kindred to their own, Lee and her followers took the opportunity to preach their sacred tenets of pacifism, communitarianism, and celibacy to the revivalists. The Shakers won many converts at this revival, but Mother Ann's preaching carried risks as well as rewards. Shaker remembrances of these early days state that "to such as loved the things of this present world, the testimony and the work accompanying it appeared like the greatest possible inconsistency and delusion."[13] Once again, Ann Lee found herself at odds with the local authorities, suspected of witchcraft, devil-worship, and worst of all, treason. In July of 1780, after only a year of public preaching, Lee and nine of her followers, representing the entirety of the Shakers' joint Anglo-American leadership, were arrested and tried before the revolutionary government at Albany. They were found guilty and imprisoned as "enemies to the country." Lee herself was singled out for special treatment and separated from the other prisoners. Convinced she was a British spy, the American Revolutionaries transported her south to Poughkeepsie, where they intended to hand her over to the British army.[14]

The charge of treason was, according to the Shakers, the product of "designing men." The Shakers themselves believed that "the real ground of enmity was in the cross," or celibacy, "a stumbling stone and rock of offense to a licentious world."[15] Yet, even the imprisonment of Ann Lee and the rest of the Shaker leadership was not enough to extinguish the zeal of the Shakers' newly won converts. Lee's New York followers successfully petitioned Governor George Clinton for her release in December of 1780, after she had spent half a year in prison.[16] Much to the dismay of her enemies, Lee's imprisonment won her more followers, not fewer. "Great numbers" of people, from not just New York but Massachusetts and Connecticut, too, flocked to

Lee's new gospel, eager to hear the preaching of a woman who had been willing to risk imprisonment rather than recant her beliefs.[17]

The Shakers became targets of religious persecution and pamphleteering in New York and New England in the 1780s and 1790s. During her missionary tour of Massachusetts, Mother Ann herself was physically attacked by a mob. There was a significant outbreak of anti-Shaker sentiment during this time period, partly in response to the very newness of the religious movement as well as the advocacy of a few key apostates. The Shaker revival of the eighteenth century was part of a larger pluralistic backlash against the Congregationalist establishment in the years following the First Great Awakening. Like the Shakers, many of these smaller sects challenged the centrality of marriage, though their tenure was much more short-lived.[18] After the initial controversy died down, the Shakers and their neighbors in New England eventually settled into a grudging tolerance as their communities grew and prospered.[19]

Despite this early rough beginning, the Shakers increased in numbers throughout the Northeast and became prosperous enough to send a mission to Ohio in 1805 following the Cane Ridge Revival. The ecstatic Christianity expressed at the revival, especially the outpouring of "gifts of the spirit" — speaking in tongues, shaking, and intense emotion — made the region seem an attractive site for a Shaker mission.[20] Even Colonel Smith's 1810 mob attack failed to deter the Shakers in their westward progress. The Shakers founded no less than seven distinct settlements in Ohio, Kentucky, and Indiana in the early 1800s. By 1830, the Shakers comprised nineteen different communities, stretching from Sabbathday Lake, Maine, to South Union, Kentucky, and numbered approximately 4,000 members. Though that number may seem small in comparison with major world religions, it is unprecedented when compared with other communitarian American religious groups, most of which never exceeded more than a few hundred members in a single location. If longevity alone is the defining criteria for success, the Shakers can be considered the "most successful" communitarian society in American history.[21]

The first half of the nineteenth century also witnessed a dramatic rise in the number of Catholic institutions in the United States — and with them Catholic men and women religious. At the time of the penning of the Declaration of Independence, not a single religious order for women existed within the boundaries of the original thirteen colonies. By 1850, there were 1,300 sisters spread across nineteen distinct orders.[22] Priests, nuns, and sisters gradually became part of the religious fabric of the early American republic.

While all three swore vows of chastity, it is important to note they all had different roles. Nuns, like the Ursuline sisters of Charlestown, took solemn vows and lived in a cloister, while sisters took simple vows and missioned to the poor and needy outside their enclosure. Together, nuns and sisters can be thought of as "women religious," while priests and monks are termed "male religious." This era saw the founding of the first seminaries, monasteries, and convents in the United States, as well as religious orders for women founded for Americans by Americans, such as Elizabeth Seton's Sisters of Charity.[23] American Catholics also built a lasting infrastructure that included voluntary and tract societies, newspapers, and orphanages and hospitals. They transformed the nation's educational landscape, constructing free schools for the poor and elite academies for the wealthy, open to Protestant and Catholic alike. Convent boarding schools for girls gained a reputation for elite, exclusive, and rigorous female education in the early nineteenth century. The most prominent were the Ursuline-run schools in Charlestown (1827) and New Orleans (1727), the Convent of the Visitation in Georgetown (1799), St. Joseph's Academy in Emmitsburg, Maryland (1809), and the Convent of the Sacred Heart in Manhattan (1848). The presence of these celibate individuals and the very real brick-and-mortar transformation they wrought on the republic provoked nothing short of a cultural crisis among middle-class Protestants.

Secular health reformer Sylvester Graham and his followers are also key to understanding identities of sexual restraint in this time period. While Graham and other health reformers never advocated total celibacy, they did argue for the limitation of sexual intercourse within marriage as well as complete sexual abstinence for the unmarried. A former temperance lecturer, Graham rose to fame in the 1830s by crusading against "the solitary vice" of masturbation. Though Sylvester Graham's lectures on sexual restraint received their fair share of bad press in Portland, Boston, Providence, and New York, the Grahamites were unique in the ways in which they utilized print to organize themselves against their opponents. By harnessing the press to publish two separate pro-Graham journals, the proceedings of their meetings, and a variety of books on the Graham philosophy, Grahamites created an apparatus to implement and sustain the physiological reforms preached by Sylvester Graham.

Less than a month after the infamous riots at Amory Hall that prevented Graham's *Lecture to Mothers* from being heard by the ladies of Boston, devoted Grahamite David Cambell turned out the first issue of the *Graham Journal of Health and Longevity* on April 4, 1837. The *Graham Journal* served the Grahamite community of reformers along with fellow publication the *Library of Health*, edited by Dr. William Andrus Alcott. Cambell and Alcott were charter members of the American Physiological Society (APS), founded in Boston in February 1837. Graham's lectures so inspired these Bostonians, they banded together to form an association to promote "physiology, or the science of life, in its most extended sense." Rather than confined to a handful of educated medical professionals, the APS believed knowledge of the human body should "be accessible, in a community like our own, to every citizen." One hundred and sixty-three members joined the initial APS, and men outnumbered women three to one.[24]

The APS and its associated publications upheld Grahamite stances on sexuality and warred against "the solitary vice" of masturbation. To that end, Grahamites promoted the Graham diet as a means to conquer the lusts of the flesh and encourage all-around good health. Graham argued that rich foods—meats, coffee, tea, alcohol, spices, and confections—inflamed the passions and diverted the body's vital energies away from staying healthy. By adapting what was essentially a strict vegetarian and low-carbohydrate diet (vegan but for the allowance of milk) Grahamites believed sexual restraint would become effortless and natural, and various diseases from indigestion to tuberculosis could be prevented. Grahamite reformers faced harsh criticism for their sexual and dietetic ideologies in an era where sexual rights within marriage as well as meat and bread were considered to be a married man's prerogative, regardless of social class. Because of constraints around censorship, Grahamites and their opponents were often prohibited from discussing Graham's more explicit pronouncements regarding sex and masturbation in public. Instead, criticisms of the Graham diet often stood in proxy for criticism of the Grahamites' sexual restraint.[25]

It is important to acknowledge that Roman Catholic, Shaker, and Grahamite practices regarding sexual abstinence have entirely different origins. The celibacy of Catholic priests and nuns became codified during the early Middle Ages. Prior to the Reformation, celibacy was set above marriage in order of saintliness.[26] Shaker sexual regulations developed out of eighteenth-century radical Quakerism as well as Mother Ann Lee's personal revelation that sexual intercourse was the root of all human suffering. Shakers and Catholic celibates did not find common ground on the basis of their sexual practices while they lived on earth—the Shakers certainly rejected Catholicism as decadent, echoing the critiques of the Reformation. In the later nineteenth century, they were not above engaging in Nativist fearmongering, arguing that as "scientific and intellectual celibates" they alone could "checkmate the dangerous growing power of the Catholic hierarchy."[27] Both groups rooted their celibacy in emulation of early Christian communities that had been leery of sex, marriage, and procreation since the time of Paul. The abolition of monasteries and convents during the Reformation had made celibacy a suspect and tainted practice in the eyes of Protestants. Yet, both groups simultaneously rose to prominence in America in the early nineteenth century in an unprecedented way. Despite their disparate origins, as religious communities that abstained from sex, Shakers and Catholics were frequently conflated by American Protestant writers and readers.[28] One travelogue, for example, proclaimed Mount Lebanon a "rural Vatican," and the Shaker elders "more despotic" than the pope.[29]

Though on the surface the Grahamites might seem miles apart from new religious movements such as the Shakers, Grahamism's intertwined dietetic and sexual principles speak to the way Grahamism functioned in a way that was very similar to a religion. Anthropologist Clifford Geertz has defined religion as "a system of symbols which acts to . . . establish powerful, pervasive, and long-lasting moods and motivations in men," giving order to human existence.[30] People may feel "religious" about aspects of culture that do not explicitly proclaim themselves so long as the believer saw the activity as embodying certain "transcendent truths" (i.e., it is possible to be "religious" about basketball if one gets a transcendent experience from playing). Grahamites certainly understood their larger system as a way of consciously choosing virtue over vice and health over disease. Opponents of Graham attacked him as a weak celibate monster and derided male Grahamites' masculinity, similar to the language used to attack Shaker brothers and Catholic priests.[31] Though most Grahamites were middle-class Protestants themselves, they faced virulent persecution for daring to challenge male sexual prerogatives within marriage. The fact that Graham's call for chastity and sexual control was rooted in the medical science of the day rather than religion complicates traditional understandings of sexual restraint as mainly a spiritual practice.[32]

It can also be useful to think about religion not in highly formalized terms but in the more expansive definition provided by French sociologist Émile Durkheim, a system of "things set apart and forbidden."[33] Sex, in various expressions, was set apart and at times forbidden by Shakers, Catholic men and women religious, and Grahamite sexual reformers. It was but one aspect of a larger system of belief, its sacredness reinforced by other practices. As many scholars of religion have observed, practices, objects, and ideals are not inherently sacred but are made so by believers.[34] The sexual practices of the groups studied here should be thought of as an aspect of "lived religion," moderated by interactions between individual believers and society at large.[35] Sexual abstinence was a devotional belief, a daily choice made with conscious intention, comparable to other religious practices like saying the rosary or keeping kosher in the home. As with any aspect of lived religion, these three groups used sexual restraint to try to shape their cultural worlds, while at the same time being shaped themselves by American society at large. Their sexual practices were sometimes in concert with larger societal forces, but more often in tension with American middle-class sexual values that privileged sex within marriage above all else.

Studying these celibate practices in comparison provides an opportunity to reconsider how historically Christianity has always been queer, and its celibate practices perhaps "the queerest thing of all."[36] Theologians and LGBTQ activists alike have debated celibacy's relationship to queerness. In a modern context, it can be problematic to identify celibacy as queer, given that some celibates both inside and outside of religious orders do not choose that term for themselves and can be seen as being "involuntarily queered."[37] This is further complicated by the fact that celibacy is the only sexuality officially permitted same-sex-oriented members in some conservative churches.[38] There is also a fear that by understanding celibacy as queer, the term "queer" itself may become watered down, further diluted of its radical origins.[39] While these concerns speak to the uneasy place of celibacy and abstinence vis-à-vis modern LGBTQ politics, "queer" can also be a useful term for understanding the challenges these practices placed in their historical context, before the emergence of modern sexual identities. Some theologians see in celibacy's origins a forgotten radical critique of heteronormativity. The presence of vowed celibates in the historical record has long presented alternative gender norms in the embodiment of men in long cassock-like dresses and nuns gifted with male names at their profession. Celibate communities found in monasteries, convents, and Shaker villages transcended both married life and singleness, the people neither partnered nor alone.[40]

Given their unique social arrangements and unusual sexual practices, it is unsurprising that these groups have long captivated the interest of historians. Scholarship on the Shakers flourished in the 1970s and 1980s alongside efforts to preserve their art and handicrafts and a broad general interest in utopian communities. In the wake of second-wave feminism, feminist scholars saw in Shaker communities greater opportunities for women as a product of their celibate mandate.[41] The notorious Maria Monk and her fellow escaped nuns have been of perennial interest since Ray Allen Billington first published his history of anti-Catholicism in the 1930s.[42] The followers of Sylvester Graham have also been examined by those curious about the intersection of health, reform, and sexuality during the Second Great Awakening.[43] Though these groups have intrigued historians for decades, new insights from the fields of queer theory and the history of sexuality make them ripe for reconsideration. Far from settled scholarship, analysis of these organizations and practices can yield new understandings when seen through an intersectional feminist lens, as demonstrated in April Haynes's recent reevaluation of black and white female moral reformers in the early republic.[44] But, as this study shows, moral reformers were not alone in using sexual abstinence as a way to challenge gender roles, and their private and public challenges to patriarchal sexual norms were shared by other men and women of the nineteenth century.

Looking at these different groups together—secular and religious, mainline denominations and outsider sects—based on their sexual beliefs and behavior is an innovative approach. Religious historiography on the Shakers has tended to study them in tandem with other emerging religious movements of the nineteenth century, notably Mormons and Oneida Perfectionists.[45] While such comparative work is valuable for understanding how these groups offered up both sexual and doctrinal challenges to mainstream Christian theology, it must also be acknowledged that celibacy, polygamy, and complex marriage are hardly alike in practice. Shakers, Catholic religious, and Grahamites, on the contrary, shared a belief that the disciplining of the body through sexual restraint could have crucial spiritual, physical, and moral consequences. Graham's health reform was tinged with an evangelical fervor, and it's important to note that Sylvester Graham trained as a minister, not a medical doctor.[46] Through their sexual abstinence, all three groups attempted to control the uncontrollable, whether that was the soul's fate in the afterlife or the health of the body in an era where the causes of disease still remained mysterious.[47] At this time in history, both advocates and critics of sexual restraint saw physical health as intertwined with sexual and spiritual virtue.

I call these behaviors "sexual restraint," which ranged from complete sexual abstinence (for Shakers) to celibacy for select groups (Catholic priests and nuns) to groups that wanted to limit the frequency of sex within marriage (Grahamites and other sexual reformers). I believe the term "sexual restraint" best encompasses this spectrum of thinking on sexual abstinence, acknowledging the similarity of these practices while also recognizing their differences. In understanding sexual restraint as an early American sexual identity and behavior, it is important to understand the difference between celibacy, chastity, and virginity. A person's religious commitment to celibacy as a Shaker or Catholic priest or nun differed from Grahamian ideals of chastity before and within marriage. It is also true that declaring oneself a Grahamite or vowed member of a religious order was different from simply being a confirmed bachelor or an unwed spinster. Proclaiming oneself a celibate person was more of a disclosure and revealed information about one's sexuality than simply being unmarried—it required a kind of "coming out."[48] Being a celibate Shaker and asserting that all those who engaged in even virtuous, married sex were damned for eternity was an organized attack on sexual values in a way that simply being unmarried was not. It was similar for male and female religious, whose specific sexual commitments gave them a culturally sanctioned religious function lay Catholics did not have.

Celibacy also was different from chastity in this historical moment. Unlike celibacy, which was attacked as unnatural and unhealthy, post-Revolutionary Americans idealized chastity, especially in women. In the post-Revolutionary era, a woman's virtue became synonymous with her chastity. Novels such as *Clarissa* and *Charlotte Temple* were tragedies precisely because when their heroines lost their chastity, they were made unfit for marriage and a place in the social order.[49] Unlike the celibacy of Shaker sisters and Catholic nuns, a young girl's virginity was seen as a temporary condition—more specifically, it was the prelude to a happy marriage. A woman's chastity was guarded by her father until it could be transferred over to the authority of her husband. In this understanding, virginity is property and something that, once lost, can never be regained. Such popular ideas were in direct contrast to Shaker communities and Catholic holy orders, which allowed the sexually experienced to regain a virginal state by taking on a new celibate identity. Grahamian medicine, too, allowed for the possibility for one who had become unwell due to sexual excess to reform and regain health. And yet hallmarks of the sexual vernacular, like *Aristotle's Masterpiece*, a popular sex manual of the day, argued that virginity also had a shelf life, comparing a "stale" virgin to "an old Almanack out of Date."[50]

To be clear, these were not the only communities in early America to include sexual abstinence as part of their credo. Several utopian communities of the nineteenth century flirted with celibacy for some or all members at least for a time, including the Harmonist and Zoar communitarian groups. Some, like the Amana communities of Iowa and the Moravians of the eighteenth century, highly regulated the sexuality of married couples and had separate cloisters for unmarried men and women.[51] Even non-utopian religions like the Methodists at times had members who advocated celibacy. Young Methodist circuit riders came under suspicion in the early republic for scorning marriage and were compared unfavorably to Catholic priests.[52] Of these other communities, those that practiced celibacy exclusively for all members were often confined to a single community or region, as with the Ephrata cloister in Pennsylvania.[53] For Methodists, celibacy was never institutionalized or formalized as it was for Catholic priests, applied only to male itinerants, and had been officially abandoned in favor of required marriage by the 1810s.[54] By contrast, Shakerism, Catholicism, and Grahamism held abstinence as a sacred principle that applied to both men and women. The three groups that are featured in this book were prominent, successful, and able to maintain a network beyond a particular community or region. They also successfully navigated and manipulated the emerging market economy, culture, and tourism industries in a deliberate and self-conscious way that other communities, though practicing some degree of sexual abstinence, did not.

Abstaining from sex was a political act that carried very real social, economic, and legal repercussions for both individuals and communities. Practicing sexual restraint in the 1800s sometimes came with harsh consequences, from horrific mob violence to legislation that sought to confiscate Shaker property or require the inspection of Catholic convents by male Protestants.[55] During the 1840s and 1850s, lurid "escaped nun" stories served as cultural propaganda for the Know-Nothing movement that had risen up in response to increased immigration from Catholic Ireland. Sexual restraint inspired political action at the local and translocal levels in the nineteenth century, from practitioners and opponents alike. This study shows yet again how the most personal and intimate of decisions (whether or not to have sex, with whom, and how often) can come with a political cost.

It is no coincidence that Shakers, Catholic priests and nuns, and Grahamite reformers became targets of violence and prejudice at the same historical moment that the American middle class came into being. Much has been written of the religious, economic, social, political, and cultural dimensions of the "new" middle-class identity that arose in America between 1820 and 1850. The market revolution dramatically transformed American society during this time period, resulting in the creation of a social order culturally and economically distinct from that which had preceded it.[56] Unlike the "middling classes" of the eighteenth century, the nineteenth-century middle class no longer represented "a point of equilibrium between two other fixed classes; to be middle class was to be, in theory, without fixed social status."[57] Because the social status of the middle class was so amorphous and undefined, it became all the more important to try to project one's class identity through outward displays of dress, sentimentality, and ritual.

Middle-class identity also has had a sexual dimension, in which sex within marriage was the ideal. Historians have illuminated how adultery, seduction, prostitution, polygamy, and free love challenged middle-class norms.[58] Lifelong sexual abstinence as a Shaker or a nun was also completely in opposition to the married sexual ideal as much as any of these more obvious examples of deviant sexuality. The presence of celibate sexual outsiders such as Shakers and Catholics disrupted middle-class sexual identity, family structure, and the gender hierarchy. And though he did not advocate complete celibacy, the outrage against Sylvester Graham is very revealing. As a middle-class Protestant reformer, Graham was himself an "insider." Graham's sexual ideology could not be dismissed as either Catholic superstition or sectarian enthusiasm, which made him all the more threatening to those who wanted to maintain the sexual privileges that came with middle-class marriage. "Marriage" is both a relationship between two individual people and an enduring social phenomenon in Western Christianity, invested with a certain moral authority. As historian Paul Johnson has written, "If a man stops fighting his wife and starts fighting his marriage, and if that event is repeated in society until 'marriage' itself is called into question, that is a religious problem."[59] Practicing sexual restraint represented yet another way to "fight" marriage and undermine cherished middle-class sexual ideals. Sexual reformers like Graham crossed a line when they advocated sexual restraint for married couples. Graham drew the ire of libertine republican newspaper editors and sporting men when he attacked a pillar of white masculine privilege under coverture: a husband's unrestricted access to his wife's body.[60] Middle-class men had in the course of roughly two generations yielded the sexual liberties their grandfathers had once enjoyed. Graham's attacks hit especially close to home for men of this class, because he asked them to forsake the limited sexual pleasures that still remained.

It may on the surface seem oxymoronic that the celibacy of Shakers, Catholic priests, and nuns and the sexual restraint of the Grahamites incited such violent and visceral reactions. The sexual restraint of otherwise normative middle-class subjects has been well documented by scholars, almost to the point where the early republic and antebellum eras could be characterized as an epoch of sexual restraint. Positioned between a bawdy eighteenth century and movements for sexual liberation in the twentieth century, the nineteenth century has been defined by its prudery, repression, and attempts to quash all forms of perceived sexual deviance—notably homosexuality, masturbation, pornography, prostitution, and polygamy. The first "sexual revolution" has been characterized as a reactionary one, as Americans became less sexually tolerant of premarital sex and state governments in places like Massachusetts disproportionately punished the sexual transgressions of black and indigenous women.[61] The transatlantic pleasure culture that flourished in cities like Philadelphia in the eighteenth century did not outlive the War of Independence.[62] Throughout the mid-nineteenth century, organized reform movements targeted deviant sexual practices—Female Moral Reform societies attempted to reform so-called fallen women and penalize male seducers, abolitionists attacked white slaveowners' sexual abuse of enslaved women, and anti-Mormon mobs decried the abuses of plural marriage.[63]

Shouldn't the American middle class have embraced those practicing celibacy and abstinence as part of their larger culture of restraint? By refusing to engage in sexual activities, those who were against sex became sexual minorities and sexual deviants in eighteenth- and nineteenth-century America. Targeting celibacy was a key component of this homogenizing push toward what would later be called heteronormativity.[64] In the years between 1780 and 1860, sexual attitudes shifted away from a toleration of various sexual behaviors toward a worldview in which only sex within marriage was posited as natural and normal.

While they may not have been prostitutes, adulterers, or sodomites, celibate Shakers and Catholics were completely nonnormative by the sexual standards of early America. Their chosen restraint must be distinguished from a larger middle-class culture that sought to force sexual restraint onto others while upholding sex within marriage as the sole ideal. The deviance of celibacy has sometimes been difficult for scholars to discern. Partly, it is due to the endurance of one of the greatest myths about human sexual behavior, what Gayle Rubin described as "sexual essentialism—the idea that sex is a natural force that exists prior to social life." In her revolutionary essay "Thinking Sex," Rubin explained that academic and popular thought on sex retains a tendency to "fall back on the notion of a natural libido subjected to inhumane repression."[65] The historical examples of Shakers, Catholic men and women religious, and Grahamites show that sexual inactivity also has historically carried cultural, political, and legal repercussions.

Examining the celibacy of American Shakers and Catholic priests and nuns can further contribute to discussions on the nature of sexual acts and sexual identities in early America. Proceeding from Foucault, prevailing thought among many in the discipline has held that "sexuality" and "sexual orientation" are "a modern invention" and should not be mapped onto the homosexual (or heterosexual) behaviors of early Americans. This argument advocates that prior to the sexological research of the 1880s, individuals did not see themselves as possessing sexual identities, only engaging in sexual acts or behaviors. Americans did not understand erotic desires as falling into a discrete rubric that we would call "sexuality," but were rather "expressions of social and moral standing," integrated into other aspects of their lives. And indeed, in colonial America there is strong evidence indicating that "women or men who were punished for unnatural sexual acts did not acquire a lifetime identity as 'homosexuals,' and they could be reintegrated into the fold." Such acts may have been labeled either acceptable and normal (sex within marriage for procreation) or deviant and sinful (masturbation, sodomy). But as long as sexual sinners committed penance for their crimes, they did not seem to acquire a lifetime stigma regarding their sexual natures.[66]

Scholars interested in the history of same-sex relationships or queer identities have been engaging a "dynamic contestation" with Foucault in the decades since his famous pronouncement.[67] Some have wished to complicate what might be too easy a dichotomy between early modern sexual acts and modern sexual identities, arguing that Foucault's understanding of sexual identities should be at least "revised" if not "reversed."[68] In scholarship on the early republic, this has taken the form of examining same-sex affairs between evangelical men and in detailing a "marriage" between two nineteenth-century New England women.[69] Thomas Foster in his introduction to the recent anthology *Long before Stonewall* writes that although "the terms *homosexual* and *heterosexual* are indeed modern . . . the *acts-versus-identities* pronouncement is an oversimplification made from the vantage point of modernity."[70] This duality favors psychological and legal understandings of sexuality over cultural representations and lived experience. There is evidence that those who were "the other," sexually and religiously, knew it and accepted it as a part of themselves, even if it bore no resemblance to the modern-heterosexual/homosexual binary.[71] *Against Sex* argues that histories of celibacy and sexual abstinence can further complicate understandings of sexual identity, especially sexual identities that exist outside of the dyad of opposite versus same-sex attraction.

Examining sexual abstinence also paradoxically provides an opportunity to expand understanding of the nature of desire. Desire should be understood to transcend sexual acts, encompassing the meanings, emotions, and relationships surrounding sex, even those sexual impulses that are not acted upon.[72] Sexual abstinence, the restraining of sexual desire, may very well fall into a category described as "twilight moments," or those "sexual acts and relationships that take place without ever being acknowledged or named."[73] Celibacy itself is often thought, especially by its critics, as the absence of all desire, a bloodless and empty void. It would be better to ask, what desires can celibacy provoke? What passions flourish in abstinence?[74] The subjects of *Against Sex* were not undesiring. By sacrificing sexual expression, they hoped to allow other desires to grow in its place—a deeper communion with God, a sacred community of believers, greater health and longevity, or even a broader connection with humanity, unencumbered by marital ties.

Against Sex examines Shakers, Catholic priests and nuns, and Grahamite reformers based on their shared belief in sexual restraint amid an American society undergoing the rapid social, demographic, and economic changes historians call "the market revolution." Their abstention from sexuality allowed all three groups to challenge dominant norms of masculinity and femininity rooted in heterosexual marriage and to experiment with alternative family structures. Their sexual principles often set them at odds with the cultural and social values of their time, but they were also thoroughly enmeshed in the rapid changes of the early nineteenth century. The revolutions in print technologies, in consumer culture, and in transportation and travel allowed advocates of sexual restraint to see and be seen in American society as never before.

Chapter 1, "Vinegar-Faced Sisters and Male Monsters" examines how sexual restraint challenged and transformed traditional gender roles. Investigating sexual restraint during the heyday of separate spheres, in the words of Jeanne Boydston, allows for "multiple understandings of gender."[75] Dominant notions of masculinity and femininity took on new meanings when they were no longer tied to marriage. Celibate masculinity was in some ways more threatening to the status quo than celibate femininity, if for no other reason than sexual restraint dovetailed neatly with normative ideas about women's "passionless" nature. Such debates demonstrate there was no one coherent definition of "masculinity"; libertines, working-class men, middle-class reformers, and utopian dreamers were all trying to articulate who was the "right" kind of man.

The predisposition to categorize those who practiced sexual restraint as somehow "other" further contributed to the development of sexual restraint as a distinct sexuality in the antebellum era. Chapter 2, "Identities of Sexual Restraint," examines what it meant to practice sexual restraint as part of one's daily lived experience. The spiritual testimonies and memoirs of these historical subjects challenge the popularly held notion that there were no sexual "identities" prior to the late nineteenth century. Individuals practicing sexual abstinence or limitation saw themselves as distinctly different from those who did not. Grahamites especially held an awareness that sexuality was not something "natural" but what we today would call "socially constructed."

Chapter 3, "Breaking and Remaking the Family," examines how people in Shaker villages, Catholic convents and seminaries, and Grahamite societies created alternative relationships when freed from the script of traditional marriage. In joining these communities, individuals were required to "come out" to their families of origin and made public the private nature of their (a)sexuality. While "particular friendships" between members of the same sex were warned against in seminaries and convents, Shakers believed homosocial bonds to be superior to heterosexual marriage. Grahamites strove to create more equitable marriages which gave wives greater sexual autonomy in regulating the couple's sex life. Moreover, all three groups explored new types of family arrangements and allowed for platonic relationships between men and women to flourish independent of either the expectation of marriage or the specter of seduction. In many ways, such friendships anticipated our modern ideas about cross-gender friendship — that men and women can be colleagues and work partners without being in a sexual relationship.

Chapter 4, "Alterative Extracts," demonstrates how a celibate sexual identity allowed the products of Shakers, Catholics, and sexual reformers to achieve a "brand-name" recognition in the emerging marketplace. The sexual distinctiveness of these products and their producers made them seem exotic to consumers. Similar to the way that racialization and Orientalism also were employed by marketers and advertisers, Shaker patent medicines and herbs, Catholic education, and the Grahamite health establishments were enhanced by claims to a mystical purity.

The final chapter, "Performing Sexual Restraint," showcases how gender disorder, sexual distinctiveness, and consumption were expressed through performance and tourism. Intrigued by what they had read in pamphlets, books, and newspapers, noncelibate Americans went to see these identities embodied. Shaker villages and Catholic convents became some of North America's earliest popular tourist attractions. Criticism mingled with curiosity when spectators watched Shakers dance or saw nuns take the veil. Just as nineteenth-century white Americans interpreted and consumed racial difference in the form of blackface minstrelsy, sexual difference was also something to be performed and commodified within the emerging culture industry.

Investigating sexual restraint gives a more comprehensive picture of the sexual landscape of early America. It allows us to better envision how Americans in the nineteenth century understood sexuality and its relationship to concepts of "natural," "normal," and even humanness itself. Sexuality was the glue that held gender identity, family structures, and even popular culture together. When Shakers, Catholics, and Grahamites refused to adhere to the sexual status quo of their time, they challenged the very foundations of American society.

CHAPTER ONE

Vinegar-Faced Sisters and Male Monsters

The Gender of Sexual Restraint

Author Godfrey Greylock neatly described celibacy's effect on the Shaker sisters and brothers he met at the Shaker settlement at Mount Lebanon, New York, "the capital of the Shaker world," for the curious readers of his travel narrative. As the Shakers prepared to commence their meeting before a "fashionable mob" of Manhattanites over from the nearby Lebanon Springs resort, "a female specimen of elongated acidity went up to certain ladies who had introduced the world's custom of carrying babies into public assemblies" and removed them. Greylock commented with a wink, "Oh, vinegar faced sister, how often in church and concert-room have we longed for a preventative police force like thine!" He further lamented the sad sight of "young girls cut off from all that sheds a charm and halo upon the years of maidenhood" and could only pray that they would one day exchange "the Shaker garb for a bridal dress." But Greylock assured readers that pretty sisters were the exception rather than the rule. Most Shaker women did not possess the physical charms capable of attracting a man: "The sallow cheeks and lackluster eyes bear sad record of the violation of Nature's laws." Greylock encouraged "any young gentleman romantically inclined, to make the attempt, and so rescue at least one enchanted damsel from the den of these celibate dragons."[1]

Lucius Sargent, a Boston-area physician, echoed the same sentiments when he visited the Hancock and Mount Lebanon Shaker villages while traveling with his wife and children. "They would persuade the world's people that all the women there are virgins . . . virgins in thought word & deed." He remarked sarcastically that if the sisters were not truly virgins, "they ought to be, that is if man in the natural, not the Shaker state, has anything to say." In his official medical opinion "they ought not to be probably if their health spirit or personal appearance are worth improving."[2] For both Sargent and Greylock, unnatural celibacy plucked the roses from a healthy girl's cheeks. Or conversely, celibate Shakerism could only be something the most sour and vinegar-faced of women could ever be attracted to, since they had no hope of gaining a husband. Finally, if pretty "damsels" resided in Shaker villages, they could not possibly be there of their own free will and were in need of red-blooded American men to rescue them away from monstrous celibate men, the "dragons" who held them in thrall.

"Escaped nun" stories popular throughout the nineteenth century provided similar representations of celibate women. This particular genre, a cross between adventure tale and anti-Catholic propaganda, portrayed nuns as pale, sick, and unhappy creatures, who because they had chosen convent life and celibacy over traditional motherhood were withering and fading. In nuns, the Protestant observer could readily see "that profound discontent, that pallid look, that meager countenance, those symptoms of wasting, declining nature."[3] The celibacy of priests and women religious was regarded not as a mark of holiness, but as dangerously contrary to "nature," marking them as abnormal and perhaps not even human. The narrator of an escaped nun story unimaginatively titled *The Escaped Nun* asked, "Can those vows which outrage the general propensity of nature be ever well observed, except by a few ill-constructed beings, in whom the germs of passion are injured, and who properly should be referred to the class of monsters?" Rather than eradicating the "animal functions" altogether, the convent, on the contrary, amplified them exponentially in its inhabitants.[4]

In popular fiction, newspaper articles, travelogues, and firsthand accounts, sexual restraint was viewed as causing gender deviance. The vast majority of Protestant middle-class consumers of these narratives, themselves outsiders to Shaker, Catholic, and Grahamite worlds, panicked at the gender trouble caused when their contemporaries promoted practices that challenged the sexual status quo.[5] These sources reveal that the act of sexual intercourse was intrinsic to nineteenth-century ideas of American womanhood and manhood. Practices of sexual restraint challenged and transformed conventional gender roles in early nineteenth-century America.[6] The era between the American Revolution and the Civil War was a society caught "between patriarchy and domesticity," two gender regimes that both posited very specific norms for men and women.[7] Masculinity and femininity took on new meaning when they were outside the heterosexual matrix of marriage and childbearing. Celibate masculinity was in some ways more threatening to the status quo than celibate femininity, because for women to practice sexual restraint dovetailed neatly with rising assumptions around women's naturally "passionless" nature.[8] For a man to practice sexual restraint, however, bordered on the impossible.

By the 1830s, the male libido had become "both naturalized and ungovernable." If a man could not express his sexuality through the approved channel of marriage, he would be forced to turn to illicit outlets such as prostitution, seduction, or the solitary vice of masturbation. A man, therefore, could not choose to be celibate without his neighbors suspecting him of being a potential seducer.[9] These attitudes are revealed in the cottage industries of anti-Shaker and anti-Catholic pamphlets and derogatory newspaper articles published in both the "flash" weeklies and the mainstream press. Such writings either feminized these men as emaciated "sawdust bread eaters" or the reverse—portrayed Catholic priests and Shaker elders as hypersexualized, demonic creatures.[10] Attempts to redefine celibate priests and Shaker elders as rakes and seducers can be understood as a way of reading these people back into the rubric of heterosexuality through the familiar tropes of the seduction narrative. The only alternative to being a seducer was being a monster, irredeemably outside the realm of humanity.

Because their middle-class antagonists could not accept the extreme sexual abstinence of these men as genuine, they instead charged them with crimes of sexual excess. By portraying priests, Shaker brothers, and Grahamites as adulterers and seducers and their female counterparts as victims and vixens, middle-class reformers attempted to bring those they saw as sexual deviants within their sphere of influence, further expanding their regulatory control over sex and mirroring their efforts to regulate prostitution.[11] These reformers sometimes did so by writing and circulating prurient tales about illicit liaisons between nuns and priests, or Shaker sisters and brothers, engaging in the literary practice termed "immoral reform."[12]

The presence of celibate persons within the historical record evokes the words of feminist theorist Monique Wittig: "The refusal to become (or to remain) heterosexual always meant to refuse to become a man or a woman."[13] Though Wittig's words were written in reference to the rise of lesbian feminism of the 1970s and 1980s, they are applicable to the Shakers, priests, nuns, and reformers of the early nineteenth century. Their opponents perceived engaging in sexual intercourse as threatening the very core of womanliness and manliness. Feminist and queer theorists have long debated the relationship between sexuality and gender identity. While nonnormative sexuality does not always equal gender deviance and vice versa, there is a strong case for understanding sexuality and gender as mutually constitutive. If "normative sexuality fortifies normative gender," according to theorist Judith Butler, it is understandable that the abnormal sexual restraint of these historical subjects may also have disrupted their performance of gender.[14] In turn, at times the perceived gender deviance of these subjects also led to allegations of sexual disorder and promiscuity, the exact opposite of the restraint and celibacy they so valued. By engaging in sexual restraint,

Catholic nuns and Shaker sisters, vegetarian reformers, and celibate Jesuits added to the patchwork definition of gender in antebellum America as surely as did more familiar images of the noble working man or the "angel in the house."

For the Grahamites, Shakers, and Catholic men and women religious who practiced sexual restraint, chastity did not render the female members unfeminine or the male practitioners monstrous. In some cases, sexual restraint did allow for more equitable ways for men and women to relate to one another in these contexts. However, gender roles within Catholic institutions, Shaker villages, and Grahamite circles also reinforced many of the traditional ideologies of gender existing in American society at large. Though outside the definition of what society considered "normal" sexuality, fringe status did not allow these groups to completely transcend the gendered assumptions around power that pervaded antebellum America.

Vinegar-Faced Sisters and Feminine Seducers

Print is where nineteenth-century readers discovered the gender deviance of sexual restraint. In return, salacious stories of gender inversion sparked an appetite for more print: prejudice against those practicing sexual restraint proved to be extremely profitable.[15] Celibacy as part of a spectacle of gender and sexual deviance was a key part of the "escaped nun" publishing boom of the antebellum era. With the riot at the Ursuline convent in 1834, the relationship between print and protest worked in reverse of what one might expect. Rather than the publication of an explosive text provoking an outbreak of violence, the burning of the convent was an occasion of violence that provoked an outbreak of print. The two anti-Catholic escaped nun narratives that became best sellers in the 1830s, Rebecca Reed's *Six Months in a Convent* and Maria Monk's *Awful Disclosures of the Hotel Dieu*, would not be published until more than a year after the convent lay in ashes. Though Reed's and Monk's narratives have the distinction of being the best-selling and most well-known escaped nun tales, the burning of the convent encouraged the flourishing of an anti-Catholic print genre that promised to expose the secret lives of nuns and priests.[16] A feeding frenzy of anti-Catholic literature ensued at every level of the literary marketplace, from cheaply printed dime novels to ornate gift books. These escaped nun stories capitalized on the horror the perceived gender and sexual deviance of nuns provoked in the Protestant imagination. Antebellum publishers spent thousands manufacturing lithograph illustrations of novices taking the veil and mass-printed stories that featured cross-dressing "female Jesuits" and Machiavellian lady superiors.

Escaped nun stories traded in sensationalism and suffering not only to titillate readers with depictions of eroticized violence but to illustrate that Catholicism was horrific and in desperate need of reform. The escaped nun tales of Monk and Reed sold, presumably, because they promised to give credible firsthand accounts of life within a secret, closed community. However, the burning of the convent encouraged such curiosity among readers and speculation among publishers that it also inspired convent tales that were explicitly and entirely fictional. *Rosamund* (1836) sold out within a week and had to issue a second run. Charles Frothingham's *Convent's Doom* (1854) claims to have sold 40,000 copies in ten days, and the obviously imitative *Six Hours in a Convent* (1854) went through eight editions in a single year. Rebecca Reed and Maria Monk spawned a host of imitators: *The American Nun* (1836); *Open Convents* (1836); *The Chronicles of Mount Benedict* (1837); *The Haunted Convent* (1854); *Maria Monk's Daughter* (1874). Other "escaped nun" but not explicitly Mount Benedict stories also became popular in the 1840s and 1850s: *Cecilia* (1845); *The Convent and the Manse* (1853); *Madelon Hawley* (1857); *Viola* (1858).[17] The strange career of *Maria Monk* and the immoral reform of escaped nun novels even exerted influence on anti-Mormon captivity narratives in the 1850s.[18]

Escaped nun novels showed celibacy was only for the naturally sour women of "elongated acidity" or a plague on otherwise lovely but wasting virgins. Contrary to these portrayals of celibate women as either sickly or helpless, just as often nuns (especially the authority figure of the mother superior) took on the role of masculinized seducer. Like other marginalized narrators, the female protagonist of such tales needed to explain why she was taken in and deceived in order to gain credibility and the reader's sympathy.[19] Frequently, the excuse given was that she was "seduced" into a convent by a two-faced charismatic female leader. In *Stanhope Burleigh: The Jesuits in Our Homes* (1855), the Lady Abbess "seduced" Agnes, a young sea captain's daughter, away from "the endearments of her home, to bury herself in a convent." The abbess is compared to a cruel general for whom "no enemy must escape the field." The Lady Superior of the Sisters of the Sacred Heart (which had a growing presence outside Manhattan at this time) was similarly described as a woman of calculating beauty with "a graceful and winning manner." She declares to the hero, "Do you think it absolutely necessary that a Lady Superior should become a hag before she is qualified to win and guide the fairest and best maidens of this heretic Republic?"[20] If the nuns were not "vinegar faced" like the Shaker sisters, it was all the better to deceive; treachery could hide behind a lovely face. The narrator of *The Escaped Nun* explained the secret behind the sisters' success: "It is the most artful and refined seduction. She thickens the surrounding darkness, she lulls you into tranquility, she decoys you into her snares, she fascinates you. Ours was particularly attached to me."[21] The lady superior was rendered mannish by her authority as well as her celibacy. Rather than simply being an unattractive woman, she was endowed with a certain kind of masculine charm. The superior was simultaneously depicted as a rake on par with the villain of the most prurient seduction novel and a wicked enchantress out of a fairy tale. In this way, the innocent heroine and scheming lady superior reconfigured the archetypes of the "Poor Unfortunate" and the "Siren" present in seduction novels like *Charlotte Temple* and penny press scandals, such as the one surrounding the 1836 murder of Helen Jewett. While the heroine "seduced" into a convent could earn the reader's sympathy as an all-too-human sinner, her counterpart, the "Siren," was a scheming villainess, a "predator, the gleeful incarnation of Original Sin who perversely sought the destruction of the social order."[22] And yet, ironically, in her role as "Siren," the lady superior's crime was not acting as procuress for a house of ill repute, but "seducing" promising young women away from traditional marriage (and often Protestantism) and into the celibate sisterhood. The sexualized language employed to describe these female seducers also gave readers more than a hint of same-sex innuendo.[23]

Nuns and sisters were masculinized to the point where some suspected them as posing as male impersonators. Many escaped nun and anti-Catholic stories warned against Irish servants being clandestine nuns, secretly teaching children Catholicism and spying on Protestant families. Two novels, *The Female Jesuit* and *Danger in the Dark*, went a step further, suggesting that nuns went about society passing as men. Even the title of *The Female Jesuit* (so successful it spawned a sequel, *The Female Jesuit Abroad*) suggested that nuns were but the equivalent of female priests—and in anti-Catholic circles, there was no priest more cunning or deceitful than a Jesuit.[24] *The Female Jesuit* deviated from the standard escaped nun narrative in that the "escaped nun" protagonist, Marie, was not a sympathetic character at all, but an unrepentant manipulator, whose "escape" from convent life turns out to be yet another ruse for her to defraud the kind Protestants who have taken her in. The book claimed that Marie was not the only one of her kind and that there were many such "female Jesuits" at large in American cities. One such person was a Philadelphian named "Theodore" who disguised him/herself and worked as a waiter. Originally educated in England, she was affiliated with the Sisters of Charity in New Orleans and Baltimore. On her superior's command,

> she cut short her hair, dressed herself in a smart-looking waiter's jacket and trousers, and, with the best recommendations for intelligence and capacity, she, in her new dress, applied for a situation as a waiter at Gadsby's Hotel in Washington city. . . . Now the Jesuit was in her glory. Now the lay sister had an opportunity of knowing many of our national secrets, as well as the private character of some of our eminent statesmen. Now it was known whether Henry Clay was a gambler; whether Daniel Webster was a libertine; whether John C Calhoun was an honorable but credulous man.[25]

The Escaped Nun claimed that the infamous Hotel Dieu of Montreal contained a room of disguises, so that nuns could costume themselves as schoolteachers, maids, and even priests. "They are often mistaken for men, especially for priests," the book alleged, because "in the evening it is not very difficult for a woman to pass for a man in a crowd, when dressed with care, and somewhat practiced beforehand, especially with one or two real men to accompany her."[26] These spurious accusations served to further render nuns as monstrous and deceptive women, beyond the pale of "normal" middle-class white femininity.

Gender deviance among women held readers of escaped nun tales transfixed with equal parts fascination and horror. The climax of many an escaped nun tale from the antebellum era was the veiling ceremony in which a prospective nun cut her hair short as a renunciation of vanity and the pleasures of the world. Protestant curiosity about this practice was not just limited to fiction. When Mary Barber made her vows at the Ursuline Convent at Charlestown in 1828, Bishop Fenwick and Superior Mary Edmond St. George Moffat invited "a number of respectable Protestant ladies" as a political move to cultivate interest in the school and the goodwill of the community. However, the Protestants in attendance were disappointed that though they were allowed to witness the prayers, blessings, and incense of the ritual, its most sensational aspect was not open to the public.[27]

This aspect of Catholic ritual was often described in highly sexualized terms. The moment of "sacrifice" was depicted in art from the shoddiest engravings found in the dime novel *The Nun of St. Ursula* (1845), to more middling gift book illustrations, to Robert Weir's high art masterpiece *Taking the Veil* (1863). The frontispiece of *The Nun of St. Ursula* (figure 1.1)

FIGURE 1.1 "Cecile Taking the Veil," *The Nun of St. Ursula* (1845). Courtesy of the University Archives, Catholic University of America.

illustrated the novel's point of climax and terror as Cecile, the damsel in distress, kneels before the altar, the abbess with "fatal scissors" in hand.[28] Notably, this scene was one of only two illustrations in the entire cheaply printed volume; the other depicted the convent engulfed in flames.

As engravings were expensive to produce, they were often reused, especially in gift book production. In one engraving, titled *The Sacrifice* (figure 1.2), a young blonde woman, teary-eyed, kneels to make her vows. One sister cuts

FIGURE 1.2 "The Sacrifice," *Cabinet of Modern Art* (1852). This image was reproduced four times in different gift books between 1849 and 1855. Courtesy of the American Antiquarian Society.

her long hair, as the abbess stands behind her with the white veil, the bridal crown discarded. This image was reproduced no less than four times between 1849 and 1855 and was used to illustrate both poems and short stories. Images of nuns taking the veil appeared beside illustrations both exotic and domestic; from Venus on her half-shell and women wearing Spanish *mantillas* to innocent and sentimental scenes of a young girl with her dog, or of a mother bathing a child. The inclusion of images like *The Sacrifice* as well as other depictions of nuns inside gift books shows that this imagery was provocative enough to be interesting, yet wholesome enough to be marketed to young women or a family audience.[29]

It is understandable why this ritual may have been so sexualized by the Protestant public. The veil ceremony was effectually a marriage ceremony, where a nun married herself to Christ the bridegroom and renounced traditional marriage and wifehood in favor of her order and the company of her sisters. If the ceremony itself was a kind of wedding, inevitably some kind of consummation must follow. Long, flowing hair was viewed in nineteenth-century Western culture as an extension of a woman's sexuality as well as an essential marker of her femininity. In the mid-nineteenth century, women's hair played a key role in performing middle-class sentimentality, used as it was as tokens of remembrance, such as the practice of keeping a lock of a close friend or family member's hair or in the hairwork jewelry crafted for mourning.[30] Anthropologists have likened the shearing of a novice's hair in the veiling ceremony to a kind of ritualized castration, while others have interpreted it as a loss of her individual identity and embrace of a collective one, symbolized by the identical habit worn by all the sisters of a given order.[31]

Antebellum Protestants seized on the cutting of a woman's hair and gave that process a profound sexual charge, to the point where the priest performing the deed seems more like a rapist than a clergyman. In *Danger in the Dark*, an anti-Catholic novel set in Cincinnati, Anna Maria and Arabella are duped into becoming nuns by their scheming confessor, Father Dupin. As they make their vows, Dupin says, "Heaven requires sacrifice! Long hair is an ornament and only fosters pride, and as pride becomes not saints, you must now be shorn." Then, "he inserted into Anna Maria's ebon locks, the sacred scissors, like his own heart relentless and remorseless! The monster ceased not to despoil until the head was made bare, and the last ringlet dropped from the temples of beauty!"[32] In the end, they are no longer women, but Dupin's "mutilated victims." In another novel, *Stanhope Burleigh*, the heroine Genevra actually dies of grief at the moment when they are about to cut her hair.[33]

These sensational novels tell us that for a woman to lose her femininity was both a spectacle to be witnessed and a fate worse than death. In cutting her hair, a nun lost one of the primary markers of femaleness at a time when gender roles were predicated on men and women's inherent distinctiveness.[34] Fears of "female Jesuits" masquerading about were but another iteration of the growing anxiety that pervaded the newfound "world of strangers." In an urbanizing society where anonymity had replaced the face-to-face relationships of an earlier era, the markers of respectability coded in manners, dress, and hairstyles carried a great deal of weight. A woman's beauty in the antebellum era was not simply a matter of aesthetics, but part and parcel of the social order because of the "regulating" and "refining" influence it had over men. For a woman to deliberately sabotage her femininity by swathing her figure in a shapeless Shaker gown or nun's habit went against "a social responsibility to cultivate her own beauty." Magazines like *Godey's Lady's Book* and other kinds of prescriptive literature emphasized women's moral beauty as well as their physical beauty, and actually argued that improving one's morality could beautify one's outward appearance. As members of what many Protestants considered a corrupt and decadent religion, women religious possessed neither physical nor moral beauty.[35]

The inherent sadism depicted in an anti-Catholic novel like *Danger in the Dark* was not singular to the escaped nun genre and was well within the antebellum era's fascination with the "pornography of pain." Classics of temperance and antislavery literature such as *Ten Nights in a Bar Room* and *Uncle Tom's Cabin* similarly deployed beatings, whippings, and other forms of violence to impress upon readers the urgency of their cause.[36] Anti-Catholic writers drew parallels with the "slavery of the mind" fostered by Catholicism and the "slavery of the body" practiced in the South, declaring the latter to actually be "less degrading" to a human being than the former.[37] Henry Hazel and other writers of escaped nun fiction used their tales to advocate for laws outlawing convents on American soil, and encouraged readers sympathetic to abolitionism to consider nunneries a kind of female slavery.[38] One pamphlet, entitled *Priest's Prisons for Women* (1856), published during the height of the sectional crisis, explained that a convent was "an institution whose object it is to kidnap their daughters, and imprison them as *free white slaves*, the property of the priests."[39] Such texts implied that while individual Catholic persons may be tolerated, Catholic institutions that trained priests and nuns had no place in America. They also re-centered white women's sexual virtue and reproductive capacity as being the most valuable to the nation, ignoring the sexual violence experienced by black women under chattel slavery.

Publishers and reviewers alike viewed escaped nun stories not as trashy adventure stories, but as reform literature. For example, reviewers of *Stanhope Burleigh* compared the book to *Uncle Tom's Cabin*, and hoped the anti-Jesuit novel would do for Know-Nothingism what Mrs. Stowe's book had done for antislavery. Frederick Douglass agreed and championed *Stanhope Burleigh*'s potential twice in his paper, *The Northern Star*. Douglass encouraged the pseudonymous author to reveal himself, calling him "a man of no ordinary powers of mind, and no uncommon daring."[40] Douglass's enthusiasm for *Stanhope Burleigh* demonstrates that escaped nun stories had wide appeal in reform circles, even across racial lines.

Perhaps because they never advocated lifelong celibacy or withdrew from conventional society like their Shaker and Catholic counterparts, far less ridicule was heaped upon the female followers of Sylvester Graham. However, the movement's frank discussion of female and male sexuality both frightened and titillated detractors. Transcendentalist Orestes Brownson lamented the preponderance of "disinterested lecturers, ready in public discourses to explain to his wife all the mysteries of the conception and birth of a human being." By granting women an equal say in the sexual politics of their households, men such as Brownson saw it as an assault on male bastions of privilege. White middle-class men like Brownson were now "bound hand and foot, and delivered up to" the likes of Graham, William Andrus Alcott, and Mary Gove, "sage Doctors and sager Doctoresses, who have volunteered their services in the management of his affairs. He has nothing he can call his own, not even his will."[41] In this logic, power could not be granted to female reformers without depriving white men of their privilege. No wonder the men attacking Graham's "Lecture to Mothers" at Boston's Amory Hall hooted and hollered and made the noises of barnyard animals when female Grahamites attempted to speak, effectively reducing them to a level less than human. In the many Graham riots, it seemed that if women were going to attempt to seize sexual knowledge, they must also be willing to face male violence. The members of Boston's Ladies' Physiological Institute (LPI), founded under the auspices of Dr. Harriot K. Hunt in 1848, recalled that "the members of the Institute were stoned on their way to meetings, and had to cover their faces with thick veils so they would not be recognized." Even though the LPI was much less radical than the Grahamite women's groups of the 1830s, the organization still received a frosty reception from Boston society for the supposed crime of teaching women about their own anatomy. Only one minister, a Reverend Jenks, would agree to officiate at their first anniversary.[42]

If anything, female Grahamites were suspected of being helplessly feminine. Like the heroines of the escaped nun tales, they were a chorus of "poor unfortunates," hopelessly enthralled by the siren songs of Mary Gove and Sylvester Graham. While reform publications such as *The Liberator* and *Zion's*

Herald championed Mary Gove's lectures to women, James Gordon Bennett of the New York *Morning Herald* had a distinct ax to grind, and ran a series of derisive articles against Gove during her New York lecture tour in the spring of 1839. A devotee of Graham, Gove had made a career for herself as a traveling lecturer, preaching the benefits of sexual restraint and the Graham system to exclusively female audiences. However, James Gordon Bennett's *Morning Herald* painted a picture of Mary Gove's lectures as a carnivalesque spectacle of gender and sexual inversion, where the most fashionable and respectable ladies of New York society eagerly listened to a strange woman tell them "of things that they heretofore have been taught to think of with dread, if not with fear and trembling; and show them parts and parcels of anatomy, many of which they have been forbidden to look upon." Mary Gove, "reputedly pious, modest and delicate," held the ladies in the audience spellbound with her knowledge of Galen and Aristotle. The newspaper reported that the unassuming Quaker matron "prepares a piquant and spicy dish of this forbidden fruit and serves it up for a dessert at 4 o'clock P.M. three times a week at 25 cents a plate full for each guest."[43]

Bennett repeatedly lumped Mary Gove in with the most scandalous women of her day, fellow "petticoat lecturers" Abby Kelley, the famous abolitionist, and free-love advocate Fanny Wright.[44] He even ran articles linking Gove to the notorious Madam Restell, despite the fact that as an advocate of sexual restraint, Mary Gove was promoting the far opposite of abortion. Bennett likened Mary Gove to the "she-serpent of old," tempting the pure and virginal Eves of the city with forbidden knowledge of "anatomy and obstetrics," which would inevitably prove their downfall. Bennett insisted, "Since the fall of man, she is the first woman who has attempted to lecture on anatomy."[45] Like Sylvester Graham, Mary Gove was characterized as a monster—no less than Satan—for daring to talk frankly about female bodies in the name of sexual restraint. And like that of the Lady Superior of the escaped nun tale, her seemingly pleasant and respectable demeanor was naught but a façade.

"The Fanatic, the Jesuit, and the Voluptuary": The Male Monsters of Sexual Restraint

If women who practiced sexual restraint were characterized as full of vinegar or as beguiling as the serpent in the Garden of Eden, men were considered even more monstrous and predatory. To be a celibate Catholic priest or a Shaker brother, disinterested in biological fatherhood and the accumulation of wealth, was contrary to every expectation for white male citizens. And for the middle-class white men who made up the majority of Grahamites, to live on "sawdust bread and water" and limit sexual intercourse with their wives to once a month at maximum, to voluntarily relinquish both privilege and pleasure, was unthinkable to the point of insanity to most of their contemporaries.[46]

It had not always been evident that men were the more passionate and libidinous sex. Prior to the nineteenth century, women were considered to be "naturally" more passionate, while men were considered in possession of greater reason and self-control. Contestations over celibacy reveal much about the early nineteenth century as a time when sexual values and behaviors were in flux. During the post-Revolutionary era, the gendered dynamics of sexual virtue shifted from women to men. In the new moralistic and didactic literature that portrayed men as seducers and women as victims, "characteristics previously associated with women, especially lust and deceit, were transposed onto men."[47] In the early republic and Jacksonian eras, new ideas of male self-discipline or "manliness" came into conflict with a much more hedonistic and rakish masculinity embraced by middle-class "libertine republicans" and working-class "jolly fellows."[48] Beginning in the 1820s, a new kind of "cult of true manhood," based on discipline and self-restraint, encouraged middle-class white men to work hard in order to get ahead in the emerging market economy.[49] Grahamite men especially fit the ideal of the reforming "manliness" that libertines and jolly fellows found anathema. This era has been characterized as a contest between "two dueling mid-century masculinities: *restrained manhood* and *martial manhood*" that at times cut across both class and regional lines. Advocates of restrained manhood grounded their identities in expertise, cherished domesticity, and abhorred violence. Those who practiced martial manhood reveled in physical displays of dominance over those they considered to be inferior—women, the enslaved, and weaker men.[50] Further complicating this paradigm, both "restrained" and "martial" men of the antebellum era objected to the celibate masculinity of priests and Shakers—the restrained wanted to reform them or use political machinations to eject them, while martial men advocated violence. Yet, restrained celibate priests often ministered to working-class jolly fellows and earned their respect as beloved leaders in urban and frontier communities. These debates illustrate there was not a singular or stable construct of masculinity in the antebellum era; Shaker brothers and Grahamite reformers attempted to define and redefine what it meant to be a "man" as much as cultural tastemakers and sporting men.

As celibacy masculinized women, some contended that it in turn effeminized men. In the eyes of their critics, sexual restraint weakened men. This was especially evident in the critiques of men who adopted the Graham system, which limited sex, proscribed masturbation, and required followers to abstain from all forms of "stimulating" food. Because of censorship around sexuality in the papers of the day, critiques of Graham's diet often stood in for his prescriptions for limiting the libido. And as Graham and his fellow reformers believed that overstimulating food led to sexual degeneracy, it was a perverse critique of the Grahamites' own logic. The *New York Review* painted a portrait of "Dietetic Charlatanry" asking readers to imagine the oxymoronic nature of a Graham house feast: "We must think one of the rarest spectacles in the world must be (what is called) a Graham board-ing house at about the dinner hour." Around the table "some thirty lean-visaged, cadaverous disciples, eyeing each other askance — their looks lit up with a certain cannibal spirit; which, if there was any chance of making a full meal off each other's bones, might perhaps break into dangerous practice. The gentlemen resemble busts cut in chalk or white flint, the lady-boarders . . . mummies preserved in saffron." Another installment portrayed a visit to David Cambell's Brattle Street Graham boarding house in Boston, where the proprietor answered the door, tall and gaunt, with a high-pitched "branny" voice.[51] The *Boston Medical and Surgical Journal*, one of the preeminent medical publications of its day, declared the Graham system poisonous to masculinity, writing, "Emasculation is the fruit of Grahamite fanaticism." Sylvester Graham himself was portrayed in terms more suited to a female hysteric: "Mr. Graham's nervous system is kept in a state of high excitation, not to say irritation, by external and internal friction, and muscular and moral exercises."[52]

GRAHAMITES DID NOT feature as often in popular fiction as priests or Shaker brothers. A serialized short story that appeared in *Brown's Literary Omnibus* titled "The Grahamite and the Irish Pilot" is unique in this regard, yet perfectly captures the oddity of the male Grahamite in the public imagination. The Grahamite is described as "thin as a whippin post" with a body like "a pair of kitchen tongs, all legs, shaft, and head, and no belly; a real gander lookin critter, as holler as a bamboo walkin cane, and twice as yaller." Like many a Grahamite, he was a professional man, a lawyer from Maine; "Thinks I, the Lord a massy on your clients, you hungry, half-starved lookin critter, you, you'll eat 'em up alive." Like the description of the Grahamite dinner party that appeared in the *New York Review*, the Grahamite is de-

FIGURE 1.3 "The Great Republican Reform Party," Louis Maurer (1856). The Grahamite is the thin man on the far left. Courtesy of the Library of Congress.

scribed as being both comically thin and deprived to the point of cannibalism. In short, a "male monster."[53]

A visual representation of a Grahamite, a true "saw-dust bread eater" appeared in the political cartoon *The Great Republican Reform Party* (figure 1.3) by lithographer Louis Maurer. Maurer's image portrayed the growing Republican Coalition in the broadest and most burlesque terms, lumping together "Fourierists" with women's rights advocates, free lovers, African Americans, and a Catholic priest. All of these figures were meant to inspire fear as they petition John C. Frémont; a Bloomer advocate of women's dress reform, wearing spurs with a whip in her hand; a free man of color dressed in ruffles and finery, an elderly woman spouting the principles of free love; and lastly, an emaciated sponsor of the new Maine Law, the first state law to outlaw liquor sales and a major victory for the temperance movement. Emboldened by temperance's recent triumph, the extremely slender gentleman now declares, "The first thing we want is a law making the use of Tobacco, Animal Food and Lager-beer a Capital crime." At first glance, it would seem that only the Catholic priest is not a caricature—he is young and handsome, neatly dressed in his long, black cassock. Given antebellum Protestants' tendency to believe all priests seducers in disguise, he would have inspired fear precisely because he is portrayed as young and handsome.

While Grahamites believed that sexual restraint enhanced health and longevity, many thought extreme sexual abstinence destroyed the male body. One can clearly see the difficulties of reconciling Shaker celibacy with male sexuality in the apostate tract written by Reuben Rathbone in 1800, *Reasons Offered for Leaving the Shakers*. Rathbone complained of his struggle "to become a *Eunuch* for the Kingdom of Heaven's sake." In trying to convince others of the dangers of the Shaker religion, Rathbone centered on the sexual unnaturalness of Shaker celibacy, which went both against traditional Protestant ideals of healthy sexuality within marriage and the new libidinous masculinity. He detailed a Shaker asceticism so severe that men like himself were subject to "involuntary evacuations" of "the seed of copulation." Rathbone also related that was sent on a missionary errand to Connecticut with the order to "go forth and circumcise as many as you can." Circumcision is a ritual practice that confirms membership within God's chosen people and can often refer to a spiritual rather than a physical state. Given how concerned Rathbone was with controlling his sexuality, the image of phallic destruction conjured up by these words was no doubt intentional.[54] Castration anxiety also surfaced in the print campaign surrounding the confrontation between the Turtle Creek Shakers and the Ohio militia in 1810. Ohio convert Richard McNemar, one of the first Shaker writers to advocate for the sect in print, found it necessary to refute accusations "that the Shakers castrated all their males." The recurring image of castration and genital mutilation in anti-Shaker accounts deserves attention. The frequent use of words like "eunuch," "castrate," and "circumcise" implied that celibacy could be possible only through the destruction of the male body. In anti-Shaker accounts, Shaker celibates were not simply people who made a personal decision not to have sexual intercourse out of religious devotion— they were incomplete people and incomplete men. As most anti-Shakers held that celibacy was impossible, the only way the Shakers could possibly achieve it was through an unhealthy and unholy destruction of the male body. In the same pamphlet, McNemar also refuted the accusation that the Shakers "divested of all modesty, stripped and danced naked, in their night meetings; blew out the candles, and went into a promiscuous debauch" during their meetings.[55]

Rumors of castration and promiscuity may have carried extra weight at this time, as Methodist circuit rider Jeremiah Minter had himself castrated in 1791 so as to avoid the sexual temptation provoked by one of his married female parishioners.[56] Minter wrote about his decision in his 1817 autobiography: "I came to a resolution from a desire . . . to devote myself entirely to the Lord in a single life, and never marry. And with this resolution . . . by the aid of a surgeon, became a *eunuch for the kingdom of heaven's sake*."[57] Those familiar with the Minter controversy may have found the celibacy of Shaker brothers, as well as Methodist circuit riders and Catholic priests, destructive and suspect. Living outside the boundaries of marriage led the public to speculate that Shaker male sexuality ran to deviant extremes: they were either eunuchs or utterly debauched. Both kinds of accusations point to the notion that genuine celibacy was less believable to non-Shakers than castration or promiscuity.

Legal and print records show that joining the Shakers effeminized male converts in ways beyond the physical. An 1807 proposal to the Ohio legislature argued that men who joined the Shakers should be considered "civilly dead." "Civilly dead" was also the phrase used to refer to the status of married women under the British common law practice of coverture, in which a woman, once married, was subsumed under the financial and legal identity of her husband. The Ohio bill would have dissolved marriages between any Shaker and his non-Shaker wife and placed the couple's children with the wife or a court-appointed guardian. It further mandated that the property of a man who converted to Shakerism be divided among the dependents he left behind, and that any "gifts, grants or divisions of money of money or property real or personal" made to such a sect would be considered "utterly void." Such a law would have effectively transformed Shaker men into the legal equivalent of women. Though the law would certainly have done a great deal to help Polly Smith recover her children and support them (and might have prevented the 1810 mob altogether), as of 1818 no such bill had been signed into Ohio law. A similar measure introduced by supporters of Eunice Chapman in the New York legislature allowed for custody of children to be awarded to the mother but did not require Shaker husbands to provide financial support. Apparently, patriarchy proved itself to be stronger than the fears aroused by Shaker celibacy's destruction of the traditional family.[58]

Aside from subverting traditional sexual standards and their roles as husbands and fathers, there were other reasons why male Shakers would have appeared effeminate to their early republican contemporaries. For one, since pacifism was integral to Shaker religious beliefs, Shaker men did not participate in militias or armies. Many male Shaker converts in the Northeast had fought in the War of Independence but refused to collect their veterans' pensions. Participating in a militia played an important role in claims to citizenship and masculinity in early America: the two groups predominantly excluded from militia duty were women and the enslaved. Colonel James Smith, a respected Continental army veteran himself, sneered at the Shakers' pacifism: "They pay their fine rather than attend musters." Smith in his pamphlets juxtaposed his own status as a proper patriarch, veteran, and citizen against that of his son and other male Shakers. In his second pamphlet, *Shakerism Detected,* he testified, "I suffered much in procuring the happy liberty we now possess. I lost my old Brother in the contest. . . . I myself was nigh unto death with camp fever." Unless the Shakers released his grandchildren, Colonel Smith warned, "the military spirit I once possessed in my youth might again arise and I would be under the disagreeable necessity of taking my children from you by force." That Smith's pamphlets inspired 500 men to march on the Shaker compound is a testament that his military spirit had not left him; he made good on his threat.[59]

Colonel Smith also spoke out against the ways James Smith Jr., had failed him as a son in joining the Shakers. Beyond his failure to be an affectionate husband and kind father, James Jr. neglected his duty as a son by being cavalier with the family property. Colonel Smith complained that after being "divested of his natural affection towards his wife Polly," James Jr. became "determined to sell his plantation in Kentucky and remove to the Shakers in Turtle Creek." Eunice Chapman also lamented how her Shaker husband "suffered his real estate which was worth about 6000 dollars to be sold for 1500." It was indeed the expectation of the Shakers that the men, women, and families who joined their communities would, after settling any outstanding debts, either sell their property and material goods or transfer them over to the Shakers for communal use. Almost all Shaker villages, including the Turtle Creek settlement, began when landed and prominent converts deeded their property to the sect. Shaker covenants refer to this as forming "a joint interest" or being "in union." The parallels to marriage and the "union" of husband and wife are significant. In joining the Shaker "union," single men and fathers again took on a feminine role. Like brides, they brought dowries of goods and property. In signing the covenant, these men married themselves to the Shaker community. While women who joined the Shakers also brought goods, often in the form of portable property, when they joined the sect, it would not seem as transgressive for them to do so. It was within early nineteenth-century norms of gendered behavior for a woman to give up her property and legal identity, whether joined in union to a husband or to the Shakers. For a man to give up his property to the control of others effeminized him and defied the ideal of the early republican yeoman farmer.[60]

Shaker celibacy ripped at the fabric of heterosexual marriage and threatened a man's ability to control family and property. Add to this a refusal to carry arms and defend the republic and the community by participating in militias, and a Shaker man's status as man and citizen would have appeared tenuous. Celibacy caused Shaker men to lose patriarchy and manliness but also opened the door to myriad accusations of "otherness." Anti-Shakers frequently repeated the accusations that Shakers were not American citizens. It was also not hard to tar them with the brush of being secret Catholics in an overwhelmingly Protestant nation. Celibacy was a foreign sexual practice of decadent European Catholic "others," in contrast to the virile Protestant men of the early American republic.[61]

Already tarred with accusations of sexual deviance, lacking in proper masculinity and patriotism, and bearing a strong resemblance to foreign Catholics, the Shakers lacked so much of what was necessary to be a citizen, even their whiteness was up for debate. Colonel Smith made an interesting comparison between the Shakers and the formerly enslaved: he asked, "If a law can be past [sic] to prevent black and mulatto persons from residing in the state of Ohio except they give bond with sufficient security, because they have been degraded and unmanned by slavery, can we not touch a treasonous nest which is hatching and breeding among us?" Smith argued that the Shakers and freedpersons were both "unmanned," one by slavery, the other by celibacy.[62] Smith and his supporters further fanned the flames of racial antagonism in Ohio territory by questioning the Shakers' relationship with Tecumseh and his band of Indians. What the Shakers interpreted as a kindred religious revival among the Shawnee, citizens of Lebanon saw as a potential war party. Colonel Smith and his supporters considered the Shakers to be less than free white men. On the one hand, the Shakers' lack of property and patriarchy left them as "unmanned" as the formerly enslaved. On the other, they were race-traitors masquerading as pious white men and women, corrupting the new nation from within.[63]

The celibacy of Catholic priests was treated with even more suspicion during this time. The figure of the lascivious priest became a standard stock character in both anti-Catholic pamphleteering and popular fiction. When a woman claiming to be the "real" Maria Monk presented herself in New York City with a babe in arms, the product of an illicit liaison with a priest at the notorious Hotel Dieu in Montreal, a great portion of the public had no trouble at all accepting Monk's story regarding the boy's paternity. And while a young unmarried woman who bore a child out of wedlock might otherwise be made an object of shame during this era, Monk, because she had been seduced and abandoned by a priest, received an outpouring of sympathy from anti-Catholic partisans. She was welcomed into the drawing rooms of the toast of Protestant society and may have even tempted Samuel F. B. Morse, noted Nativist and inventor of the telegraph, to contemplate a marriage proposal.[64] Monk's tale purported that for nuns, the vow of obedience superseded the vow of chastity, so that lustful priests could compel virginal sisters into sexual relations, claiming it was no sin. Monk claimed a priest told her "anything he did to her would sanctify her."[65] Though an investigation by the journalist W. L. Stone revealed Monk to be a fraud and her tale concocted by anti-Catholic ministers and greedy publishers, her story continued to be widely read and circulated as fact by antebellum Protestant readers.[66]

Rebecca Reed's *Six Months in a Convent* (1835) was much less salacious on this count, yet still asserted that because priests lived outside of marriage, they corrupted the sexual morals of the women around them. Reed wrote that priests used the influence of the confessional to ask nuns and otherwise virtuous female parishioners "various improper questions, the meaning of which I did not *then* understand, and which I decline mentioning."[67] On the heels of the Maria Monk scandal, Samuel Morse published the supposed *Confessions of a French Catholic Priest*, in which he claimed priests sowed the seeds of debauchery in women in the confessional. The ex-priest claimed, with a pretty girl, a priest will start by asking if she has had "bad thoughts," "bad desires," or "bad actions" and then pressure her that if she does not answer, she'll damn her soul to hell. In doing so, the curate actually taught young men and women the corrupt vices they were meant to avoid.[68] Texts like Reed's and the *Confessions* again provided that titillating, voyeuristic glimpse into a hidden culture, pornography wearing the respectable garb of reform literature. It should also be noted that Morse's sensational *Confessions* has been revealed by scholars to be just as fraudulent as Maria Monk's convent tale. Large portions of *Confessions of a French Catholic Priest*, especially the priest's confession of lust for his young female parishioners, was translated nearly word for word from the French version of Victor Hugo's *The Hunchback of Notre Dame*.[69] Rebecca Reed's testimony should be taken with more credibility, as she was an actual postulant among the Ursulines. What passed between Reed and her confessor cannot be known for certain and the possibility of sexual abuse or coercion cannot be entirely dismissed. Regardless of the validity of Reed's claims, her narrative helped make the confessional synonymous with seduction in the Protestant imagination.[70]

Examples of less-than-celibate Shaker brothers abounded in antebellum popular fiction and drama as well. Similar to the escaped nun tales, there was a cottage industry of anti-Shaker romances written during this time. The plot was fairly formulaic: a young Shaker brother falls for a pretty Shaker sister; they decide to run away together but are stopped by a villainous Shaker elder who wants the girl for himself. The short story, "The Shaker Lovers," later turned into a stage melodrama, made the comparison between greedy and selfish Shaker brothers and cunning and lascivious Catholic priests explicit rather than implicit. When the titular Shaker lovers, Martha and Seth, attempt to run away, they are stopped by the interference of the menacing Elder Higgins, "whose manner was as hateful as his countenance was repulsive, and whose character was a strange compound of the fanatic, the Jesuit, and the voluptuary." "The Shaker Lovers" claimed to have been based on a true story. While it is true that many Shakers, male and female, who had been brought up as children in the community left when they reached the age of majority, and some of these ex-Shakers did indeed marry, this tale cannot be matched to actual events within any early nineteenth-century Shaker community. Seth, the ex-Shaker hero, warns that the Shakers are neither more virtuous nor more angelic than most, and "could you lift the curtain, and see all that this sober and wonderfully honest exterior is sometimes made to conceal, you might, perhaps, be a little less inclined to exempt them from the common feelings and frailties of other people."[71]

What emerges from the writings of Protestant authors, journalists, and consumers attempting to uphold the sexual status quo is a strange gender dichotomy around the subject of sexual restraint. In this logic, men and women who practiced sexual restraint were either rakes or monsters. In portraying priests and Shaker brothers as lascivious seducers of women, they were quite literally rewriting these celibate men back into their own familiar narratives, specifically the familiarity of the seduction novel. Even if the figure of the rake was a hated one at a time when Female Moral Reform associations were actively campaigning against men who visited prostitutes and seduced young women, he still had a place within the heterosexual matrix as a villainous foil for the virtuous hero.[72] It is notable that the other depiction of those practicing sexual restraint was the figure of the "monster," which was leveled at those who were perceived as deviating most from gender norms. So, effeminate men like the Grahamites were monsters in the forms of cadaverous cannibals. Masculinized women were also monsters: the characterization of Mary Gove as a "she serpent" or of the lady superior as a siren, a creature that was half female, half-beast. In these written attacks against celibate persons, the Protestant middle class attempted to police not only the boundaries of what constituted normal gender and sexuality but also what it meant to be human.

The Persistence of Separate Spheres

Though sexual restraint and celibacy conjured up visions of masculinized women and effeminate men, in practice gender roles within Shaker, Catholic, and Grahamite communities conformed to antebellum social and cultural expectations as much as they transgressed them. Though these groups granted greater influence for women in the realms of spirituality and education, they also upheld antebellum notions of separate spheres and the gendered division of labor. All three groups likewise offered opportunities for women to pursue leadership—as Shaker deaconesses and elderesses, as teachers and nurses within Catholic schools and hospitals, and as lecturers and officers within Grahamite physiological societies. However, women were rarely allowed to exercise power over men in these organizations. In the case of certain Catholic orders and Grahamite groups, women also struggled against the attempts of their male counterparts to usurp the limited authority they had.

The antebellum concept of separate spheres actually aided Catholic orders and Shaker communities in their pursuit of celibacy. By keeping men and women apart during work as well as recreation, these groups discouraged heterosocial bonds from forming between men and women. Catholic sisters within convents and schools lived in all-female communities, often with the exception of a bishop, who was attached to the community to act as confessor and adviser. At the convent of the Sisters of the Visitation in Kaskaskia, Illinois, for example, the bishop was the only white man allowed to stay within the convent walls overnight. Though this rule was put in place presumably to quell suspicions of *Maria Monk*–like allegations, it was often impractical in the frontier environment of the Old Northwest. In 1840, Superior Mary Seraphina Wickham wrote to Father John Timon, provincial of the Congregation of the Mission, in great distress over whether or not a priest visiting her school for examination day could be allowed to lodge at the convent. "We wish to know if we invite him to occupy the bishop's bedroom whilst he remains here? Please answer, the question, as we are embarrassed & know not how to act on account of obedience. The Bsp gave us viz that no one of your sex excepting a Bishop may lodge in the Academy."[73] However, this proscription only seemed to apply to white men. Convents in slaveholding states such as the Sisters of Charity of Nazareth in Kentucky, the Ursulines in New Orleans, and the various orders operating in Missouri all had numerous enslaved people, male and female.[74] In this case, the racial hierarchy between the sisters and the enslaved dispelled any notions of sexual impropriety.

Shaker sisters and brothers by contrast lived together and worshipped together within the same community and often slept under the same roof. They embedded their celibate principles within their architecture. Dormitories at Hancock, Massachusetts, and Enfield, New Hampshire, had separate wings, staircases, and entrances for men and women. These separate wings were joined in the middle by shared common spaces, like the refectory, where men and women ate at separate tables. Meetinghouses, too, had separate entrances for men and women. Even the Shaker school year was ordered to keep men and women separate; girls were educated in the summer by Shaker sisters, boys by Shaker brothers in the winter when they could be spared from agricultural work.[75]

LABOR WITHIN CATHOLIC and Shaker communities also conformed to antebellum expectations. Shakers were unafraid to challenge some of the most fundamental aspects of American society—military service, private property, and marriage. They did not, however, attempt to overthrow the gendered division of labor, presumably because it suited their needs.[76] During the first 100 years of Shakerism in America, there were no attempts to ask Shaker sisters to learn trades such as carpentry or blacksmithing and no calls for Shaker brothers to darn socks or prepare food in the kitchens. When parents indentured children to the Shakers, it was with the expectation that boys would be taught a trade and girls the basics of needlework and housewifery.[77] It is also telling that as Shaker presence in the antebellum marketplace grew, Shaker brothers represented the community in financial and legal matters. While Shaker sisters worked in the herb houses, gardens, and dairies, their names were never attached to seed labels or packaging, nor did they represent the Shakers in agricultural competitions such as the Boston Mechanics' Association.[78] Despite Ann Lee's legacy and status as the second incarnation of Christ in the form of a woman, Shaker sisters did not preach publicly as often as Shaker men in the meetings attended by the "world's people." Later Shaker tracts written by Shaker theologians actually attempted to bury Lee's influence and central role within the religion entirely. In this way, arguably Shakers follow the pattern of many other "fringe" religious groups, which often begin with egalitarian values but embrace male dominance as they seek legitimacy in their second and third generations.[79] So while following the gendered status quo may have been very practical, it also limited the roles men and women could perform even on the utopian fringe. In Catholic communities, women performed occupations that were seemingly natural outgrowths of women's roles as caretakers: teaching, nursing, and caring for orphans. Nuns and sisters did not attempt to preach publicly, and priests did not teach young ladies needlepoint. In some cases, nuns were attached to seminaries and monasteries specifically to feed and clothe their male counterparts.

It should be noted that Catholic sisters had a remarkable amount of autonomy and self-governance for women in this period. Catholic sisters lived in exclusively female communities, and the leadership of these orders was exclusively female as well, from the lady superior (sometimes called Reverend Mother) on downward to the mistress of novices, the school administrators, to the treasurer and procuratrix (convent steward). Protestant white women did not have the right to elect representatives in American government in the early nineteenth century, but most Catholic orders gave women the right to elect their superiors. In Shaker villages, by contrast, elders of the men's and women's orders were not elected but seem to have been chosen in secret among the established leadership of the community, often in conference with the central ministry at Mount Lebanon. Many orders, such as the Sisters of Charity, had regulations put in place to see that power was distributed somewhat evenly, limiting a superior to no more than two consecutive terms of three years each.[80] When a novice made her vows and entered a religious community, she swore obedience to the female leaders of her order, not to any male priests or bishops. In a missionary order like the Sisters of Charity, this vow meant a willingness to serve wherever a sister might be needed. In contrast to many secular female seminaries, the teachers at convent schools were also exclusively female. Catholic charity schools and hospitals in the early republic and antebellum periods were "highly visible, self-supported, self-directed enterprises" that "made obvious the lack of an equality between the sexes."[81]

The unique autonomy of Catholic women religious was provocative not only to Protestant outsiders but to the priests and bishops who were supposed to be their compatriots. Conflicts over sex-segregated environments and male presumptions of power caused a schism within the American

Catholic community in the 1840s when bishops in New York and Nashville tried to force sisters within their diocese to swear a vow of obedience to them instead of to their respective orders.[82] The sisters saw this as rooted in the bishops' desire to keep the generous donations the Sisters of Charity received within their dioceses rather than sending them back to Emmitsburg. Bishops and priests also butted heads with sisters about the administration of schools and convent affairs. Despite the fact that women in religious orders elected their own leaders, bishops and priests did have authority over the administration of schools and hospitals within their diocese and seemed to have closely monitored the election of lady superiors. In some cases, the bishop's vision for a school or an academy clashed with the sisters' own experience as with the "strange misunderstanding" that occurred between the Sisters of Charity of Nazareth and Bishop David of Bardstown, Kentucky.[83] The bishop felt one sister, Ellen O'Connell, "dominated" the newly elected Mother Angela in the running of the academy at Bardstown, so he sent Sister Ellen away on a mission to found a new school in the frontier settlement of White Sulfur, Kentucky. The sisters themselves, including Mother Angela, protested his decision. Sister Ellen had received a fine education as the daughter of a middle-class Baltimore family, while Mother Angela had grown up in the backwoods of Kentucky. Mother Angela felt her limited education inadequately prepared her to run the academy on her own and vowed she would resign if Bishop David insisted on sending Sister Ellen away. This was no idle threat, for when Bishop David failed to heed her wishes, Mother Angela quit in protest. Due to the ill feelings that stemmed from this incident, Bishop David never lived in the spacious new brick residence that had been built for him at the Nazareth convent.[84] The "strange misunderstanding" illustrates the degree to which priests and bishops tried to mold the will of women religious to suit their liking, and the ways, in turn, sisters negotiated to keep the autonomy they had been granted.

In their role as father-confessors, priests exercised paternal authority over sisters, whom they referred to as "daughters" regardless of actual age. Letters between nuns and their confessors clearly demonstrate a balance of power that was tilted toward the priests. Sisters often signed their letters "I am your Obedient Child." Even Mary Seraphina Wickham, superior of the Kaskaskia convent, signed her letter to Father Timon, "With filial affection and gratitude, Beloved Father, I remain your unworthy daughter in Xt (Christ)." Often the letters themselves read as quite assertive, with such signatures used only to maintain the illusion of deference. In no case was this clearer than with Mary Edmond St. George Moffat, superior of the Ursuline Convent in Charlestown, who often signed her letters "The Superior" in bold script, double the size of her deferential claim to be "your most humble and obedient servant."[85]

Paternalistic and even misogynistic attitudes could be found in Grahamite circles as well. Despite the presence of organizations such as the Ladies Physiological Society and the prominence of Mary Gove within the movement's ranks, letters and articles within Grahamite publications often portrayed wives as frivolous hindrances to a husband's successful adoption of Grahamism. And indeed, the culinary principles on which Grahamism rested required cooperation from the wives, daughters, and domestics who would be preparing these vegetarian meals. As men usually did not cook or supervise the preparation of meals in the 1830s, a man who wished to follow the Graham diet would have to seek his wife's toleration, if not her enthusiastic participation. Husbands would have to negotiate with their wives in the practice of Grahamite sexual restraint as well. Grahamite publications show that male Grahamites resented the authority their wives had over domestic affairs in this regard; though as white men, they enjoyed full political and economic rights, narrow definitions of masculinity kept them out of the kitchen. David Cambell, editor of the *Graham Journal of Health and Longevity*, stressed the necessity of finding a Grahamite wife who would be a "help-meet" rather than a hindrance to her Grahamite husband. He cautioned against Graham men so anxious to be wed that they marry not fully Grahamite wives who seduce their husbands back into non-Grahamism. First, "her flesh began to smoke upon the table"; then, "the flirting against his friends the Grahamites, commenced, till, finally, she hated them because they had influenced her husband to become a fool."[86]

Grahamite women, too, directed misogynistic attacks at non-Grahamite women. Asenath Nicholson, keeper of a Graham boarding house in New York City, wrote into Cambell's *Graham Journal* denouncing non-Grahamite wives. "The wife, if she have been educated a city miss, flirts, and tauntingly talks of bran bread, salt and potatoes, while she eats her flesh and sips her tea, telling her husband, the same time, if he chooses, he may starve on sawdust, she will not," while a more "industrious" wife "puts on a graver face and talks of the necessity of something to strengthen." Nicholson asked female readers hyperbolically if they would rather be the wives of drunkards or the wives of Grahamites.[87] Another article, "What Shall We Have for Dinner," presented a scene at the breakfast table between a Grahamite husband and his non-Grahamite wife. It is truly a case of "father knows best," where the reasonable Grahamite husband must educate his ignorant wife, who dares to want hot tea and lobster for dinner. He is forced to tell her that she is no different from a drunkard who desires a pint of rum every day because it "feels good." And yet, in the same issue, when a wife wrote asking for advice on how to persuade her husband to adopt the Graham system, the editor advised her to win him over gently with "patience" and "kindness."[88] Such portrayals fit the antebellum ideal of woman's use of "moral suasion" over direct confrontation, similar to the advice given to female reformers active in the temperance and antislavery movements.[89]

Sexual restraint was viewed as reducing women to pale, sickly shadows and Grahamite men to emaciated walking cadavers. It could transform seemingly respectable people like Mary Gove into seductive sirens and celibate priests into hypersexualized scoundrels. Perhaps most notable is the fact that critics of sexual restraint myopically saw gender deviance, while the lived experience of Shakers, priests, nuns, and Grahamite reformers showed a remarkable degree of conformity. Critics seized on and magnified the differences that did exist, and often imagined monstrous divergences to mark practitioners of sexual restraint as far outside the norm, and in some cases, not human. In doing so, they were blind to the very real ways these groups conformed to antebellum expectations of gendered labor and male dominance. The predisposition to categorize those who practiced sexual restraint as somehow "other" and outside definitions of "normal" further contributed to the development of celibacy as a distinct sexual identity in the antebellum era. Shakers and Catholic priests and nuns understood their celibacy as a key component of their identity, and they, along with Grahamite reformers, used sexual restraint to challenge and critique heterosexuality and the institution of marriage.

CHAPTER TWO

Identities of Sexual Restraint

In 1828, Noah Webster's landmark *An American Dictionary of the English Language* defined celibacy as "an unmarried state; a single life. It is most frequently applied to males, or to a voluntary single life."[1] This definition differs greatly from modern understandings of the word, where celibacy implies not only an "unmarried state" but also "abstention from sexual intercourse." The modern definition of celibacy that includes both abstention from sex and abstention from marriage first appeared in Webster's in 1970, reflecting perhaps the expanded opportunities for Americans to have sex outside of marriage following the sexual revolution of the 1960s.[2] In Webster's time, by contrast, it was possible to be "celibate" but also sexually active, especially if one was an unmarried man. Chastity, too, had a different meaning than in the present. Americans of the Jacksonian era understood that both married and unmarried persons could be chaste. Chastity meant "Pure from all lawful commerce of sexes. *Applied to persons before marriage,* it signifies pure from all sexual commerce, undefiled; *applied to married persons,* true to the marriage bed."[3] In this latter case, it was entirely possible for a married person to be chaste, as long as sexual activity was confined to one's lawfully wedded spouse. That one could be "celibate" but still impure, and married yet still "chaste" left practitioners of sexual restraint in a bit of a "Catch-22." Such ambiguity was doubtlessly what made the celibacy of Shakers and Catholic priests and nuns controversial, for there was no guarantee that their unmarried lives were chaste ones. Language itself did not allow them to define themselves as such.

In embracing celibacy, Shaker sisters and brothers and Catholic nuns and priests practiced a sexual identity for which nineteenth-century American society did not even have a name. This chapter will explore what it meant to practice sexual restraint as part of one's lived experience. I understand "lived experience" to be the product of a particular historical and cultural moment.[4] The spiritual testimonies and memoirs of these historical subjects can further discussions on the development of sexual "identities" prior to the late nineteenth century.[5] In focusing solely on binaries of premodern versus modern or homosexual versus heterosexual, a great many other sexual behaviors and identities are left in the shadows. Most historians of sexuality would agree that there are a wide variety of sexual behaviors beyond the heterosexual-homosexual binary, some of which (married, with opposite sex partners, in private, with only one partner) have been culturally and legally privileged.[6] Even though celibacy is often omitted from this analysis, in the decades of the early to mid-nineteenth century featured in this study as well as our present moment, engaging in sexual behavior within the context of marriage was considered normal. Complete sexual abstinence was not.

Celibacy and chastity, sexual identities based on abstinence, were consciously chosen identities to the Shakers, Catholics, and sexual reformers who embraced these ideals. Sexual restraint was at once an individual identity based on one's personal sexual abstinence as well as a requirement for membership in a larger group, whether that be a Catholic religious order or a Grahamite physiological society. Furthermore, opponents of sexual restraint heaped ridicule and gendered stereotypes upon Shaker sisters, Catholic nuns and priests, and Grahamites, promoting the belief that sexual restraint made one's manner and body unhealthy and abnormal. Individuals practicing extreme sexual abstinence also saw themselves as distinctly different from those who did not. Unlike modern-day sexual identities which are often justified by a "born-this-way" biological imperative, these groups and individuals often prided themselves on the unnaturalness of their restraint.[7] In this sense, the subjects of this study understood desire to be what we would consider to be "socially constructed," the product of cultural conventions and religious traditions.

Letting individuals speak in their own words of the experiential dimensions of their sexually abstinent identities presents a challenge for historians. Though much has been done to recover sources on sexual experience from the so-called Victorian age, manuscript sources in which sexuality is discussed in explicit terms remain somewhat rare. Private diaries, hymns, prescriptive literature, meeting minutes, and letters to Grahamite journals allow Shaker and Grahamite understandings of their sexuality to become visible. Unfortunately, Catholic records on how priests and sisters experienced and understood celibacy in this era are much more opaque and elusive. It could be that such sources either do not exist or did not survive or perhaps that conversations of such a delicate nature were likely confined to the confessional and not recorded.

This chapter examines four individuals' experiences with celibacy and abstinence as a form of sexual identity. These narratives allow what from the outside seems like a harsh and unnatural regimen to emerge as deeply personal, individualized, and meaningful. The most frank records come from three white men: a Shaker brother, a reform-minded Grahamite man, and a young Catholic priest. It is not surprising that those who wrote most explicitly about their experiences of sexual abstinence were men. Silence in the historical record on this issue from women further underscores the degree to which nineteenth-century women may have internalized their own ideas of women's naturally "passionless" nature.[8] Still, these diaries remained a private matter and were not intended for public view, as evidenced by the choice of two diarists to express their sexual struggles only in code. What emerges from these narratives is an idea that a celibate sexual identity was complex and complicated, actively wrestled with and chosen rather than the product of unthinking dogma. The fourth narrative, by a black Shaker sister, Rebecca Cox Jackson, can be read in contrast and in rebuke to these white male experiences. Jackson's life provides a window into racialized experiences of bodily autonomy, sexuality, and personal freedom.

Trying to Learn the "New Tongue": Living Shaker Celibacy

For Shakers, celibacy was a practice that formed a larger part of their identity as followers of Mother Ann Lee. Celibacy was just one of a wide variety of customs the Shakers endorsed that set them at odds with the status quo. Pacifism, communal ownership of property, and belief in a female deity, Holy Mother Wisdom, formed the fundamentals of Shakerism as much as sexual abstinence. And yet, the writings of Shakers, from printed pamphlets to private correspondence, show that celibacy was the most frequently cited matter of difference between the Believers in Christ's Second Appearing and those they called "the world's people." Such a high degree of importance was placed upon celibacy and the dissolution of marriage that the Shakers refused to abandon this most prized principle even as the sect dwindled to near-extinction in the twentieth century. Even when beloved elders and prominent leaders of the community left to marry, the Shakers refused to compromise.[9] In short, to be a Shaker was to be a celibate person.

Spiritual autobiographies of prominent Shakers reveal that overcoming the lusts of the flesh was not something that came easily to men or to women. Some of Shakerism's most successful leaders during the early years of the religion, such as missionary Issachar Bates, theologians John Dunlavy and Richard McNemar, and even elders Ann Lee and Lucy Wright, had once been married. Accepting celibacy was an essential part of the Shaker conversion narrative, and it was never something one undertook lightly.[10]

Even the most devout and enthusiastic members understood that the Shaker cross of self-denial was a hard one to bear. Missionary Issachar Bates saved his most spiteful words for those Believers who turned apostates, who returned to the lusts of the flesh "like the dog to his vomit again." He wrote, "I have often labored with such people, and it is like throwing water against a goose's breast; it cannot enter." The problem with the lustful was "they do not wish their hearts broken, they choose to keep them whole." The Shaker way of life, and celibacy, required in Bates's opinion the breaking of one's heart, "to pieces, because it is deceitful above all and desperately wicked;—and have a new heart, such as God has promised to give to the honest." Only the most humble and submissive to God's will could make such an unnatural sacrifice.[11] Eldress Antoinette Doolittle, by contrast, possessed considerably more empathy for those converts who tried and failed. She knew the Shaker way to be "narrow and straight" and that even those who come with sincere motives "find great work to do; for there is a mixture of good and bad, truth and error, in every human heart."[12]

Shaker hymn lyrics often reveal more about how the Shakers understood and cultivated celibacy than their journals or letters. These hymns were never explicit, but frequently referenced "the cross," "self-denial," and a rejection of all things "carnal." Music and dance were both vibrant and vital parts of Shaker spirituality. The repetition of such words and phrases reified them in a Believer's mind and gave them a way to understand their faith, as surely as concepts of sin and salvation were used in Protestant services. One hymn, called "The Direct Road to Happiness," contrasted the "narrow path" of the Shakers with the "broad" road of the people of the world. Shakers find Christ's burden of self-denial light, but "Few souls desire Christ's way to go / It crucifies their natures so." However, the hymn stated the broader avenue leads misguided Christians further and further astray from God's true path. Only "the upright honest soul / Who every passion does control," would enjoy true blessedness.[13]

Another hymn, "Solemn Work," stressed that in order to maintain self-denial, Shakers must cultivate a "searching self" that was as watchful and vigilant about one's own sins as it was about noticing the faults of others. A "searching self" was not something a Shaker was born with, but was described as the titular "solemn work."[14] Contrary to modern understandings of sexual identity which are often predicated in naturalness or rooted in a biologically inclined orientation, Shakers held their celibate identity as something that was indeed unnatural. It was the product of effort, work, and sacrifice. The fact that it was born of artifice and not nature made it all the more valuable to them, as superior as a finished ladder-backed chair is to a pile of lumber.

One of the most concise understandings of how Shakers understood their celibacy can be found in the hymn "A New Tongue," in which the challenges of learning the Shaker faith are compared to the challenges of speaking a foreign language. The Shaker "language" and all it encompassed—celibacy, pacifism, communitarianism—was the language of heaven. The hymn urged Believers to "Quit Satan's hateful language / Come speak in the new tongue." Celibacy was presented as the language of Christ himself and his first followers as well the language the Shakers expected would be spoken in the afterlife, where people neither marry nor are given in marriage. This guarantee of salvation was something the Shakers held more precious "than mines of purest gold." Contrary to what outsiders might believe, the hymn assured listeners, "The brethren and the sisters / The aged and the young / Find sweetest consolation / In speaking the new tongue."[15]

The Shakers possessed a self-conscious and deliberate celibate identity; they believed that taking up "the cross of self-denial" was necessary for salvation. In becoming "eunuchs for the kingdom of heaven's sake," as referred to in the Gospel of Matthew, Shakers sacrificed sexual expression to ensure their heavenly reward. Just as the "sacred theater" of spirit possession, glossolalia, trances, and visions provided concrete proof of the existence of God among the Shakers, celibacy provided an equally concrete means of ensuring one's salvation.[16] Compared with Calvinist doctrines of predestination, where only an unknown "elect" would be saved, Shaker theology was much more open and democratic: salvation was open to anyone who joined their community and accepted the Shaker's cross of self-denial. While strict Calvinists had rejected a "gospel of works," Shakers rejected the elitism inherent in predestination. Their celibacy was a lifelong work intended to both open heaven's gates in the afterlife and create a sacred community within each Shaker village. The Shakers believed in a celibate Christ. They also believed that in becoming celibate themselves and living communally, they emulated the earliest Christians. Simultaneously, they saw themselves as living in the post-millennial age promised by the book of Revelation. Celibacy allowed the Shakers to feel that they were a part of both elite groups — the earliest, purist Christians and those who witnessed the second coming.[17] Sociological studies of religion have argued that sacrifice and abstinence are not simply features of successful utopian societies, but requirements. Sacrifice makes membership "more valuable and meaningful." The more it "costs" an individual to do something, the more "value" he or she will assign to the activity.[18]

Despite the assurances that celibacy was a pearl of great price, the Shakers knew all too well that the lusts of the flesh were hard to quit. For while some remained Believers for life, for others Shakerism was more of a passing phase, an enthusiasm to be tried until a person tired of it or could find a better situation. Though the Shakers were prepared to absorb the ebb and flow of curious inquirers and casual turnoffs, the loss of Believers of long standing, especially those who had been appointed to positions of leadership, hit a given community especially hard. To see a dear friend lose his faith could often trouble the spiritual foundations of even the most ardent Shaker.[19]

The diary of Isaac Newton Youngs, a lifelong New Lebanon brother as well as a craftsman, teacher, and musician, provides a glimpse of how these apostasies affected the Shakers' rank and file. It is also remarkably candid on the difficulties of practicing celibacy. Youngs kept many public diaries of the New Lebanon Shakers and compiled a history of the sect completed in the 1850s. But his struggles to accept the Shakers' rule of celibacy come not in plain prose, but coded diary entries that would have been unintelligible to the casual observer.

Youngs lived from 1793 to 1865 and witnessed the heyday of Shaker society. He had the rare distinction of being a Shaker nearly since birth—his father "opened his mind" to the Shaker elders at Watervliet in January of 1794, when Youngs was only a few months old. The elder Youngs was known to have possessed many spiritual gifts that the Shakers prized, such as the ability to speak in tongues, yet struggled with the Shakers' commitment to celibacy, leaving and returning to the community several times during Isaac's childhood. Spiritually adrift and destitute, Isaac's father committed suicide when Isaac was only eighteen years old.[20]

His father's untimely death no doubt made an impression on Youngs as he entered manhood about the consequences of failing to attain Shaker standards of spiritual and sexual perfection. And according to his biographer, there was no doubt that Youngs was a perfectionist among perfectionists, evidenced in the material and written artefacts he left behind. Youngs's idealism and internalization of Shaker virtues can be glimpsed in a handmade music pen in its lacquered rosewood box or in the perfectly matched rhyme and meter of his poems and songs. Though often rebuked for being lazy and idle as a boy, Youngs showed great spiritual precocity by Shaker standards. He was admitted into the Church Family at Mount Lebanon and signed the

Shakers' covenant at only thirteen years of age.[21] Church Family member-ship was reserved for those Shakers who possessed the greatest spiritual commitment—and Church Family membership within the Shakers' central ministry at Mount Lebanon was the most elite of the elite. Most Shakers, even those who had been "gathered in" the society as children, were not permitted to sign the covenant until they had reached the age of majority, approximately twenty-one. For such an exception to be made indicates that young Isaac must have shown a great deal of sincerity in his religious con-victions. It also meant that he had committed himself to a life of celibacy without perhaps understanding the depth of his sacrifice or the difficulties of restraining his sexual desires.[22]

Young adulthood brought trials of faith and struggles with celibacy for Youngs. As Youngs entered manhood, "Satan oft laid his tempting snare / & cross'd my track, most everywhere," he wrote in his autobiography. His sex-ual crisis was sparked one day in 1815 when he glimpsed a party of young men and women close to his own age bathing in the North Family's pond.[23] That very same day, his close friend Bushnell Fitch apostatized, driving young Isaac into his own dark night of the soul.

Seeing a peer, especially one as close as Bushnell Fitch, choose a differ-ent path threatened to unravel Youngs's own faith. Most distressing of all was when apostate Bushnell Fitch returned to the village for a final time in 1817 with the intention of carrying off "a Shaker wife." Fitch talked to sev-eral of the sisters, trying to entice at least one of them to elope with him. He repeated the careworn rumor "that their girls were held in bondage &c." But truly, it was not the well-being of the Shaker sisters that motivated Bushnell Fitch, but his own financial self-interest: "he told them that his father told him that he would not give him any of his interest if he did not come back and get him a Shaker wife." The following day he came back with a one-horse wagon to carry off an unnamed Shaker bride, who at that moment refused to go along with his plan. Bushnell protested, refused to leave, and created quite a scene. Youngs recorded, "He seemed to think it strange that they would not let him have a wife! He seemed to think they might let him have [name crossed out] as she was not much accounted of, and would never make a believer &c." At the last, Fitch told the elders "that if they had any sort of feeling for him, they would let him have some one and seemed to be quite effected to take at it very hard." His longtime friend Isaac Youngs was horrified and thought Fitch had quite lost all his wits, la-menting, "A Shaker Wife!! O who would have once thot that of you Bush-nell? I should have that you would have been too shamed."[24]

The episode of Bushnell Fitch and his attempt to acquire "a Shaker wife" is significant. It shows how deeply ingrained notions of compulsory hetero-sexuality were even among those who had once been Shakers themselves. It was not unusual for ex-Shakers to try to reclaim back wages or property after they left the community, even though in signing the Shaker covenant, they had renounced all claims to either. Bushnell Fitch stands alone in feeling he was entitled to a *wife* in return for all his years of labor and faithful Shaker celibacy. Fitch tried to force the Shakers to adhere to standards of patriarchy, where women were property. His masculine pride demanded he should be given "some one," even a woman "not much accounted of" as reparations, as the elders might let another apostate have an extra bolt of cloth or some spare carpentry tools.

Shortly after Fitch's apostasy, Isaac Youngs found himself immersed in his own trial of faith, which pitted the aspirations of his soul against the desires of his body. Contrary to what their critics thought or what even present-day individuals might believe about a sect that practiced sexual abstinence, Shakers were not made of stone. While Mother Lucy Wright preached in meeting to "labour more within us to take up our cross against our own natural dispositions and ways," Youngs suffered temptation and torment in secret. A young man in his prime, Isaac felt tempted by the plea-sures of the world, a world he had renounced before he even understood what it had to offer. He wrote, "My natural part within me says 'shall I live here on earth all my days and not know any thing of this world or under-stand the evil with the good—O let me give way a little, what can be the harm to feel after knowledge?" He wondered if it was truly possible for a person to live a life completely free of sin and temptation. Youngs struggled with involuntary physical functions beyond his control, most likely noctur-nal emissions: "!! I experience I know what—But how long! How long shall I remain subjected to weakness, why is it? Why can't I break out and be a free soul. . . . O if I could once get my head out, I would hate the flesh with all my feelings & never get . . . with it again." What might have seemed to some a mere embarrassment was to this young Shaker man nothing less than a battle for his soul. He wrote in great despair, "!!! For some cause it appears that my soul & body is bound & I do those things that I would not. . . . I feel exceedingly shiftless & good for nothing." Copies of Sylves-ter Graham's *A Lecture to Young Men on Chastity* and Dio Lewis's *Our Secret Sins*, texts that warned of the dangers of masturbation and sexual overstim-ulation, were present in Shaker libraries, though they were published de-cades after Youngs's spiritual crisis. While official Shaker records and private diaries are meticulous about recording the weather and sales of Shaker goods, they remain silent about the sexual growing pains of adolescence.[25]

Brother Isaac's sexual and spiritual struggles went on for years. His felt his nature to be "an evil plant," one he wished he could "pluck" from the very bottom of his soul.[26] He was reprimanded for going too often to the sisters' rooms and seemed to have developed an infatuation with one unnamed sister in particular. He tried confessing his sins to the elders, as was the remedy for such behavior, but they seemed at a loss at how to deal with Brother Isaac's persistent lust. They finally told him he must talk to Mother Lucy or Eldress Ruth about it. The suggestion that he speak of his troublesome lusts to the highest-ranking women in the Shaker sect shamed Youngs so much, he never wrote of his sexual struggles in his diary again.[27] It is unclear how Isaac Youngs made peace with the "cross" of celibacy, though he must have, as he chose to remain in the society for another forty years, until his death. For Youngs to forsake celibacy would mean he could no longer be a Shaker and would be cast out from the only true family he had ever known. He would become a failure like his father. For this young Shaker brother, the benefits of continuing to live as a Shaker outweighed the sacrifices.

Living the Graham System

Unlike the Shakers, who believed celibacy was necessary for spiritual salvation, Grahamite sexual reformers believed the benefits of sexual restraint would be reaped in this life, not the next. Early histories of the movement have interpreted Graham's advocacy surrounding hygiene and chastity as a metaphor for the entire American antebellum age.[28] These studies envision sexual reform as a metaphor for modernization, where adapting Grahamite values about culinary and sexual excesses led to the internalization of middle-class identity. But in the words of one historian, people turned to Graham "not in order to enter the emergent middle class" but because "they were sick, and they wished to become well."[29] Graham's system—which encompassed not just sex but diet, sleep, and temperance—provided a needed "regimen" to antebellum middle-class men, displaced from the traditions of home and village to the urban center. Grahamism was also immensely popular among female reformers. Nor was Graham's appeal strictly confined to urban centers—Grahamite publications were distributed in the South and rural areas as well as the industrializing North. By the end of 1837, there were twenty agents selling *The Graham Journal of Health and Longevity* in

Massachusetts alone as well as in states far beyond Graham's northeastern lecture circuit — Michigan, Ohio, and Georgia. By 1839, the *Journal* could be bought as far away as South Carolina and Mississippi.[30]

The diary of Worcester horticulturalist George Jacques reveals that followers of Sylvester Graham at times struggled with prescriptions for health and vitality bought at the cost of sexual restraint. George Jacques was a young man of about twenty-four years of age when he began keeping his diary in 1841. Like many of the men attracted to Grahamism, he was an educated New Englander of the middle class, having graduated from Brown University in 1836. Like leading Graham lecturer William Andrus Alcott, he was a former schoolmaster, having taught in Rhode Island and Virginia for three years prior to returning home to participate in his family's nursery business in 1840. Jacques was an intellectually curious and intelligent man; he spoke French, Italian, Spanish, and German and as of 1841 was teaching himself to read Hebrew. He was also an avid reader and fan of Samuel Coleridge, Charles Dickens, and Harriet Beecher Stowe. Most importantly, Jacques was a devoted Washingtonian and attended meetings of the society in both Worcester and Boston.[31]

Despite his cleverness and perhaps because of it, George Jacques considered himself to be sickly, weak, and of a nervous disposition. As a Washingtonian, rather than just an ordinary temperance advocate, Jacques likely struggled with an addiction to alcohol, as the Washingtonian Society was established for and by self-identified "drunkards" in a Baltimore tavern in 1841.[32] It is possible Washingtonian connections introduced him to Grahamism and sexual reform; Jacques referenced Samuel Woodward's latest book on solitary vice in his diary after attending the annual Washingtonian Convention.[33] Certainly, Graham's ban on alcohol and stimulating drinks would have complemented his temperance pledge. But he also may have converted to Grahamism for health-related reasons: "If Phrenol[ogy] Is true, I am constantly inclined to underrate myself, self-esteem being the smallest organ in my head *My temperament being strongly nervous*, I have too much sprightliness and physical activity for my strength — teeth liable to decay — extreme sensitiveness to physical suffering — sensibility." Jacques believed himself predisposed to consumption, dyspepsia, sleeplessness, and mental insanity and subject to extremes of feeling. He fretted over trouble with his eyesight, his weakness for liquor, and his general ill health to the extent that at one point he wondered if he should commit himself totally to celibacy, for fear of passing these unhealthy traits along to his own children.

"Would it not be best to live un vieux celibate? Would it not have been better for me had mon pere done the same? Infinitely! Infinitely! Oh Dieu that it had been so!" he wrote in his journal.[34]

George Jacques may have been attracted to the promises of the Graham system to treat his melancholy and nervous disposition, but he struggled against its prohibitions against solitary vice, and the expectations antebellum reform culture had regarding the male libido. He wrote tips to himself on how his life might be improved: "Remedy for Melancholy. 1 Early Rising; 2. Plain nourishing food; 3. Exercise in the open air. Also associate with the cheerful—Study the scriptures—Avoid Sin— . . . —Prayer." Next to this he also wrote, "Remedy pour l'autre chose—1. Keep employed, body or mind; 2. Guard the senses . . . to these may be added 4 Guard the Imagination and avoid every thing that excites it or the senses . . . Tabac, intoxicating drinks. Indulgence . . . 5. Take regular exercise, wholesome food, bathe occasionally—ex. Mod & gen cold bath. . . . dormissait solitaire . . . Noth short of total abst. can save those addicted to it." While the "remedy for melancholy" certainly followed the directions of Graham and Alcott, "remedy pour l'autre chose," or "the other thing," the issue he declined to name, was the universal sexual reform prescription against masturbation.[35] These most private entries about "l'autre chose" were written in Jacques's unique code, which substituted Greek letters for Roman ones, undecipherable to a curious parent or servant who did not have the benefit of a classical education.

In his mid-twenties, George Jacques also struggled with the prescriptions of antebellum middle-class white masculinity. Social norms dictated that Jacques find a wife and marry, yet the reform circles he moved in also required Jacques to practice sexual restraint while he remained a bachelor. Courtship was difficult for Jacques, and his diary entries on the subject reflect the sorrows of an unhappy man twice spurned by potential brides. In Worcester, Jacques again attempted courtship and risked rejection. In his coded diary entries, he chronicled his courtship with one Miss Louisa Inman. He first mentioned her in October of 1843: "Played backgammon with Miss I and got beat every time." For the next two years, he continued to visit with and play backgammon against Miss Inman. Once in 1844, he recorded having "loved with L alone on the sofa." Despite his intense fondness for Louisa, his health and recovering drunkard status made him doubt whether or not he was fit for marriage: "Objections to my marriage—1st—incapacity to get a living. 2nd should not be loved by my wife—3rd my children would inherit mon defects."[36]

It is unclear whether these were Jacques's own fears or the objections of Louisa and her family. In April of 1845, he seemed to have asked her father's permission to marry her and was rebuffed; he wrote of his frustration, "the great want of my life — ergo must ergo will get married!" He kept up his acquaintance with Louisa throughout 1845 and tried to propose again several months later. She tried to let him down easy, telling Jacques she could not accept him as a husband, "only in the light of a friend." Despairing, he resolved to take the moral high ground and not seek revenge against Louisa and her family for spurning him, in hope that he would one day find another woman to marry.[37] Unfortunately for George Jacques, this also was not to be. He remained a bachelor until his death in 1872. The second volume of his diary, begun more than ten years later in 1852, reveals a much more somber and misanthropic man.

What conclusions can be drawn from George Jacques's experiences with sexual restraint? He was neither a priest nor a Shaker, but a somewhat average, white, middle-class man of his time, who believed Grahamite principles would improve his health. He sought to free himself of solitary vice as well as a weakness for alcohol, and may have believed the two were interrelated. And yet, though he vowed to get plenty of exercise, leave off stimulating food and drink, and think pure and pious thoughts, he never wholly embraced the vegetarian aspect of the Graham diet. There were many avenues individuals pursued to Grahamite sexual restraint. Some came to it out of concern for their health. For others, sexual restraint was always the end goal, and the prevention of disease was secondary. The example of George Jacques shows that those who subscribed to Grahamism were not the dogmatic, blind followers the popular press imagined them to be. It was more of an "à la carte" ideology for someone like Jacques; he practiced the parts that seemed most relevant and beneficial to him.

Though sexual abstinence and limitation were as much a part of the Graham system as bran bread and a vegetarian diet, the few testimonies that remain are hardly as explicit as those of George Jacques. In the case of published testimonies, whenever sex was discussed explicitly it was done so anonymously. Conversely, wherever anyone was willing to attach his or her name to an endorsement of Graham's system, they spoke openly of Graham's diet but not of his sexual prescriptions. This even carried over into the privately recorded meeting minutes of the Ladies Physiological Society of Boston (LPS). As part of their constitution, the female members of the LPS promised to "to give some account of their health before and since adopting the Graham system" when called upon. Furthermore, no member should "feel at liberty to refuse when called upon" to discuss her experience, presumably including her sexual experiences.[38] During a meeting in which they hosted Sylvester Graham himself, Graham instructed the ladies to speak frankly with one another; "all restraint being laid aside in this society and the meeting as a band of sisters."[39] And though the secretary dutifully noted occasions on which LPS members spoke openly of their experiences on the Graham system, their words were never recorded.

In print, Grahamites were more likely to speak in more general terms of their miraculous recovery on the Graham system. Adeline Brooks's letter to the *Health Journal* was typical. Brooks blamed her ill health on her work as a dressmaker from the age of fourteen to twenty-one: "During this time I thought I had pretty good health, but took almost no exercise, lived on rich food, attended a great many evening parties." Brooks was plagued by a great many ailments, including at her lowest point, the stoppage of her menses. After two years on the Graham system, including frequent cold-water bathing, she experienced a total recovery. She wrote to the editor, "My system now possesses a capability of endurance and resistance which it never did before."[40] Reading between the lines of Brooks's published letter, with its mention of "evening parties" (presumably spent in the company of the opposite sex) and her strict adherence to Graham's regime of both diet and bathing, it is fair to assume she most likely practiced sexual restraint as well. And as she lived near Oberlin College, which at the time ran its dining system entirely on the Graham diet, managed by former *Graham Journal* editor David Cambell, she lived in a community with many kindred spirits.[41] Sylvia Cambell, a charter member of the Ladies Physiological Society, would have been there as well. If Cambell met with Adeline Brooks and other interested women to discuss those controversial tenets of Graham's "Lecture to Mothers," no record exists. Such conversations were likely deemed too indelicate to be printed in the newspaper.

Celibacy and Catholic Religious Life

As difficult as it is to uncover the experiential dimensions of sexual restraint for Shaker and Grahamite subjects, it has been even more so for the Catholic priests and nuns who feature in this study. Such sources (if they ever existed) either may have been purged from the historical record or remain highly restricted in terms of access. In this way, writing about nineteenth-century subjects' feelings about not engaging in sexual activity mirrors many of the difficulties historians of sexuality have in obtaining their sources.

This quotation from the biographer of Mother Elizabeth Boyle, first mother superior of the Sisters of Charity of New York, sums up the challenges of this research neatly: "A sister's life, however, although before the world, is intended to be shielded from observation."[42]

Like the Shakers' commitment to celibacy, in its most idealized form a nun or priest's vow of chastity was intended to be a sacrifice. It was not a state that was supposed to come easily or naturally, but something consciously chosen in emulation of a celibate Christ. Rather than a rejection of desire, the vow of celibacy reflected a desire to become closer to God by rejecting earthly concerns and pleasures. It was considered analogous and of equal weight to vows of poverty and obedience, which were also intended to be difficult sacrificial behaviors. Priests and women religious rejected personal comfort and personal freedom in hope of gaining eternal treasure and love in the afterlife. Nineteenth-century Catholics, like their Shaker counterparts, believed celibacy allowed a person to emulate the life of the angels; "chastity crucifies sensual life and makes one participate in the angelic nature as far as is possible with this mortal state."[43] Chastity worked in concert with poverty and obedience as a spiritual discipline that perfected human nature.

While many men gave their lives to the service of the church and agreed to live by the priesthood's rules, it did not mean they always did so unquestioningly. Doubts about celibacy and its continued necessity in the new American priesthood can be found in the writings of Richard L. Burtsell, who served as a Catholic priest in New York City during the mid-nineteenth century. Burtsell was born in 1840 to a wealthy New York Catholic family who could trace their ancestry back to Maryland's first colonial settlers. His family had high hopes for him and sent him at the age of ten to study at the Sulpician seminary in Montreal. At the age of only thirteen, it was decided he would become a priest, and he traveled alone to Rome to study at the Urban College of Propaganda, sponsored by John Hughes, archbishop of New York. Burtsell spent over a decade at the prestigious Collegio Urbano, where he earned both a doctor of philosophy and a doctor of theology degree. In Rome he studied alongside the church's best and brightest, gathered from all over the world—fellow English speakers from Scotland and Ireland but also priests from Russia, Tasmania, Egypt, Guinea, Baghdad, Copenhagen, and Sudan—as well as a handful of fellow Americans.[44] Though he had been intended for the priesthood since childhood, he was not formally ordained until the age of twenty-two. In November of 1862, Burtsell returned to his native New York City as the assistant pastor to St. Ann's Church in Astor Place.[45]

Still fresh from the seminary in 1865, Burtsell and his colleagues from Collegio Urbano safely concluded that celibacy was still in the "great characteristic" of the priesthood despite "many individuals' frailty." In their opinion, marriage made their Protestant counterparts selfish and narrow-minded, while celibacy allowed the priest to care for the whole human race.[46] Yet only a year later, the young priest questioned whether the celibate priesthood was in the best interests of the church. On a steamboat trip from Saratoga Springs to New York, Burtsell and two of his fellow priests spent the afternoon debating the merits of celibacy for priests. "We discussed on the propriety of letting the clergy marry: and we agreed on its propriety." The reasoning of Burtsell and his two companions, Dr. McSweeny and Father Nilan, was that "celibacy never allows priests to become men. . . . Celibacy brings lonesome hours to the priest: marriage would give him a perpetual object to be loved: Celibacy makes priests selfish, marriage would make him more social."[47] Father Burtsell and his colleagues in the priesthood knew of fellow priests who had failed to keep the vow of chastity. They spoke in hushed tones of rumors of a fellow New York priest caught buying venereal medication and of priests "taking liberties with girls of well-to-do families."[48] While hardly the stuff of Know-Nothing pamphlets, Burtsell's words echoed many Protestant criticisms against celibacy and public opinion on bachelorhood in general.[49]

Richard Burtsell had spent almost half his life in Catholic institutions, yet he was hardly dogmatic. Many of his own arguments against celibacy seem more suited to the post–Vatican II era than the middle of the nineteenth century. He left Rome where priests were abundant to return to an urban metropolis that had a desperate need of priests to minister to the city's growing population of Catholic immigrants. Burtsell felt these demands keenly and wished for more priests to meet the spiritual and material needs of the city's Catholics. In his opinion, "so few choose celibacy, that few smart and good men become priests" and "any one, however vulgar or untalented becomes a priest, if a celibate." Not only did Burtsell feel that celibacy kept good candidates away from the priesthood, he also felt it interfered with his mission as a priest and kept him from ministering to his parishioners. Burtsell saw his influence on his flock deriving from a "superstitious reverence" that was rooted in his own separation from his fellow human beings. He also argued that celibacy kept a priest from exercising any true social and political influence, as he was required to "fly a woman as the very devil."[50] On the surface, Burtsell might appear sheltered, but he was savvy to the balance of political power and social capital in urban New York; he knew priests could not hope to cultivate influence and participate in organized benevolence if they were not allowed to collaborate with women. As Burtsell was an abolitionist, his frustration undoubtedly stemmed from personal experience as a priest in largely Protestant and heavily female reform circles.[51] One of his colleagues, Dr. McGlynn, disagreed and insisted celibacy was "the divine characteristic of the Catholic clergy." In response, Burtsell wrote derisively that such men would rather allow "many individuals to go to hell than deprive the church of this beauty."[52] For Burtsell, celibacy had become ornamental rather than functional.

Despite his misgivings around celibacy, Richard Burtsell remained a priest until his death in 1912. One can't help but read his words and wonder if Burtsell, a young man, had begun to regret what he had given up to gain his calling. His feelings seem to mirror in many ways the doubts of Isaac Youngs, who had been a Shaker since childhood. Burtsell, ensconced within first the seminary at Montreal and later the Collegio Urbano, had, like Youngs, come of age in a community where celibacy was both idealized and the norm. Later, in his mid-twenties and surrounded by the hustle and bustle of urban New York, it is easy to imagine Burtsell becoming aware of the possibilities, especially for family life, that had been closed to him when he chose to become a priest. Or perhaps equally, Burtsell's doubts were the musings of a pragmatist who wished to attract the best and the brightest men to the service of the church. Overworked and spread thin, Burtsell and his liberal-minded colleagues understandably desired policies that would allow the church to do the greatest good for the greatest number. For all his extraordinary activity, he confessed to feelings of melancholy, "excessive gloom," and loneliness, which he attempted to dispel with "artificial engagements" to fill his hours.[53] In his diary, Burtsell never seemed to question his vocation as a priest, but he does seem to have wished at times that being a priest did not require celibacy.

Richard Burtsell's diary is remarkable for its candor on the subject of celibacy. Most extant Catholic sources are much less forthright. One of the things that can be gleaned from these opaque sources is that becoming a nun or a priest was something done with extreme care and intention. Contrary to the picture presented in escaped nun stories of mother superiors and scheming Jesuits looking for wealthy naïve Protestant women to "seduce" into convent life, Catholic records of religious orders reveal that it was actually very difficult to become a priest or a nun in the antebellum era. While these tales of intrigue and seduction may have sold books and pamphlets, they were a far cry from what novice priests or nuns experienced as they formed their vocations. Even at a time when Catholic orders in the United States were in desperate need of men and women to serve in their missions, convents and seminaries were very discriminating in admitting new members. Rather than trying to recruit Protestant heiresses, no one in the records of the Sisters of Charity of Nazareth, Kentucky, or in the convents at Kaskaskia, Illinois, or St. Genevieve, Missouri, was taken without being a professed Roman Catholic.

Working-class women like Bridget Brophy labored for many years to acquire the funds necessary to present themselves as sisters. Becoming a nun for someone like Brophy was not happenstance, but a goal several years in the making. Father de Luynes of New York gave his wholehearted endorsement of her vocation, writing, "She would have long since availed herself of her having been received as Postulant by you and the good Sisters at Nazareth to go to her new home, but want of means detained her. She has, by her labor, earned every penny she needed for her travelling expenses and I mention the circumstances as indicative of perseverance and sincerity on her part."[54] The convents usually favored women who were young, literate, and without family ties. Father de Luynes of New York City presented several such women to the Sisters of Charity of Nazareth over the years. One Rose Devlin he described as twenty-three years of age, healthy, "small sized, nothing disagreeable in her appearance, can read and write, has no other intention but the purest motive of the love of God, in asking to be received, will make a wonderful sister." De Luynes made sure to acknowledge that "by her own industry she has $300," and could therefore pay her own way to Kentucky.[55] A rare case of an older postulant was Miss Mary Byrne. Though at thirty she would have been older than the majority of postulants, Byrne "was never married" and had not "encumbrance of parents, brothers or sisters dependent on her." Mary Byrne was indeed given a trial and became Sister Dominica only two months after she departed for Kentucky in November 1859 and remained until her death in 1908.[56]

Even in the cases of those women who seemed to meet all of the requirements of the sisterhood—youth, vitality, education, and spiritual zeal— orders took great pains to vet prospective members. When Miss Theresa Eberle of Cincinnati presented herself as a postulant to the Sisters of Charity of Nazareth in 1841, she carried with her testimonials of good character and capacity to teach. But since she was not local and did not present "a letter from her confessor or some responsible person," she could not be accepted as a postulant until such a recommendation was presented.[57] In some cases, even a wholehearted endorsement from a confessor did not guarantee that a woman was fit for the sisterhood. Rose Devlin, who Father de Luynes had thought possessed the makings of "a wonderful sister," was not admitted to the order after her two years of novitiate expired. De Luynes was sorry to hear of it but acknowledged that when a candidate showed a "deficiency of piety or in sense, or health," they should not be admitted. He himself supposed that "defects latent in the world, are evolved in a religious community."[58]

This level of scrutiny also applied to male applicants to the priesthood. The Domestic Councils Minutes kept at the St. Mary's of the Barrens Seminary in Perrysville, Missouri, reveal that prospective priests were carefully screened both before and after admission to the seminary. A want of piety, humility, or aptitude for liturgical study was enough to disqualify a candidate from the priesthood.[59] After a year of study, a seminarian was allowed to "make the good purposes," or declare his intention to enter the priesthood according to the rules of the Vincentian order. He then entered into a novitiate period in which his character would be examined to see that he possessed the necessary poverty, chastity, piety, and obedience his vocation required. A student from the seminary wishing to apply to the priesthood might be put off several times before he was finally accepted, as a way of testing the sincerity of his calling. Rather than beguiling innocents into their ranks, the seminary leadership at St. Mary's seemed to feel it was necessary that a young man gain maturity before making such an important commitment. The seminary leaders denied admission twice to an otherwise pious and "exemplary" scholar, simply because they felt he was not yet old enough.[60]

Seminary records also indicate that there was more to being a priest than just celibacy. Prospective priests needed to be bright enough to acquire the Latin and Greek necessary for the makings of solid theologians, yet not too vain about their intelligence. An otherwise enthusiastic novice who had the misfortune of being a bit dim was refused after two years "on a want of talent & energy necessary to acquire the science required for the exercise of our functions." Meanwhile, the vows of an extremely bright novice were delayed because of "having studies more at heart than piety."[61] Among the priests themselves, vanity and lack of obedience were considered serious obstacles to becoming a good priest, as much as the difficulties of keeping the vow of celibacy, although on one instance they did dismiss a novice after they found letters in his possession whose content was scandalous enough for the council to conclude "he has no vocation." This same novice was guilty of "transgressing the rules & keeping particular friendships."[62]

Guarding against "particular friendships" was a warning issued at both convents and seminaries. It has often been interpreted as a proscription against same-sex relationships.[63] Even if it was platonic, a "particular friendship," or an exclusive bond between two individuals, interfered with a sister or priest achieving the expansive Christ-like love she or he was supposed to feel toward all persons. Convents and seminaries established a number of rules and regulations to guard against both heterosexual and homosexual attachments. The rules for seminarians at St. Mary's of the Barrens in 1844 were as strict as, if not more so than, any of the Millennial Laws adhered to by the Shakers. They were designed to discourage both physical and emotional intimacy between fellow seminarians as well as priests and their male pupils. For example, students were forbidden from calling each other anything other "than their proper names" even during times of recreation. Seminarians and priests were told to exercise modesty and "diligently avoid that kind of levity and curiosity of looking about in the church or in other holy places, such as the chapel, the sacristy." This also carried over into the schoolroom, where making jokes and passing notes were expressly forbidden. A seminary student could not enter a fellow student's room without the permission of his superior. Contact with the outside world was closely monitored; seminarians were forbidden from talking to strangers during recreation, and books sent to them were subject to the superior's inspection, lest they contain material that might interfere with a student's desire to become a priest. Students should also "avoid most carefully laying their hands on one another without necessity. Neither will they lie down in an indecent posture, in summertime especially." Such behaviors were "quite contrary to holy Modesty."[64] While celibacy was the ideal, seminary rules implied that it might be disturbed as much by same-sex attachments as by opposite-sex ones. This acknowledgment of same-sex attraction is remarkable for the time period, in which such desires were rarely acknowledged to exist in even the most risqué "flash press" weeklies.[65]

Over the next twenty years, the rules for the seminarians at St. Mary's only increased in severity. One possible reason is that the intermingling of lay scholars and seminarians at the school was regarded as highly suspect by the order's motherhouse in Paris.[66] The back of the 1844 pamphlet for the seminarians included such rules as number 14, "Do not touch one another, even through jokes nor entertain yourselves alone with one another," and number 15, "Do not make yourselves familiar with women, though they be some relation to you." The need for such rules gives the sense that the vow of chastity was a fragile and temperamental thing that could easily be swayed or broken by the merest connection with another person. In this regard, these rules actually lend credence to the many anti-Catholic and escaped nun stories that made seminaries and convents out as cruel places, filled with coldhearted people. It also ran contrary to the lived experiences of many priests and sisters whose letters show a great affection for each other and for the people of their community.[67]

The "Holy Living" of Rebecca Cox Jackson

The lives of Isaac Youngs, George Jacques, and Richard Burtsell provide important insight into how men struggled with identities of sexual restraint. Yet another powerful example is the life of Shaker eldress Rebecca Cox Jackson. Jackson's life calls into question what celibacy might have meant in the context of antebellum racial ideology. Rebecca Cox Jackson was born a free woman of color outside of Philadelphia in 1795. She spent most of the early years of her life in the home of her brother, Joseph Cox, a high-ranking member of Philadelphia's Bethel African Methodist Episcopal (AME) Church. She was briefly married to a man named Samuel S. Jackson, with whom she had no children. Jackson's spiritual awakening came in 1830, when she began to experience the prophetic dreams and visions that would form the foundation of her preaching in the decades to come. She soon became an active participant in both the AME Holiness and Sanctification movements underway at the time. Jackson began holding small meetings in her home and preaching before large numbers of black men and women. Her unsanctioned preaching and especially her belief in celibacy soon brought her into conflict with the AME establishment, including her own brother. She attacked what she saw as the "carnality" of the AME church and held that the only way to achieve true sanctification was through "holy living," which included celibacy. In 1837, these radical beliefs led to her being accused of heresy by the leading lights of Philadelphia's black religious community.[68]

Rebecca Cox Jackson embraced celibacy as part of her own spiritual discipline long before she ever came into contact with Shaker theology. Though her beliefs sparked outrage among the AME Church of Philadelphia, she found a community of kindred spirits among the South Family Shakers in Watervliet, New York. She first visited them in 1836 and would return to stay in 1847 as a full member. Though the Shakers' religious beliefs forbade them from voting, military service, and other outward displays of political activism, the Shakers were sympathetic to antislavery causes and integrated black believers into their order as full and equal members alongside white ones. When Rebecca Jackson joined the Watervliet Shaker community, she was allowed to preach publicly both in Shaker meetings and in those the Shakers opened to "the world's people." The Shakers were quite taken with her preaching style and recorded how on September 10, 1848, "Sister Rebecca Jackson rose up and spoke beautiful of the good way of God."[69]

While satisfied with the Shakers' commitment to celibacy and their recognition of her spiritual gifts, Jackson eventually grew discontented with their inaction on "gathering in" more free black members like herself. Partly this was due to reluctance of the Shakers to engage in missionary activity beyond the confines of their established settlements—the last village had been founded in Sodus Bay, New York, in 1826.[70] In 1851, Jackson and her lifelong spiritual companion, Rebecca Perot, departed Watervliet of their own volition to start a Shaker ministry in Philadelphia among the free black community without the blessings of the official Shaker ministry. Though the Watervliet Shakers seem to have greatly valued Jackson and her preaching, they were governed by a strict hierarchy. They also greatly feared the intermingling of Shakers with "the world's people," another reason they may have been hesitant to sanction Jackson's Philadelphia venture. Eventually, Jackson's evangelical efforts persuaded the Shaker leadership to officially recognize the Philadelphia "out-community" in 1858. They appointed Jackson as eldress, and she went forth to spread the Shaker gospel with the sect's full endorsement. Jackson's urban Shaker community was the only one of its kind in the sect's 230-year history.[71]

The Philadelphia Shaker community that Jackson founded was predominantly composed of black women and ranged from thirteen to twenty members at any given time. Letters to and from Jackson's Philadelphia community reflected that there were a smattering of white sisters and black brothers gathered in as well in the 1870s. The community continued to endure after Jackson's death in 1871, and could boast a small gathering of members living in two houses as late as 1908. The Philadelphia sisters lived together in one house, and often worked as seamstresses or laundresses to support themselves. Though they visited and received visits from the other established Shaker communities throughout the late nineteenth century, they likely did not receive the same level of financial support as did the larger majority white Shaker settlements. Jackson was taken back to be buried at the Shakers' Central Ministry at Mount Lebanon.[72] Her burial at Mount Lebanon marked her as fully a member of the Shakers' ministerial elite yet also separated her in death from the remarkable interracial community she founded.

It is important to consider what Rebecca Jackson's celibacy meant in the context of attitudes toward black female sexuality in the antebellum era. Aside from being a spiritual discipline that helped Jackson and her followers lead (in her words) a "sanctified" life, it also challenged antebellum racial ideologies that held black women to be sexually available and sexually promiscuous—the stereotype of the "Jezebel."[73] Jackson and her band of free black women defied the expectations of both antebellum whites and fellow churchgoing blacks, such as Jackson's own minister brother. The AME church located African American women's virtue in respectable Republican motherhood, not in a religiously based sexual abstinence.[74] While many Americans, white and black, found the Shakers' celibacy unnatural and disturbing, the black Shaker sisters of Philadelphia showed that chastity was not merely the provenance of "passionless" white womanhood.[75] Male converts like Isaac Newton Youngs may have struggled to live up to Shaker ideals, but Rebecca Jackson's celibacy, by contrast, was her own independent revelation.

Eldress Rebecca Cox Jackson and her "little band" were not the only women of color attracted to celibacy and sexual restraint. The Oblate Sisters of Providence, an order of African American nuns founded in Baltimore in 1829, also provided an example of celibate black womanhood. The Oblate Sisters were "trebly scrutinized as black, Roman Catholic, and women religious," and their convent and school faced threats of violence in the 1830s, a decade that saw a spike in both antiblack and anti-Catholic violence. While the white, cloistered Carmelite nuns were more likely to provoke the ire of the Nativist press, especially in the wake of "escaped nun" Olivia Neale, the black Oblates felt extra pressure to conform to ideals of chastity and respectability.[76] The white male clergy of Baltimore, for example, instructed the Oblate Sisters to raise the neckline of their collars to extreme levels of modesty.[77]

As free black women, the Oblate Sisters of Providence faced discrimination both from without and within the Catholic Church. They were forced to accept segregated seating within their own chapel to keep the peace in slaveholding antebellum Maryland. Notably, in an interesting reversal of norms, white parishioners were confined to the back six rows instead of the front. The Oblates were members of a church that proclaimed black and white spiritually equal in the eyes of God but did not object to either slavery or racial discrimination while on earth. Some white Catholics questioned whether free black women even had the right to enter religious life. Attempts to found racially integrated orders of women religious in New Orleans had been quickly quashed by the antebellum Catholic Church. There were concerns within the Baltimore diocese that the presence of ordained black women like the Oblate Sisters of Providence profaned the habit. To become a vowed sister or nun was to demand a place of dignity and respect within the Catholic community. Catholic sisters repeatedly asserted their "ladyhood" in promotional brochures for their convent schools and presented their institutions as places of refinement and gentility.[78] In the minds of most white antebellum Americans, being a lady was incompatible with black womanhood. The black women who joined the Oblate Sisters of Providence and taught young black girls in their school asserted their right to be seen as dignified women religious, even in opposition to white members of their own faith.[79]

Free women of color also attended anti-masturbation lectures of sexual reformer Sylvester Graham and participated in the Female Moral Reform movements of the 1820s and 1830s. As with Rebecca Cox Jackson and the Oblate Sisters, the stakes for these free black women in adopting Grahamite ideas of sexual restraint were in some ways higher and the strategies different than for their white counterparts. Black female moral reformers challenged notions of white purity and replaced them with their own definition of virtue. Virtue was different than the passive "passionlessness" many white middle-class women laid claim to, as it was intentional. Free black women's participation in Grahamite circles was not about respectability politics or mere prudery, but a "strategic counterdiscourse" to a culture that denied black women, free and enslaved, sexual autonomy.[80] Organizations like the Zion Female Moral Reform Society urged their white allies not only to refuse to associate with known "seducers" and men who patronized prostitutes but also to shun enslavers. They made visible the sexual violence experienced by enslaved black women as well as the "licentiousness" perpetuated by white men against domestic servants even within northern homes.[81] Educators Amy Cassey and Sarah Mapps Douglass also taught Grahamite principles of physiology and shared anatomical knowledge with young black girls. While Douglass on the one hand condemned "solitary vice" and warned against self-pollution, she also encouraged her pupils to see their bodies as beautiful and deserving of respect in a culture that devalued them.[82]

Though Rebecca Jackson and the free women who joined the Oblate Sisters and the Zion Female Moral Reform Society were not enslaved, it would have been impossible for them to escape knowledge of the sexual degradation and violence black women experienced under slavery. The so-called pornography of pain, especially the sexual violence perpetrated against female slaves by white masters, saturated abolitionist discourse at the time.[83] In light of this, the choice of Jackson and other black women to practice celibacy and advocate for sexual abstinence should be seen as a right to sexual and bodily autonomy as well as a form of spiritual discipline.

The lived experience of the individuals discussed in this chapter show that celibacy and sexual abstinence were sexual identities to nineteenth-century Shakers, priests, nuns, and Grahamites. If the struggles of Issachar Bates, George Jacques, and Richard Burtsell are any indication, sexual restraint was not an identity that came "naturally" or easily. The individuals featured in this chapter add a face and a humanness to a sexual behavior that was demonized and thought strange by the majority of their contemporaries. Their lives also show the complexity of celibate experience in Shaker and Catholic religious orders. Celibacy and chastity also had the power to challenge degrading racial stereotypes, especially when practiced by black women.

Practicing sexual restraint may have put strict limitations on sexual expression, but it did not mean a life devoid of love or affection. Catholic sisters formed relationships with their confessors and pupils and Shaker missionaries forged affectionate lifelong bonds while still practicing celibacy. In doing so, these individuals challenged marriage and the normative biological family by cherishing platonic friendship as the purest form of love.

CHAPTER THREE

Breaking and Remaking the Family

To be against sex in the nineteenth century was not only to challenge gender norms and sexual conventions but to propose a radical reorganization of society as nineteenth-century Americans knew it. Heterosexual sex was a lynchpin of marriage, and by extension a lynchpin of the family. Those who questioned the centrality of sex to human existence directly attacked the fundamental social conventions of their time. For Shaker and Catholic celibates, distance from one's biological family could mean the creation of what gay humorist Armistead Maupin once termed "the logical family"—a community of people with shared values, or a family of choice.[1] Families of choice have long been considered a cornerstone of queer culture.[2] Prior to the legalization of same-sex marriage, these intentional families, networks of friends, lovers, and ex-lovers were celebrated by queer scholars and activists for their "extrafamilial, counter-heteronormative nature." Other religious groups of the nineteenth century, notably Methodists, also used familial language such as "sister" and "brother" with one another to create an extended family of believers in a given community. Yet, these other religions did not put the same emphasis on dismantling and reconstituting the biological family as was done in Shaker villages and Catholic religious orders.[3]

The families of choice found within Shaker villages and Catholic religious communities provide important historical antecedents for understanding families of choice. Scholars within the fields of public policy and sociology have also recently pushed to decenter the nuclear family as the primary unit of study, recognizing that a great portion of our modern lives is spent outside family units, with friends, colleagues, and neighbors.[4] Breaking away from families of origin and remaking them into families of choice were not incidental for Shakers and Catholic men and women religious, but should be understood as a deeply political act. The alternative structures of Shaker and monastic family life and the intimacies they created without sex built an explicit, nonnormative sexual culture in a society which rigidly presented heterosexual love and family as the only legitimate and legal option.[5]

The out-and-proud sexual abstinence of these groups also challenged dichotomies of public and private. Making their celibacy and sexual restraint an explicit aspect of group membership, rather than a privately held belief, allowed these subjects to create alternate institutions and family structures. Sexual behavior in the nineteenth century was relegated to part of the private sphere, and was in many cases considered too scandalous to be discussed openly, especially for those seeking membership in the middle class. This can be seen in the outcry against the lectures of Grahamite reformer Mary Gove for discussing childbirth and anatomy with married women, knowledge that editor James Gordon Bennett described as "forbidden fruit."[6] Immoral reformers talked about sex to further their points about the moral dangers of prostitution, slavery, and in the case of the escaped nun stories, Catholicism, but their sexual frankness was often equally employed as a way to detract from their arguments by their conservative opponents.[7] Historically, not all sexual behaviors get to be public and private in the same way.[8] Groups and individuals who positioned themselves as against sex made the private nature of sexuality part of their public identities. To be a member of one of these groups required a kind of "coming out" as Shaker, Grahamite, priest, or nun, and a disclosure about one's (lack of) sexual life. It was a deliberate marking of sexual identity that would not have been visible otherwise.[9]

Some of these communities openly emphasized same-sex intimacies over heterosexual ones—situating them both inside and outside nineteenth-century conventions. While Grahamite sexual reformers did not seek to destroy the family, their reforms to heterosexual marriage could be considered more insidious and radical. Reformers like Henry Clarke Wright sought to remake heterosexual marriage to give women greater control over their own bodies and bent patriarchal conventions without breaking the family unit. All of these groups that challenged sex and its role within the family sought more equitable gender relations and attacked men's presumed ownership of women's bodies. It is also important to note that within these remade and reformed families, abstinence from sex did not mean abstinence from love or affection.

Advocates of sexual restraint promoted a sexual identity based on abstinence and did so during a century that saw a dramatic increase in the number of never-married adults. During the colonial era, it was nearly unheard of for women especially not to marry. Men in some locales faced economic discrimination for remaining unwed in the form of a "bachelor tax."[10] The growth in opportunities for women to support themselves as teachers and for men to participate in the new managerial and industrial economy, far beyond parental influence, meant that in 1830 it was more possible to remain unmarried than ever before. Over the course of the century, the percentage of native-born never-married women would increase from 7.3 percent in 1830 to 10.9 percent in 1870. In New England, home to many of the Catholic convents, Shaker villages, and Grahamite societies that feature in this study, these trends were dramatically more pronounced. In 1830, 14.6 percent of Massachusetts women never married; by 1870, the number had climbed to 22.6 percent, nearly double the national average.[11] Bachelors and spinsters received some of the same ridicule heaped upon Shakers and members of Catholic orders. Bachelors were stereotyped as alternately lecherous and cold. Spinsters were believed to be hag-like and ornery, or, conversely, desperate husband-hunters. And yet, they were never victims of widespread violence or organized pamphleteering. The bachelors and spinsters who were their neighbors and relatives were tolerated and sometimes even championed by their married friends in the newspapers and advice literature of the day. There are several possible reasons for this. For one, unlike Shakers who sought to separate themselves from the "world's people," bachelors and spinsters remained within and contributed to the development of their communities. Though they had not chosen marriage themselves, they also did not actively campaign for its dissolution. Their unmarried state was not the same proclaimed chastity of the Shaker or Catholic celibates; there was always the possibility that one would eventually join the ranks of the married upon meeting the right woman or man. Though they lived outside of marriage, bachelors and old maids did not pose the same kind of threat to the family as celibate communitarians. Nor were they as loud or as well organized as Grahamites in challenging heterosexual conventions within marriage.

Breaking the Family: Shaker Communities

For a great number of those who joined celibate communities, membership often meant severing ties with one's family of origin. In the most extreme cases, it meant the destruction of marriages and the separation of parents from children. This was most commonly seen in the earliest days of Shakerism, when entire families joined the sect and were dissolved, with wives, husbands, and children being placed in separate orders and at times separate villages. Even those who remained on good terms with non-Shaker family members still endured a physical separation from their biological families. Both those who resided in Shaker villages and Catholic convents practiced similar forms of separation from the world, the most extreme being nuns in orders, such as the Ursulines or Carmelites, which practiced enclosure. In enclosed communities, nuns met their visitors in a parlor and spoke to them through a grate, which allowed them to maintain their cloister. Yet, joining these communities did not mean a complete renunciation of affection or familial ties. Rather, freed from conventional heterosexual family structures, Shaker brothers and sisters and Catholic men and women religious created and re-created new variations of the family within their communities.

The autobiography of Shaker missionary Issachar Bates gives a detailed description of how difficult one man found it to accept celibacy and loss of the biological family as part of the Shaker faith. Bates had been born in Hingham, Massachusetts to a family of spiritual searchers in 1758. As a young man, he had been a fifer at Bunker Hill and had later been among the soldiers present at West Point when Benedict Arnold betrayed the fort to the British. Bates's firsthand experiences of the brutality of war made a strong impression upon him and later attracted him to the Shakers and their pacifism. After the Revolution, Bates married Lovina Maynard and became the father of eleven children, nine of whom lived to adulthood. Even years after the war, Issachar could not shake the sense that he had done wrong: "The disease was in my heart, & that had to be broken up from the foundation."[12] What followed was a powerful conversion experience.[13] For a short three weeks, he felt at peace and swore, "I was as happy as I could wish to be, and did not feel one motion of fleshy lust all that time, & never expected to feel it any more forever."[14] Bates reacted to his newfound spiritual state by becoming a Baptist preacher but soon came to realize that the Baptist religion lacked the answers he craved. After his three weeks of spiritual bliss, "the motions of the flesh began to return, which felt more deathly to me than the bite of a rattlesnake." When he tried to discuss this with fellow Baptist elders, they had no recourse for him, and would not even let him "confess" what he described as his "secret sins."[15]

Issachar Bates toiled in this fashion for seven years, wearing the Baptist faith like a garment that didn't quite fit. He chased after salvation with every new revival, but found "they all ended in the flesh." It seemed all around him lived in sin "but the Shakers, and there I hated to go." When Bates tried to discuss the merits of Shakerism with his friends and neighbors, he was warned "to keep away from those deluded creatures." Finally, he contrived to visit the Shakers at New Lebanon, more than seventy miles away. There he confessed his secret sins at long last. When he heard the elders' testimony for the first time, it spoke to his deepest spiritual desires.[16]

But the future Shaker's trials were only half-done. Bates returned to his family and found, "My greatest trouble was at home, with those of mine old household." His fellow Baptists poured "floods" of words into his ears against the Shakers and brought every preacher within sixty miles to battle for his soul. Finally, in August of 1801, Issachar Bates made the decision to quit his family for good and take up with the Shakers at Mount Lebanon. He was resolute, yet his faith was bought at great personal cost: "Not one in my family that would unite with me, nor one in the neighborhood but what was opposed to me: even the children in the street, who used to reverence me, now mocked me. Then like Job I had to take it."[17] Issachar Bates remained a Shaker until his death in 1837. Though his family at first rejected him, eventually his wife and some of his children would be "gathered in" as well. Bates's family stayed behind at the Watervliet and New Lebanon societies while he went on a missionary errand to the Old Northwest in 1805.

It was fortunate for Issachar Bates that his wife, Lovina, was so obliging, though arguably, she may not have had much of a choice between becoming a Shaker or being left without financial support. When men like Issachar Bates left their families to become Shakers, it had very real economic consequences not only for their wives and children but for their entire community. States had very stringent divorce statutes in the eighteenth and nineteenth centuries, the rationale being that if divorce was made easily obtainable, it would destroy the family by letting individuals shirk the responsibilities of marriage. Anti-Shaker advocate Mary Dyer did not obtain her divorce until 1824, only after New Hampshire passed a targeted statute that allowed for divorce when one spouse joined a sect that disavowed the bond between husband and wife.[18] Men who decided to embrace a life of celibacy undoubtedly created hardship for their unbelieving family members and communities in an era when divorce was nearly unobtainable. And yet, their status *as* men gave them liberties that women in similar circumstances did not have.

Women who wished to become Shakers also faced trials of faith, yet with the added burden that their lives were not their own to command, subject as they were to the will of their fathers, if unmarried, or their husbands, if married under coverture. Eldress Mary Antoinette Doolittle (figure 3.1) wrote a candid memoir of her life as a Shaker and the way her family struggled with her conversion. She was born in 1810 to middling parents who ran a farm and a dairy in Lebanon Springs, New York. A mere stone's throw away from the seat of the Shakers' central ministry, the Shakers had appeared in Doolittle's peripheral vision since childhood. At the age of fourteen, with-

FIGURE 3.1 Photograph of Mary Antoinette Doolittle, Shaker Eldress, ca. 1870. Courtesy of the Winterthur Library: The Edward Deming Andrews Memorial Shaker Collection.

out her parents' permission, Doolittle attended the Shakers' Sabbath meeting in secret and confessed, "I felt drawn to the sisters by a power that I could not comprehend, and could not explain. I finally took courage and said to my parents 'I thought I could be very happy among the Shakers.'" Her parents laughed and in jest said, "Yes, you had better go."[19]

The amusement of Mary Antoinette's parents was short-lived. She took her father up on his offer and returned to spend a week at Mount Lebanon among the Shaker sisters. After four days they became alarmed: "They laughed at me, argued with me and tried to reason with me; and at last gathered up all the absurd stories they had ever heard about the Shakers, and repeated them; but all to no purpose." Realizing their daughter was in earnest, Mr. and Mrs. Doolittle panicked, going so far as to arrange for her to spend several weeks at the home of a young man "to whom in early childhood I was strongly attached." Even though her sweetheart's family treated her very kindly, Doolittle was discontented; she felt her body was in one place and her heart was in another. She was torn over whether she should "drown my feelings, and accept the advice of those who had nurtured me in infancy, provided for me in childhood and youth," or "strive to carry out my strong convictions."[20] Mary Antoinette Doolittle's friends and neighbors reacted to her conversion to Shakerism in different ways. Her uncle was supportive and told her, "Mary, if I wanted to be a Shaker, I would be one regardless of opposition." The local Presbyterian minister, however, had a much more negative reaction and preached in his sermon, "If I were his daughter, he would head me up in a hogshead sooner than let me go to the Shakers. I gave thanks that I was not a creed-bound minister's daughter."[21]

The adolescent Doolittle finally persuaded her parents that Shakerism was her heart's desire. Quite understandably, they feared she was too young to truly comprehend the gravity of her choice. The future Shaker eldress remembered her father sat her down and talked with her for two hours: "He reasoned, but did not chide" with a seriousness that "seemed as if it would break my heart." Mr. Doolittle feared his daughter was making a youthful and impulsive decision that she would later come to regret. Though he knew the Shakers to be nothing but honest in their business dealings, he found their religious beliefs strange and perhaps delusional. He told her:

> Mary, if I thought you could go, and always remain, I would not try
> to hold you. . . . Now if you go there and stay awhile, then return
> to me saying, "Father, I do not like to live with the Shakers as well as
> I thought I should, I want to come home again" I will still be your
> friend, and as long as I have a loaf of bread you shall share in it; but
> I could not feel towards you as I would have done had you accepted
> my advice.[22]

Doolittle and her father both shared a sense that Shakerism was an all-or-nothing proposition. The worst fate was not to be a Shaker, but to be a failed one, for those who tried to live the chosen life and left it were regarded as somehow tainted by the experience. Amid many tears, Mary Antoinette Doolittle chose to leave her parents' home and trotted up the hill to Mount Lebanon to begin her new life as a Shaker. "Time rolled on, and my conscience did not upbraid me for the choice I had made," she wrote. She admitted her conversion made quite a stir in her small corner of the world. Later when her family got swept up in the revivals of the Second Great Awakening, "a heavy pressure was brought to bear on me, and many severe reflections were cast upon my parents." Still, Doolittle felt that in time her parents believed granting their daughter the freedom to make her own choices "was a solace to them in their declining years, and one of the crowning joys of their earthly life."[23]

Mary Antoinette Doolittle was fortunate that her family eventually came to support her decision to become a Shaker. Many parents did, including those who indentured young children they themselves could not support.[24] At a time before social welfare services, Shaker villages took in hundreds of unwanted children, in rural areas far removed from the foundling asylums and orphan hospitals that were mostly found only in cities. Shaker indentures usually lasted until the age of eighteen or twenty-one, at which point a child would be free to go or stay as he or she pleased. Once an indenture was made, it was a legally binding document and could not be broken. It was sometimes the case that women and children—those seen as dependents—who would have liked to remain were removed against their will. For every husband who abandoned his wife to become a Shaker brother, there can be found just as many (if not more) female converts who were simply not allowed the same self-determination based on a legal system that regarded women and children as property. Wealthy Storer, a Shaker sister at Hancock, Massachusetts, recorded how in 1851, one John Irving "came while the Family were at dinner with a Sheriff and a rit of replevin [writ of replevin] Elmira Irving his daughter piloted them into the dining room where they seized Jestiner & Elizabeth Irving very contrary to their feelings they tried to resist but to little or no affect, they had to go, but their bitter cries was enough to melt the hardest heart." A writ of replevin is a legal document that obligates the return of goods or property, and the Irving sisters were their father's property. The Shakers' lawyers managed to overturn John Irving's writ of replevin, and the sheriff came again to the village a few days later with the girls who "were much pleased to get home."[25] Two years previously, Enoch Haskins came to the North Family at Enfield, Connecticut, with the intention of kidnapping his daughter Jane, whom he had previously bound. Jane Haskins quite literally had to fight her father for the right to stay a Shaker: "He clinched her but he met with so much opposition from her & others that he had to give back, but not without reluctance and heavy threats, but no one feared him in the least."[26] In short, while the Shaker family was a family of choice, male believers often had more freedom to choose than female ones.

Breaking the Family: *Connelly vs. Connelly*

Not unlike the Shakers, Catholic men and women who entered religious life similarly migrated away from their families of origin toward a family of choice. The life of Cornelia Connelly is one example of how an American Catholic woman broke from her family and remade it within convent walls. Connelly was born in Pennsylvania, married an Episcopal priest, and through unusual and extraordinary circumstances became the founder of a Catholic religious order for women, the Society of the Holy Child Jesus.[27] Late in life she told the sister who would be her biographer that her order "was founded on a breaking heart."[28] Connelly's heart broke on an October day in 1840 when her husband, Pierce, told her he wished to forsake his marriage vows to her to be ordained as a Roman Catholic priest. Though they had both contemplated the possibility of Pierce becoming a priest, there had been some small part of her that had hoped she would not be asked to make this sacrifice. Cornelia had even converted in New Orleans prior to their trip to the Vatican in 1836. Pierce could not be a priest while married to Cornelia. Though members of the church hierarchy had advised him to remain married, he would accept nothing less than full ordination. Pierce asked Cornelia, then pregnant with the couple's fourth child, to "live in constant and perfect chastity, abstaining from sexual intercourse with each other . . . more fully devoting themselves to the service of God." She begged her husband to think about this grave decision "twice over."[29] With that, the Connellys again journeyed to Rome—Pierce to study among the Jesuits and Cornelia to take up residence within the convent walls of the Society of the Sacred Heart (RSCJ) as a lay woman.

Most biographies of Cornelia Connelly have been written by sister scholars of the order she founded. While they acknowledge the challenges and trials Cornelia faced as a young wife and mother abandoned by her husband, they tend to interpret her sacrifices as part of a larger plan that led to the founding of an order that would one day minister to thousands, spread over four continents. It is hard, however, to ignore the parallels between Cornelia Connelly and Shaker women like Lovina Bates, who were faced with a difficult choice when their husbands sought to dissolve marriages in favor of a celibate religious life. Not to doubt the vocation or faith of Cornelia Connelly or Shaker ex-wives, but their status as women, especially as mothers of young children, meant that their options for financial support were limited. Divorce, in the case of the Connellys, was even less permissible than it was for the ex-wives of Shaker brothers, as the Catholic Church of the time regarded civil divorce as a sin. Though Pope Gregory did not make Pierce's ordination conditional on her joining a religious order, Cornelia still would have been required to make a vow of perpetual chastity regardless, forbidding any possibility of remarriage. In Holy Week of 1844, the Connellys signed a mutual "Deed of Separation" in which they agreed to live in perfect chastity and gave each other consent to enter into religious life. It was not a legally binding divorce, but it was enough in the eyes of the church in Rome. Throughout this process, Cornelia was promised that she would retain access to her children.[30]

Though the call to religious life had been initiated by Pierce, Cornelia soon surpassed him in her vocation. Three years among the Sacred Heart sisters, though hospitable, had convinced Cornelia that the order was not the right fit for her, or for the early American republic. The Vatican cultivated both Connellys, believing their status as high-profile Protestant converts would allow the church to make new inroads in the United States. Cornelia was encouraged to found an order of her own in England, devoted to the education of young women, with the aim of eventually expanding it back in her native country.[31] Cornelia formally made her vows in 1845, and as she contemplated the rule of her new order the words "Society of the Holy Child Jesus" echoed in her mind again and again.[32]

Pierce, by contrast, struggled with life among the Jesuits and had fallen out of love with the order within only a few months of making the Deed of Separation. Cornelia offered to release Pierce of his vow of chastity so that they both might return to married life, but he refused. One of Cornelia's biographers suspects that Pierce resented the Jesuits for their rules and high standards of obedience—he had apparently been reprimanded for visiting his former wife too often in her convent. Pierce may have also been angling for a plum position at a wealthy parish in England that would give him the prestige and influence that he craved, rather than a life of hardship and strict obedience within the Jesuits.[33]

Pierce Connelly wanted to have it both ways. He wanted the prestige of priestly influence and the emotional support of his wife. He was not willing to let his heart break as Cornelia had done. He wanted to be both priest and husband, and when neither Cornelia nor the church would allow this, he raised hell. When he was not permitted to see Cornelia at her new English convent, he took away her children and placed them in boarding schools on the Continent. Pierce did so on purpose, knowing the pain it would cause her; her confessor Bishop Wiseman wrote, "He tells Mrs. C[onnelly] he has done it deliberately, *as the only way to get hold of her through them.*"[34] Rather than let her children be used as emotional blackmail or give up her hard-won vocation, Cornelia made a tremendous sacrifice. She vowed in her journal "to have no future intercourse with my children & their Father." She would remain estranged from them for nearly the rest of her life.[35]

Not content with separating Cornelia from her biological children, Pierce turned his attention to her spiritual creation, the Society of the Holy Child Jesus. He wrote to Rome, presenting himself as the founder of "a small

Congregation which the good God had for a long time inspired me to found with the aid of a holy woman who was most docile to me."[36] When this, too, failed to get the attention he desired, Pierce journeyed once more to Cornelia's English convent and demanded to be let in. Under advisement from her spiritual director, Cornelia refused, though her former husband cried in the convent's parlor for six hours.[37]

Pierce then appealed to the courts when the church and Cornelia would no longer oblige him. He turned his coat once more—the converted ex-Protestant minister now became an anti-Catholic zealot. Pierce served Cornelia a writ on January 25, 1849 for restitution of his conjugal rights and boasted that through the courts Cornelia would "be compelled by force to return to my bed."[38] Under English law at the time, married women had very few rights, and Cornelia was considered to be her husband's property. The best Cornelia could hope for was a judicial separation which would free her from the marriage but leave her children in Pierce's hands.[39]

During the first trial, the courts sided with Pierce in the case of *Connelly vs. Connelly*, holding that the agreement of separation that the couple had signed in Rome did not legally dissolve their marriage. All throughout the trial, Pierce campaigned in the court of public opinion. He published several anti-Catholic and anti-convent tracts, as lurid as any escaped nun novel.[40] Pierce and his Protestant allies alleged that Cornelia was being held prisoner in a convent, her conversion the product of "lynx-eyed Jesuits and designing nuns" rather than something mutually agreed upon.[41] Cornelia and her allies appealed and hoped for a more favorable verdict. All the while she lived in fear of being abducted, keeping a disguise in her cell at all times.[42] Eventually, on appeal, the Privy Council reversed the court's decision in 1851, remanding the case back to the state of Pennsylvania, where Pierce and Cornelia were first married. By that time, financial support from Pierce's anti-Catholic backers had dried up and he no longer had the resources to further pursue Cornelia through the legal system. In 1856, Cornelia and her order paid Pierce's legal fees to keep him from debtor's prison, presumably for her children's sake.[43]

It was the loss of Cornelia Connelly's biological family that led to the birth of her most enduring creation, the Society of the Holy Child Jesus. Though religious life meant a renunciation on Cornelia's part of the wifehood and motherhood, her prior experiences as a wife and mother explicitly informed the order she founded. Because she was a founder of a religious community, Cornelia Connelly's expanded role allowed her an autonomy in crafting the rule and charism of her order that the average sister or nun did not exercise. The name of her community, Society of the Holy Child Jesus, was both in honor of Christ the child and an acknowledgment of the lessons her own children, now lost to her, had taught her as a mother. The Society's Rule emphasized that Christ was once a suffering child, "one whose life was ordinary, hidden within him, loving, obedient; who showed those in his company how to grow as he grew."[44] As foundress, Cornelia encouraged the women in her order to embrace a childlike spirit among themselves and the young girls who were their pupils. They ran races in the laundry and turned chores into a game. In Cornelia's eyes, her order was the Holy Child's family, and by nurturing virtues of humility, simplicity, and childlike joy "in a humble way they would become saints."[45]

It is hard not to see in the creation of this community a re-creation of the life that Cornelia Connelly had sacrificed. Cornelia, and the women who followed her, had traded their biological earthly families for a spiritual one. And yet they did not entirely reject concepts of familial love and motherhood, instead redirecting those impulses toward one another, as well as the children in their care. Rather than strictness or order, in Cornelia's philosophy, Holy Child schools were to be places of love, where "hearts were not driven, but drawn." She believed that love was a creative force and that the presence of happy children made God visible among them. The sisters took pupils on picnics, prepared plays with them, and taught them needlework in sunny summer fields. Though some of their Victorian contemporaries regarded Cornelia's pedagogy as lax, it proved to be successful.[46] There are currently over thirty Holy Child schools and colleges operating in the Americas, Europe, and Africa.[47]

Cornelia Connelly and the religious order she founded put special emphasis on children, motherhood, and family within their charism. Yet, their order was not singular in the ways that ideas of family and marriage were challenged and remade. Each individual order may have its own rule or charism, but there were many generalities that applied broadly to women religious at the time. Notably, when sisters made a vow of chastity and entered religious life, they also simultaneously became "brides of Christ." This was often ritually enacted in a literal marriage ceremony, where a prospective nun, dressed in bridal attire, made her vows and married herself to Jesus Christ and the rest of her religious community. The ceremony of Profession performed by the Sisters of Our Lady of Mercy included a psalm with lyrics based on the Song of Solomon. Its words gave the occasion a distinctly marital feel: "Who is she, that cometh up from the desert, flowing with delights, leaning upon her beloved? Thou art all fair, my beloved, meek and beautiful. Come my spouse, from Libanus; come thou shalt be crowned." The ceremony also called for the superior to affix a wedding ring on the newly professed sister's hand.[48] Nuns thought of themselves (and Catholics thought of them) as the brides of Christ. And in this state they were expected to be as faithful and as submissive to the will of the church as any nineteenth-century wife living under coverture was expected to be to her husband. Elizabeth Boyle, a Protestant convert and the first novice to be received by Elizabeth Seton's Sisters of Charity, was instructed to think of herself as a submissive bride by her male mentor and confessor, Father Moranvillé. When she informed him of her decision to become a sister against her mother's will, he told her that her mother's feelings were to be expected but "you ought not to give way. Mind that the Spouse of your soul is a jealous lover. . . . Never hesitate to give the preference to your dear Lord and to seek for your comfort in your generous submission to His blessed will. It is not you who have chosen Him but it is He who has chosen you."[49] Although Elizabeth Boyle may have shown agency and initiative to pursue her spiritual calling as a Sister of Charity, Catholic doctrine and male priests like Father Moranvillé urged her to make herself passive to Christ's will. She had not chosen Christ; he had chosen her, as surely as any jealous husband chose a young, innocent wife.

Catholic tracts made a strong case for the religious life as a valid and fulfilling option for young women, equal to the calling of wife and mother. One tract asked Protestant critics, "If they imagine that they will correspond better to their holy vocation, by living in retirement, with companions of their own sex, should such a liberty be denied them? Is there any law divine or human compelling women to marry? . . . Is there more virtue in idling away our time in visits, balls, frequenting the theater, &c &c than in living in the company of pious friends."[50] While such tracts on the one hand championed women's religious liberty and right not to marry, on the other they took an equally controlling and male-dominated view toward women who had already entered religious life. Catholic authorities insisted that a nun's vows were based on trial and experience of the novitiate years, unlike a youthful bride who married with foolish "desires and hopes." At the same time, a sister's vows were as irrevocable and binding as any nineteenth-century marriage. For the convent to have a revolving door would have constituted chaos and would be detrimental to the individual as well as her community as a whole. She would become "half a fashionable lady in her convent, as she was a formal old maid in the world, —an object of compassion and trouble to her religious sisters, and of contempt and raillery to her worldly friends."[51] These words seem to echo the warning of Mary Antoinette Doolittle's father—that those who joined the Shakers and left them seemed to be fit for neither the Shakers' utopia nor the vicissitudes of ordinary life. So, while these Catholic pamphleteers were willing to allow women freedom from marriage, they were also unwilling to allow them the right to divorce, or to live a single life unaffiliated with either a husband or a convent. In that regard, Catholics and the most conservative Protestant moralists would have probably agreed: women did not have a right to autonomy as single women.

Notably the Catholic Church did not ask priests to conceive of themselves as "married" to the church in the same fashion they did for their female counterparts. Male priests were also expected to give their lives to the church and make vows of poverty and obedience, but they were not considered "brides" of Christ, nor were they married to the Virgin Mary. Marriage in no way served as a metaphor for joining the priesthood. These men were members of an ancient religious fraternity, unbroken in lineage all the way back to Christ himself and the first male apostles. In the hierarchy of the church, priests may have been celibate, but they were still men, and endowed with an independent status female religious did not possess. They were obedient, but not submissive.

Official rules and regulations may have proscribed displays of physical affection for both sisters and priests, but lived experience was another matter. Letters between former pupils and teachers show that strong emotional bonds were formed between the sisters and the students placed in their care at these institutions, away from their biological family. One former pupil of the Sisters of Charity of Nazareth's school in Kentucky, Clara Bowen, felt moved to write to Mother Catherine Spaulding, the headmistress of the school, two years after her departure. Bowen had entered the school a Protestant at the age of twelve. At one point during her three years at school, she became extremely ill, so close to death they gave her the last rites. Believing she was on her deathbed, Bowen converted to Catholicism. Now fully recovered and back home with her parents in Cincinnati, Bowen wrote to Mother Spaulding, "Your dear face has always claimed a prominent place among the pictures memory loves to paint."[52] One incident in particular stood out in Bowen's mind: "Mother, do you recall one evening when I was just recovering, you were alone in the infirmary with me, and throwing your arms around me, you suddenly knelt down and kissed me? I have never forgotten it, for until then I thought you cold, but after that, I knew you loved me." Bowen closed her letter saying, "I follow the principle that so much love must need a little return, and therefore, I cannot help being just a bit dear to you."[53]

Mother Catherine Spaulding took the instruction of her pupils very seriously and had a reputation for befriending the most troublesome and recalcitrant girls in the school, perhaps in Christian emulation of the shepherd who wanders after the lost sheep. As head of her order, Spaulding would also have been the one charged with rebuking sisters who transgressed the rules. Perhaps we can conclude that in regard to emotional intimacy, much was left up to the discretion of a particular superior and that there were many shades of gray in terms of what was permitted. Mother Catherine Spaulding was clearly on the indulgent side of the spectrum. Her vow of celibacy and sacrifice of traditional family life did not prevent her from opening her heart to the students placed in her care. In fact, it may have been what allowed her to do so.

Remaking the Traditional Family

As the example of Mother Catherine Spaulding and her pupil Clara Bowen indicate, Catholic sisters and priests created relationships outside those of the traditional family structure that were nevertheless meaningful and important. Though bonds between confessors and sisters or superiors and sisters often seem to have replicated a parent-child relationship (as evidenced by use of titles like "Father" and "Mother"), religious also connected across gender lines as colleagues and comrades. Such bonds were indeed emotionally, if not physically, intimate, and were perhaps right to spark the antebellum Protestant imagination. Eulalia Kelly, a Sister of Loretto, was sent to found a free school in rural Jefferson County, Arkansas, in 1840. By all appearances, Sister Eulalia enjoyed religious life. But she hated to be parted from her confessor, Father Timon, whom she had met as a young nun in Missouri. She explained in a letter, "To leave the house of my Parents was, for me, a great sacrifice, but to be deprived of your council [sic] and advice, is one much greater. Maryland is long since forgotten by me, but the kindnesses I have received from you are not forgotten." Sister Eulalia concluded wistfully, "I believe I would be very happy here could I see you, say only once a year," though she knew the hundred-mile journey between frontier Arkansas and Timon's post in Perrysville made even such a small wish unlikely to come true.[54]

Shakers, too, formed intense, lifelong bonds with each other. As both Catholic priests and nuns and Shaker sisters and brothers lived in sex-segregated environments, it is not at all surprising that many of these close friendships were with members of the same sex. As nineteenth-century culture itself cultivated "a female world of love and ritual," such friendships would not have been out of place in "the world."[55] In the autobiography written toward the end of his life, Issachar Bates saved his fondest remembrances for his missionary partner, Benjamin Youngs, not his wife or children, though they were Shakers, too. Bates and Youngs logged thousands of miles together preaching in the Old Northwest. "Little Benjamin" was Bates's "beloved companion," and though he admitted he learned something from all of those with whom he traveled, Benjamin Youngs was special: "I am persuaded that there never were any David's & Jonathan's hearts more closely knit together."[56] Unlike Catholic communities that guarded against "particular friendships," Shakers seem to have held close same-sex bonds in high esteem. At the age of seventy-five, the western society Shakers arranged for this David and Jonathan pair to meet one last time before Issachar made his way back east to Mount Lebanon. "The people at Pleasant Hill were determined to see us both together once more in this world," Bates recorded, so in August 1833, the two men made a joint farewell tour of Kentucky "and visited every family, Benjamin and Issachar together once more, like former times, which was a great satisfaction." On September 6, 1833, they parted on the banks of the Ohio: "My beloved Elder Benjamin and others accompanied us across the river, and we then exchanged a few kisses, and bid, as I supposed, a last farewell."[57]

Contrary to what one might expect among Shakers, for whom opposite-sex attraction was both a taboo and a grave sin, there seems to have been an understanding that pure expressions of affection between members of the same sex were both necessary and desirable. In this regard, they again differ from the harsh regimes of the Catholic seminaries, whose rules strived to prevent any kind of intimacy, regardless of gender. When two brothers from Mount Lebanon were sent on a friendship tour of the western Shaker societies in 1834, their Ohio counterparts were glad to receive them. Yet, they were dismayed that no sisters from the east accompanied them and expressed their displeasure to the central ministry at Mount Lebanon. The "poor sisters," they reported, "looked so lonesome and wishful to be obliged to stand and see the brethren hugging, shaking hands, and even kissing without being suitably represented, so as to afford them a like opportunity was grievous to be borne, and indeed who can blame them for feeling this?" While brothers Rufus and Isaac did their best to include the sisters in conversation and were happy to visit the sisters' workshops, because of the taboos around opposite-sex interaction in Shaker communities, the Shakers themselves knew it was not the same. The Ohioans strongly urged the ministry to send both brothers and sisters next time, adding, "We have open doors and inviting hearts."[58] Shakers may have interpreted same-sex bonds of affection as evidence for the divine love they aimed to share with all members. Rather than the "fleshy" or selfish love that existed between husband and wife or parent and child, the love between spiritual partners like Issachar Bates and Benjamin Youngs appeared pure, platonic, and transcendent.

Relationships like that between Bates and Youngs exemplified the Shakers' spiritual ideal. Yet, the sect also carved out spaces for emotional and spiritual intimacy between men and women within their communities. Shaker sisters and brothers routinely came together for conversation in a ritual known as the "union meeting," which developed during the earliest years of the sect and continued throughout the nineteenth century. In 1792, Father David Meacham, successor to Ann Lee, conceived of a "Union of the Sexes," which would benefit the society both spiritually and pragmatically. As each Shaker society was ordered into families, and separate male and female orders within each family, it was necessary to find a way for the male and female Shaker leadership to come together to discuss the spiritual and temporal needs of the community. Beyond that, it was Meacham's opinion that if Shaker men and women "had not a spiritual union, they would have a carnal" one.[59] The union meeting was his solution to this problem. Every Shaker was assigned a union meeting partner of the opposite sex. They would meet regularly for conversation: sisters lined up opposite their assigned brothers no closer than "five feet apart" and took care to "not to be too profuse, contracted, or particular in their freedom & union with the opposite sex."[60] In addition to engaging in conversation on "any familiar suitable subjects," union meeting partners were expected to fulfill gender-specific tasks for one another. So the female half of a union meeting partnership mended the clothes of her assigned brother. The brother, in turn, aided his female meeting partner in any tasks she needed doing that required manual labor or craftsmanship.

The platonic affection and bonds developed between union meeting partners did not threaten the Shakers' gospel of celibacy—they enhanced it. Union meetings allowed "for mutual comfort & protection" but were also seen as "a preventative against all disorderly and unchaste union." The need for union meetings again points to the gendered and sexual assumptions that prevailed even under the Shakers' regime of celibacy. Rather than have brothers sew or sisters make furniture (a premise that would have allowed

FIGURE 3.2 Shaker sewing case, 1840s. A sewing table like this one might have been made by a Shaker brother for his female union meeting partner. The low sides were meant to allow for sisters to sit as they sewed and the small drawers were intended to hold various sewing implements. Courtesy of the Collection of Hancock Shaker Village, Pittsfield, Massachusetts (1962.157.0002). Gift of Dr. Edward Deming Andrews and Faith Andrews.

for stricter separation between the sexes), they created an allowance for heterosocial if not heterosexual partnerships. That public union meetings between men and women would discourage any kind of private "unchaste union" again affirms that Shakers did not believe their celibacy was anything "natural." On the contrary, the need for union meetings show that the Shakers assumed that the sexes were naturally drawn to one another, and would seek out illicit opportunities to interact if they were not provided them through official ministry-approved channels.[61] Union meeting partnerships were more than just a kind of "safety release valve" for heterosociality—they often created genuine loving platonic attachments. One former Shaker at Watervliet recalled how occasionally "one brother sometimes eulogized a sister whom he thought to be the best cook, and who could make the best 'Johnny cake.'"[62] The types of furniture a Shaker brother might make for his female counterpart, such as a sewing desk or chair, were specifically tailored to the task at hand (figure 3.2). These tools and objects, simple but well made, were crafted with a perfectionistic attention to detail that was an expression of the Shakers' spirituality. It has often been said that the "peculiar grace" of a Shaker chair stems from its maker's belief "that an angel might come and sit on it."[63] Gifts of pie and furniture between union meeting partners, and between Shaker sisters and brothers, should not be read as anything less than expressions of divine love in material form. The furniture, highly prized by collectors, remains, but unfortunately the pies and johnny cakes do not. Both the example of the union meetings and the loving friendship of Bates and Youngs demonstrate that embracing celibacy did not mean abandoning human affection and attachment altogether.

Reforming the Family: Henry Clarke Wright

Sylvester Graham was most well-known for his lectures against the evils of masturbation, as found in his series *Lectures to Young Men on Chastity*. But Graham's sexual prescriptions were not limited to warring against solitary vice, and broadly targeted all forms of licentious behavior. Perhaps the most controversial of all Graham's guidelines (and the one male libertines mocked most) was his idea that married couples, too, could be damaged by sexual overindulgence. Graham advised that middle-class married couples engage in intercourse no more than once per month, though husbands who worked as laborers "can safely indulge more freely than other men." While many in nineteenth-century polite society might agree that sex should be restrained among the unmarried, limiting sex within marriage was a bridge too far.[64]

By the early 1850s, Graham himself was gone, dead at the age of fifty-seven of a wasting illness that his official physician diagnosed as "exhaustion." His critics were quick to point out his system of health and longevity had produced neither for the man himself.[65] Graham may have been dead, but his ideas were not, and had instead been absorbed by the minds of many of the reform-minded northern middle class. The evolution of these ideas can be found in the career of abolitionist and marriage reformer Henry Clarke Wright. Like Graham, Wright was a minister, educated at Andover Seminary, and had made a career as a professional reformer and circuit lecturer. In 1854, Wright published his most well-known work, *Marriage and Parentage or the Reproductive Element of Man*, with the help of Bela Marsh, a former Grahamite and onetime member of Boston's American Physiological Society. Marsh had previously published *The Graham Journal of Health and Longevity*, and his bookstore on Franklin Street had been a hub of physiological reform in the 1830s. There was a clear lineage between Graham,

Marsh, and subsequent reformers like Henry Clarke Wright. Leading reform publications like *The Liberator* endorsed *Marriage and Parentage*, calling it "an appropriate bridal present" and "worthy of . . . the most attentive perusal."[66]

In *Marriage and Parentage*, Wright provided a step-by-step guide as to how and why Grahamite sexual reforms should be implemented in marriage. His vision can best be described as a kind of radical prudery—an extreme sexual restraint in the service of greater equality between the sexes. He included the familiar dire warnings about the results of married licentiousness—"Violation of Nature's laws constitute man's only source of disease to body and soul," he wrote, citing sexual overindulgence as the chief cause of "scrofula, consumption, insanity, and idiocy."[67] Like Graham before him, Wright did not shy away from using scare tactics to convince his audience, providing numerous examples of diseased and malformed children who were the product of their parents' sexual sins. He told of one couple, previously healthy before marriage, who "became diseased by abuse of their sexual nature after marriage, he in the lungs, she became deranged in the nervous system." According to Wright, sex during pregnancy (which he termed "abuse") resulted in miscarriage for the couple.[68]

Wright encouraged sexual restraint within marriage as a way of giving women greater sexual autonomy. Like many of his contemporaries, Wright upheld ideas about women's naturally "passionless" nature, believing that their desires were related to motherhood, not sensuality. Because Wright recognized that childbearing and lactation could overtake a woman's body for a year of her life, he believed therefore that wives, not husbands, should control the frequency of a couple's sexual relations. As in the animal kingdom, Wright argued, the husband should answer to "the call of the female."[69] However, where Wright stood apart from his contemporaries was in the frankness with which he addressed the issue of marital rape, in many ways decades ahead of his time. It would be over a century before feminists succeeded in making marital rape a crime—North Carolina and Oklahoma were the last states to do so in 1993.[70] Both legally and colloquially, a wife's body belonged to her husband under coverture. As an avid abolitionist and a supporter of women's rights, Wright challenged the presumed sexual privileges of husbands. Sex without a wife's enthusiastic consent was no better than "solitary indulgence," and a husband who "demands sensual gratification, against the wishes of his wife, then so is he to be so considered who commits the crime of rape."[71] Wright encouraged his fellow supporters of women's rights to see that all of their efforts for women's political and economic liberty would be in vain unless women also had sexual autonomy within their marriages. Though Wright likely would have been horrified at the idea of sex for pleasure, he did recognize that reproductive freedom was central to women's personal freedom. Wright's answer was to advocate extreme sexual restraint within marriage, rather than contraception, in order to ensure it.[72]

Henry Clarke Wright's thoughts on remaking the family were indeed in service of a literal "re-making" in which happier, better sex between married spouses produced healthier, better babies in the next generation. His thoughts prefigured the kind of eugenicist discourse that would inspire reformers like Margaret Sanger to argue that birth control was for the betterment of the race.[73] Wright believed that children inherited not only "social, political and religious maxims and institutions of their parents, but also their *bodies* and *souls*."[74] Diseased and malformed children were the direct product of diseased parentage. Men and women may be able to reproduce from acts of "passion" and "gross sensualism," according to Wright, but their offspring would be "defiled."[75] He encouraged parents to raise their own children with their future reproductive capacity in mind, knowing that any kind of sensualism or degeneracy could be passed on to future generations.[76]

Marriage and Parentage presented an idealized version of a Grahamite-inflected companionate marriage. It even included an imagined correspondence from a fictitious couple, Ernest and Nina, as they tried to implement sexual restraint within their own marriage. Wright may have gained notoriety as a marriage specialist, but his own married life was far from the ideal he presented in his works. In 1823, at the age of twenty-six, he married a wealthy widow, Elizabeth Stickney, seventeen years his senior. Stickney had already four children of her own, which provided the young minister with a ready-made family and the patriarchal authority he craved. But as she was forty-three, his new wife was unlikely to provide him with his own biological offspring, a fact that greatly dismayed Wright as time went on. Elizabeth Stickney shared his reform sensibilities, and her wealth allowed him the freedom to spend his hours poring over scripture or traveling on the lecture circuit.[77] And yet, Wright was profoundly unhappy and lonely within his marriage, which was far from the blissful love match he promoted in print. In 1843, he wrote in his diary that he and his wife had not had sexual relations in fifteen years. Wright practiced what he preached; knowing that his wife could not produce children, he forswore sexual intimacy with her.[78] Wright was still drawn to other women, and perhaps may have had out-of-wedlock liaisons with them, especially while he was away in Europe. Though his biographer Lewis Perry acknowledges that it is unclear whether these flirtations with other women were ever consummated, these relationships did have a profound effect on Wright. It was through these young women that Wright learned of wives being sexually abused during marriage by their husbands and confirmed Wright's belief that loveless marriages were no better than prostitution.[79] Henry Clarke Wright was a complicated and contradictory man, and one can see how his own experiences of a celibate marriage may have led to his promotion of a married life that was restrained sexually but not emotionally.

Those who joined these intentional communities might have broken with their families of origin, but celibacy did not require an embargo on affection or emotional intimacy. Catholic sisters formed relationships with their confessors and pupils, and Shaker missionaries forged affectionate lifelong bonds while still practicing celibacy. In doing so, these individuals exalted platonic friendship as the purest form of love in a society that privileged the biological family. Though their beliefs encouraged them to transcend, or in the case of sexual reformers, master the desires of the flesh, they were still desiring—of love, family, friendship, and community. These desires may have been invisible to a middle-class Protestant public, outsiders whose knowledge was limited to what they read in escaped nun novels or anti-Shaker pamphlets. Those who practiced sexual restraint marked themselves and in turn were seen as marked by others. Their sexual identity made them distinct. The sexual uniqueness of Shakers, Catholic sisters, and Grahamite sexual reformers would be an advantage as they entered the antebellum marketplace. The very behavior that made them targets of violence and ridicule also helped them develop a "brand name" recognition among consumers.

CHAPTER FOUR

Alterative Extracts

Sexual Restraint in the Antebellum Marketplace

Sexual restraint for Shakers, Catholic priests and nuns, and physiological reformers not only was an identity and a behavioral practice but also functioned as a brand which helped distinguish their goods and services in an ever-expanding marketplace. Shaker seeds, medicines, and bonnets as well as the convent schools and nursing care provided by Catholic women religious were enhanced by the aura of celibacy. Advocates of sexual restraint were not bystanders, but active participants in the ongoing market revolution and capitalist transition.[1] American society was dramatically transformed in the early republic from a land-based to a market-based economy. New wealth became concentrated in America's growing port cities, spurring the birth of a middle class of white-collar businessmen, lawyers, and clerks.[2] Grahamite sexual reform, based as it was upon a distinct course of diet and behavior developed by Sylvester Graham himself, was ostensibly its own "brand" from the very start, distinct from more traditional allopathic medicine and newer medical fads like Thompsonianism. The strictures of the "Graham system" and the victimization Grahamites received in the popular press allowed Grahamism to take on many of the aspects of a religious movement, complete with a charismatic leader in Sylvester Graham.

At a time when the marketplace was being flooded with manufactured goods as well as a growth of educational services, sexual restraint became the brand by which Shaker, Catholic, and Grahamite products distinguished themselves from competitors. Given the communitarian nature of Shaker villages and Catholic religious orders, their participation in emerging markets for goods and services may on the surface appear contrarian. Though all three groups articulated a worldview that was in many ways opposed to the kind of unfettered capitalism that drove the expansion of the United States in the nineteenth century, they could not afford to absent themselves from the marketplace. In some cases, it was a deliberate self-commodification, which not only provided economic gains but also made celibacy seem less threatening, and even desirable, as it became attached to products instead of people.

Shaker medicines and seeds, Catholic schools and nursing care, and Grahamite products branded sexual virtue at a time period when the commodification of vice was becoming increasingly visible in America's urban centers. This time period has often been described as the heyday of commercial sex, a time when sex work was visible and rampant in American cities like New York and Boston and sex workers themselves approached a kind of infamous celebrity in the "flash press" and sporting newspapers of the day.[3] But more than just the physical act of sex, upscale brothels in the nineteenth century also sold illusions of intimacy and romance as sex workers charmed their clientele with wine and witty conversation in lavishly appointed parlors.[4] If sexual intimacy could have an exchange value, why not sexual virtue? The commodification of licentiousness and the commodification of purity were two sides of the same coin, part of a marketplace in which commodities were becoming increasingly abstracted from their origins.[5]

In the words of one scholar, "If you do not commodify your religion yourself, someone will do it for you."[6] These three groups occupied the intersection of religion and market capitalism in ways that were often similar yet in their own way distinct. Sexual restraint endowed Shaker goods and Catholic services with a purity that American consumers sought to buy and gave Grahamites a market solution to the social reorganizations created by the triumph of that same market.

Shaker Goods in the Antebellum Marketplace

In the Edward Deming Andrews Collection at the Winterthur Museum and Library, there is a broadside advertising "Shaker Medicines, Approved by the Regular Faculty, For Sale Here" in bold, five-inch-high capitals (figure 4.1). Given that the broadside was printed in Boston and the medicines advertised were made at the Shaker community in Enfield, New Hampshire, it was most likely hung in a shop window in eastern New England.[7] The broadside told customers that these medicines were indeed prepared by a medical professional, Dr. Jerub Dyer, who in addition to being a Shaker deacon had also trained at Dartmouth Medical College only twelve miles northwest of the Enfield Shaker settlement. Five medicines were advertised—"Arnikate of Tannin"; "Shaker Family Cough Syrup"; an "Alterative Syrup," a cure-all for everything from pimples to gout and leprosy; "Vegetable Pills . . . for "Bilious Complaints"; and finally the Shakers' "Pure Fluid Extract of ENGLISH VALERIAN," a distillation of valerian

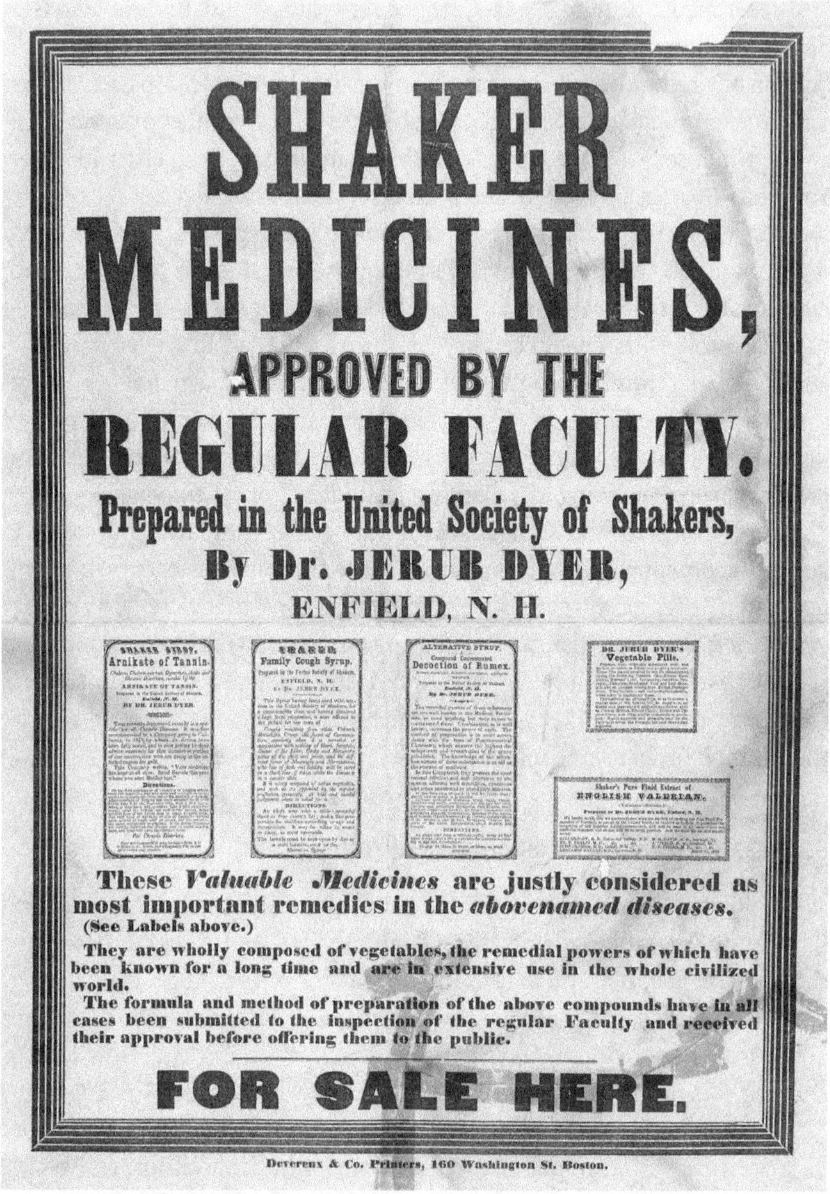

FIGURE 4.1 Broadside for Shaker medicines (ca. 1850). Courtesy of the Winterthur Library: The Edward Deming Andrews Memorial Shaker Collection.

roots, known for its sedative properties. In addition to their descriptions and claims, the extract of valerian in particular featured testimony from no fewer than seven doctors, including two on the faculty of Dartmouth Medical College. Similar advertisements from the period reveal that they were most likely the "regular faculty" that approved of these medicines.

This broadside provides a small window into the Shakers and the antebellum marketplace in which they sold their nostrums and extracts. "Shaker Medicines," being the largest and boldest printed text on this poster, reveals that the sellers of these products wanted to highlight, rather than hide, their association with the utopian sect. Medical doctors (even ones affiliated with well-known colleges) believed in the efficacy of these products enough to have their names appear in print alongside Shaker goods. And the Shakers themselves were willing to share their own medical recipes and partner with second-party dealers to market their products, despite their own desire to live separately from those they considered to be "the world's people."

More than some of their Protestant counterparts, the Shakers succeeded in merging the demands of their religion with commercial enterprise; they were renowned for their seeds, medicines, furniture, baskets, cloaks, and foodstuffs. While the realm of fiction may have portrayed Shaker women as damsels in distress or "vinegar-faced sisters," in the realm of the marketplace, there was a widespread attraction to the goods manufactured by the Shakers. This was especially true of their extracts and herbal medicines.[8] The tag of "Shaker" and its connotations of religious and sexual otherness when applied to herbs, seeds, and medicines further exoticized these products. There was a connection between the unique sexual practices of the Shakers and their ability to establish a kind of "brand name" recognition in the emerging marketplace. In the same way other patent medicines and tonics made use of racialized and Orientalist monikers to aspire to "authenticity," Shaker goods carried a sexual distinctiveness that gave their products a mystical purity. The Shakers' strange practice of celibacy allowed their products to be both wholesomely pure and tinged with the exotic at the same time.

By the time the broadside advertising Jerub Dyer's Shaker medicines was printed, the Shakers had been growing herbs for half a century.[9] While the Shakers had already pioneered a successful traffic in garden seeds in the early decades of the nineteenth century, they did not begin selling herbs in large quantities to the general public until the late 1820s and printed their first catalog of herbal medicines in 1830.[10] This initial catalog included 127 different kinds of roots and herbs, and seven extracts and twelve medicinal preparations that ran the gamut from compounds of sarsaparilla and black cohosh, to flour of slippery elm bark and rose water—all prepared by the Shakers at Mount Lebanon in New York's Hudson Valley. In 1850 the Shaker herbal repertoire had grown to include 186 herbs, twenty-seven extracts, seventy-three varieties of garden seeds, four ointments, five pulverized herbs for cooking, and one kind of snuff.[11] Shaker herbalists were revered by the French botanist Constantine Samuel Raffinesque, who proclaimed theirs the finest medical gardens in the United States. The California Gold Rush provoked a strong uptick in sales. By midcentury the Shakers regularly shipped herbs and medicines to San Francisco, Vancouver, Australia, and London, as well as locations throughout the American South and Midwest.[12]

Advertisements for early Shaker herbs and medicines capitalized on the sect's difference and uniqueness to sell Shaker products. Shaker herbs and medicines were available for sale directly at Shaker villages scattered throughout the Northeast and upper Midwest or by catalog order beginning in 1830. Mount Lebanon in New York's Hudson Valley, Canterbury and Enfield in New Hampshire, Harvard, Massachusetts (close to Boston), and Union Village, Ohio (outside of Cincinnati), specialized in producing botanical medicines. These particular villages took advantage of their proximity to key transportation networks (steamboat lines, post roads, and eventually railroads) and growing urban centers to sell their products. Shakers also relied on relationships with second-party dealers and consignment sales. Shopkeepers, apothecaries, and grocers bought Shaker goods at a wholesale price in bulk quantities and then resold them at retail price in their own establishments.[13] In the case of consignment sales, Shakers left a certain amount of product with a shop owner and returned at the end of the season to collect a percentage of the sale and any unsold merchandise. Consignment sales were not unique to the Shakers and were employed to sell everything from books to tobacco in the eighteenth and nineteenth centuries.[14] They were especially useful in those cases where goods were sold far from where they were produced. Since the market opportunities near rural Shaker villages were limited and the Shakers themselves had no desire to relocate to be closer to urban markets, consignment and second-party sales provided ideal solutions. The Shakers had first pioneered this business model with their garden seeds; Shaker peddlers developed distinct routes—down the Hudson to Poughkeepsie from Mt. Lebanon, or up north as far as Pawtet, Vermont. In a few days' journey, a Shaker peddler could do as much as $300 in sales, reaching roughly sixty individual customers.[15]

It was these second-party shopkeepers who were primarily responsible for marketing Shaker products to the general public. The earliest advertisements for Shaker herbs and medicines were placed in newspapers "close to home" as it were, and offered little in the way of grandiose claims associated with most patent medicines; they were honest and to the point, much like the Shakers themselves. One Dr. John Wadsworth, apothecary of Providence, Rhode Island, offered "A General Assortment of Drugs, Medicines, Shakers' Herbs, Roots and Extracts, Dye Stuffs, Spices, Perfumes . . . constantly on hand and for sale, for cash only, at the sign of the Great Mortar." Another salesman, Elijah Porter of Salem, New Hampshire, promised "Pressed Herbs, Extracts, &c *Prepared by the United Society (called Shakers).* The Herbs, Flowers, Bark, and Roots are set in papers of one pound each, and of the first quality." An 1846 ad in the New Orleans paper, *The Jeffersonian,* illustrates perfectly how broadly and how deeply Shaker medicines had permeated the market; the words "Flowers, Herbs and Roots from the Shakers, for sale at Shakers' prices," do not offer much description, but the laconic nature of the ad is telling. In many of these advertisements, the tag "Shaker" alone was enough of a selling point and needed no further explanation. It is significant that Wadsworth the Providence apothecary, though he offered a variety of medicines for sale, only mentioned "Shakers' Herbs" by name. The appellation "Shaker" was used in these advertisements in a way similar to a brand, or a region of origin. As dry goods dealers would advertise "St. Croix Rum" or "best Cognac Brandy," so did they advertise Shaker medicinals and garden seeds. The development of post roads and print catalogues in the beginning of the nineteenth century made it easier to sell products farther away from their place of production. Under these circumstances, brand identity became more important than ever before. The Shakers' celibacy was their brand.[16]

Limitations on printing technologies during the antebellum era meant that advertisers of Shaker medicines were forced to rely on words rather than images to attract a customer's attention.[17] Marketers of Shaker products instead used words to paint a picture. Significantly, these shopkeepers assumed that the Shaker origin of medicines (and other products) would help and not hurt sales. As with the aforementioned broadside, often "Shaker" is the most prominent word on the advertisement, printed in the largest type or in all caps, and would have been the most visible at a distance to a casual passerby. Marketers also employed a subtle, almost subtextual reference to the Shakers' unusual celibacy in these advertisements. Shaker medicines were often described as "pure" and indeed one of their products was named "Shakers' Pure Fluid Extract of English Valerian." One doctor made sure to call the Valerian extract a *pure article* and another claimed it was in "a *purer*, more simple and concentrated state, than *any other* preparation of this root with which I am acquainted." Likewise, Shaker medicines such as their compound of sarsaparilla and alterative extract promised to alleviate "impurities of the blood." At the Sixth Annual Exposition of the Massachusetts Charitable Mechanics Association, Dr. Charles Jackson awarded the Shakers a medal for their sarsaparilla syrup and said, "The Committee have entire confidence in the fidelity of the Shakers in the preparation of this mixture."[18]

To a modern observer, raised in an era where the FDA (ideally) requires strict laboratory conditions and clinical trials before a drug can be approved for sale, the association of "pure" with "medicine" seems obvious and expected. It is surprising to note that of all advertisements in the Downs Collection of Advertising Ephemera at the Winterthur Museum and Library, no other patent medicines were marketed in this same way. Antebellum patent medicines in these advertisements were described as "safe" or "delightful." They promised to "regulate," or in the case of "Kickapoo Indian Sagwa," give one's system an eponymous "kick," but they did not claim to be pure or faithful. While shopkeepers may have used the "Shaker" tag to catch a buyer's eye, much as others used Indians, "Hindoos," or "Egyptians" (figures 4.2 and 4.3), Shaker medicines employed a marketing that was unique to them and their distinctive celibate practices.[19] Shakers had many qualities. They were known for their simplicity as well as for their strange religious fanaticism and ecstatic worship. But advertisers never used the words "simple," "divine," or "exciting" to market Shaker goods. It was their "purity"—and by extension their celibacy—that was their most distinguishing characteristic for consumers.

The word "pure" did make an appearance in one very telling category of advertisements: so-called blood purifiers promised to cleanse the system of venereal diseases. While often just advertised as a "blood purifier" or "sarsaparilla tonic," an advertisement in the "flash press" sporting paper *Life in Boston* for "Dr. Gay's Blood Purifier" shows that advertisements for "blood purifier" may have been code for the treatment of syphilis and other venereal diseases. "Dr. Gay's," an obvious pseudonym, using the slang term for sex worker ("gay girls"), guaranteed to remove syphilis entirely from the system, "making the blood perfectly pure."[20] Outside of the *demimonde*, blood purifiers, such as "Goodwin India Vegetable and Sarsaparilla Bitters" and "Ayer's Sarsaparilla," promised to "Purify the blood!" without explicit

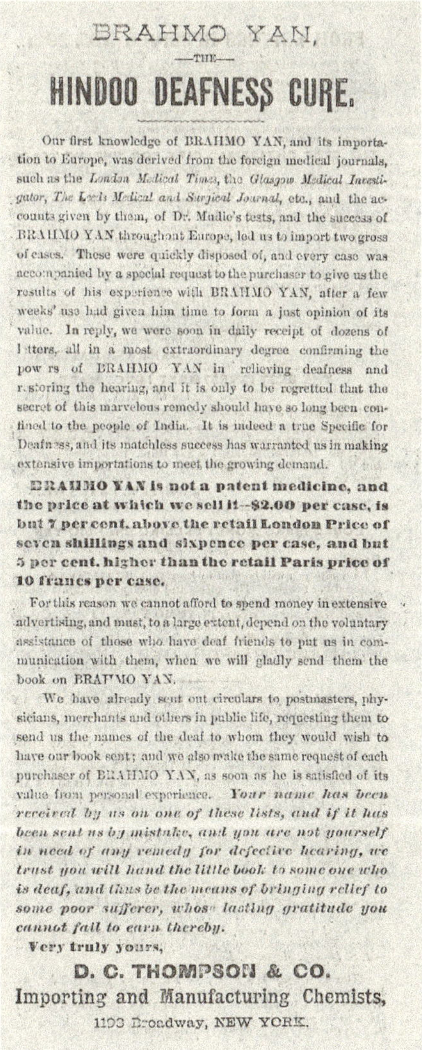

FIGURE 4.2 AND FIGURE 4.3
Mid-nineteenth-century medical advertisements. Courtesy of the Winterthur Library: Joseph Downs Collection of Manuscripts and Printed Ephemera.

reference to venereal disease.[21] Aside from the extract of valerian, the Shakers were most regarded for Canterbury Shaker Thomas Corbett's "Sarsaparilla Syrup." It, too, promised to purify the blood, and was among the Shaker products awarded a medal by the Boston Charitable Mechanics Association in 1847; the committee pronounced it "the best preparation of sarsaparilla syrup yet known." Sarsaparilla was a popular ingredient in many nineteenth-century patent medicines, and indeed, Corbett's syrup promised to treat everything from syphilis to indigestion, asthma, bad skin, diarrhea, and consumption. But it is possible that those most in need of blood purification, especially as the result of a sexually transmitted disease, may have regarded the Shakers' sarsaparilla syrup as being infused with an extra purifying punch.[22] The sarsaparilla syrup was also marketed as an "Alterative Extract." Consumers who bought the medicine presumably believed it had the power to "alter" them physically, and perhaps even morally. The Shakers also sold and processed large quantities of tansy and pennyroyal in their phenomenally successful herb business. Their celibate brand may have extended to these known botanical abortifacients.[23]

If, as some have suggested, patent medicine advertisers sought to "modernize magic," offering the promise of metamorphosis and physical and spiritual rejuvenation, the Shakers seem to have engaged in a bit of reverse psychology.[24] One would imagine that as a religious sect, often couched in terms of the mysterious and secretive, the Shakers would have played up their inherently mystical angle. Instead, they tacked in the opposite direction and sought the endorsements of scientists and medical professionals. They did so at a time when medicine itself was consolidating through professionalization—the American Medical Association was founded in 1847.[25] Though the Shakers adhered to simplicity and eschewed ornamentation, they were not the Amish, and they did not yearn to turn back the clock of innovation. The Shakers welcomed new technologies and labor-saving devices and were among the first to add an outer layer of coating to pills, increasing their shelf-life and potency. The herb house at Mount Lebanon was state of the art and was described in lavish detail in a midcentury piece for *Harper's Magazine*.[26] Rather than trying to keep their formulas a closely guarded secret, they sent their recipes off to doctors and chemists at Dartmouth and Harvard, inviting them to check their work and soliciting advice on how to improve their formulas. In return, these doctors felt confident enough to testify, "It is no *mystic* compound."[27]

Perhaps the Shakers and their business partners shrewdly detected that the Shaker origin was mystical enough and did not require further flash.

But more likely, it was the Shakers' own spiritual values of simplicity, honesty, and perfection at work. To wrap a product in smoke and mirrors, gilt and adornment, was not only poor marketing—it was heresy. The Shaker valuation of simplicity can be seen in the labels used on the packets of medicine bottles.[28] These labels for sage and marjoram show the Shaker aesthetic in labeling and packaging—they are clear and straightforward, with little ornamentation (figure 4.4). Block-printed Shaker labels of black text on colored paper are still considered iconic for their minimalism.[29] And though the Shaker name is not quite as prominent as in other forms of advertisement, it is not hidden, either.

The Shakers' celibacy endowed their products with a distinctive aura of purity that was in its own way sexually exotic in the way that "Kickapoo Indian Sagwa" and "Egyptian Regulator Tea" were racially and ethnically exotic. Shaker marketers also cultivated their products' American origins, allowing their medicines and extracts to be both foreign and familiar at the same time. Prior to the American Revolution, American colonists imported the majority of their medical compounds, pills, and powders from Europe. The boycott of British goods accelerated a trend—instead of importing British patent medicines, apothecaries mixed British formulas in the colonies, refilling and using British bottles and labels with American ingredients. Post-revolution, British medicine sales were never as strong as before. Nationalism spurred the creation of "made-in-America" remedies and an interest in using American-grown botanicals and native plants.[30] The Shakers were well positioned to take advantage of this sentiment. The first Shaker herb catalogue printed contained this verse on its cover: "Why send to Europe's bloody shores / For plants which grow by our own doors?"[31] At a moment when fears of foreign contagion were running high, provoked by the recent outbreak of cholera in New York City in the 1830s, the Shakers were able to make their products look American, wholesome, and trustworthy.

Name brand recognition extended to other Shaker products beyond medicines and seeds. Despite the persistent belief that Shaker celibacy masculinized women, turning them into sickly, dried-up shrews, during the 1850s, Shaker cloaks and bonnets were heralded as the height of fashion for young women. The distinctive Shaker-style bonnets were made of straw or palm leaf and often adorned or covered with silk ribbon. They fit closely toward the back of the head but had a deep brim that circled the face. Shaker sisters wore the bonnets themselves over their own modest muslin caps. They were ideally suited to frame the "worldly" hairstyles of the 1830s and 1850s, in which elaborate arrangements of braids and ringlets framed the face. In

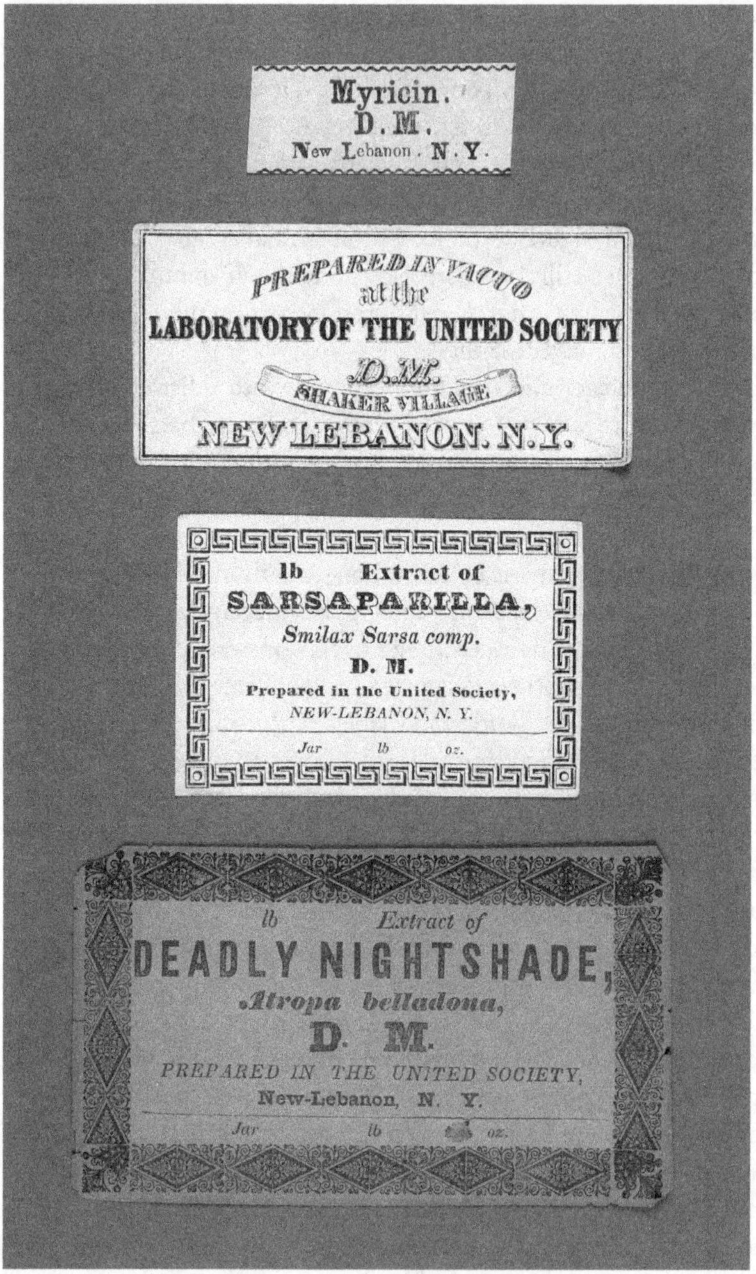

FIGURE 4.4 Shaker labels. Courtesy of the Winterthur Library: The Edward Deming Andrews Memorial Shaker Collection.

turn, Shaker cloaks, usually made of a vibrant cardinal red wool, had wide hoods which could easily be worn over the bonnet's large brim. These "Dorothy" cloaks came in and out of fashion throughout the nineteenth and early twentieth centuries; they soared to popularity again in the 1890s after First Lady Frances Cleveland commissioned a dove gray one for the Inaugural Ball.[32] Ladies' magazines of the antebellum era, such as *Godey's*, informed readers in the fall of 1853, "The Shaker bonnets came into fashion again the past summer for school children."[33] In 1858, *Godey's* suggested that with traveling season upon them, "Shaker straws, also for the country, offer the most complete protection to the complexion." Shaker bonnets and cloaks were so ubiquitous and popular, they were often referred to as simply "Shakers," as in the short story "Mrs. Vining's Help" featured in *Godey's*. In the story, the heroine "crowned her straight figure with a long, deep caped Shaker" at the end of her long day of housework.[34]

While these cloaks and bonnets were considered fashionable (and the Shakers themselves anything but), it is notable that they were most often worn by young girls. These fashions were simple and modest and perhaps, like the medicines, carried an aura of chastity around them—all attractive and admirable qualities for an unmarried young woman to possess. Among Shaker women themselves, the thin muslin caps were emblems of an adult Shaker woman's modesty and virtue, and it was considered almost obscene to go about without one.[35] Shaker men also had distinctive dress and fashion. They were known especially for their low, broad-brimmed hats and for an unusual haircut, short in the front and sides, long in the back, a kind of nineteenth-century mullet. Male Shaker fashions never caught on among the "world's people," and indeed a majority of their contemporaries found the Shaker mullet very unattractive. The appeal of chaste and prim Shaker fashions for women was indicative of the ways female "passionlessness" had become thoroughly normalized by the 1850s. Conversely, fashions for men that conveyed chastity were unmarketable.

While the tag "Shaker" was used to sell and market medicines, seeds, and other products, the reverse was also true. The Shaker brand sold herbs and extracts, but these products also helped sell the Shaker religion to a public that was at best curious, and at worst prejudiced and hostile. Evidence of using medicine to familiarize people with Shakerism survives in a printed booklet, *The Shaker Manual*, which contained testimonies about the efficacy of Shaker medicines paired with articles explaining Shaker religious beliefs. *The Shaker Manual* was intended to be kept on hand by druggists and apothecaries that carried the products advertised, the award-winning Corbett's

Shaker Compound of Sarsaparilla and Brown's Shaker Fluid Valerian Extract.[36] The odd-numbered pages contained the usual claims of the sarsaparilla compound's ability to cure a variety of ills as well as testimony from a Mexican War veteran, a Lowell mill girl, a bourgeois housewife, and a sexton from Boston's Mariner's Church, in addition to that of doctors and apothecaries. The other half of the booklet taught the public about Shaker customs, gave the location of all the different Shaker communities from Maine to Indiana, and told the history of the sect's founding under Ann Lee. Most importantly, the pamphlet detailed the sect's "moral principles," the first of which was "A life of innocence, strict temperance, and *virgin purity*, according to the example of Jesus Christ . . . entire abstinence from all sensual and carnal gratifications."[37] The Shakers deliberately took advantage of the public's enthusiasm for their products to evangelize their customers.

Given the decline in numbers in Shaker converts following the Civil War, it would seem that the Shakers were less successful in marketing their religion than they were in selling their medicines and bonnets.[38] Scholars of Jacksonian and antebellum America have thoroughly examined the use of racial difference to sell products, like food and medicine, as well as performance in the case of blackface minstrelsy or "Playing Indian"–type melodramas.[39] Though the majority of Shakers were overwhelmingly white, the consumption of their consumer goods reveals an enthusiasm for their sexual otherness. Shopkeepers were willing to sell, doctors were willing to prescribe, and most importantly, consumers were willing to buy these medicines, concocted by a religious sect whose spiritual beliefs and sexual practices ranged far from the norm. Antebellum patent medicines promised excitement, delight, and instantaneous renewal in a bottle. Should we be surprised that sexual purity was also something to distill, extract, and consume?

"Catholic Envy" and the Caring Professions

While the Shakers' sexual distinctiveness led to a branding of their products, antebellum Catholic women religious attained distinction by excelling in the service professions of education and nursing. Convent schools, charity hospitals, and orphan asylums affiliated with Catholic orders became synonymous with quality education, nursing, and social services in an era before formal state regulation of these fields. While the sexual restraint of the women and men providing instruction was certainly not the only factor in the success of these various institutions, it did play a role in how these institutions were marketed to a non-Catholic public. The effect of celibacy on traditional gender roles, especially the way it caused celibate women to be perceived as more masculine, prepared Catholic sisters to take on roles outside the home that required bravery and stoicism. Celibacy also defined Catholic sisters as "off-limits" to men in a way their Protestant counterparts were not. And yet their status not only as women but as "ladies" positioned nuns and sisters as holders of traditionally feminine virtues like compassion and tenderness, making them appear ideally suited to nursing or charity work.

Convent boarding schools for girls run by women religious gained a reputation for elite, exclusive, and rigorous female education in the early nineteenth century. The most prominent were the Ursuline-run schools in Charlestown (1827) and New Orleans (1727), the Convent of the Visitation in Georgetown (1799), St. Joseph's Academy in Emmitsburg, Maryland (1809), and the Convent of the Sacred Heart in Manhattan (1848). Ostensibly for the education of Catholic girls, such institutions often catered more to the daughters of wealthy Protestants. For while they often took on charity pupils, these schools were very elite and expensive. Convent schools emerged as places where upper-middle-class girls were schooled in the traditional ladies' "accomplishments" as well as the liberal arts, amid picturesque and peaceful surroundings, removed from the hustle and bustle of the nation's growing cities. Unlike some traditional ladies' academies that often employed male dancing masters, language instructors, or headmasters, the leadership and instruction at the convent schools were entirely female.[40]

Sarah Josepha Hale wrote of the fondness for sending daughters to convent schools as "a new thing" for Protestant parents. She supposed "the romance connected with the idea of living in a convent with real nuns who had taken the vows and wore black veils, and kept themselves apart from the world" enticed both pupils and parents.[41] The brochures and advertisements for these convent schools emphasized the grandeur of these environments and exemplified the antebellum phenomenon art historian John Davis has termed "Catholic envy." American Protestants of the early nineteenth century were simultaneously repulsed by and drawn to the ritual culture of Catholicism, which they experienced as "religious tourists." While they often feared Catholic churches and convents in their midst, during this time Protestant church design also began to incorporate Catholic elements. Gothic steeples, stained glass, even Easter flowers were used as markers of wealth by flush Protestant congregations.[42] Protestants consumed Catholicism vicariously by visiting churches and convents, by viewing paintings of Catholic settings, and by reading the harrowing escaped nun stories of Maria Monk and her ilk. Antebellum Protestants were drawn to Catholicism's emphasis on achieving spirituality through the body versus Protestantism's emphasis on "the word" alone. In Catholic ritual, the worshipper experiences religion through the five senses; the harmony of vespers, the visual iconography of statues and stained glass, the smell of incense, the taste of wine and communion wafer, and even the physicality of kneeling during the mass. A convent education provided a more prolonged exposure to the material culture of Catholicism, and yet, like a visit to a cathedral or monastery, it was intended by Protestant parents to be a liminal experience for their daughters with a clear endpoint.[43] It may seem strange to reconcile Catholic envy with the sensationalist anti-Catholic literature of this period, but they were actually intertwined. Catholic envy was precisely what gave the escaped nun novels their teeth. Fears about women being "seduced" into convents would not be enough to provoke a riot or sustain a publishing phenomenon like *Awful Disclosures* if Protestants did not believe on some level that there was something dangerously seductive about Catholicism.

Given Protestant tendencies toward Catholic envy, it is no coincidence that brochures for Catholic academies took pains to emphasize the aesthetic beauty of their surroundings. Brochures issued to promote these institutions included engravings featuring the school buildings and grounds, remarkable at a time when commissioning an engraving was expensive. The St. Joseph's School's prospectus proclaimed, "The Institution is pleasantly situated in a healthy and picturesque part of Frederick County, Maryland," with "convenient and spacious buildings." The Georgetown Academy of the Visitation announced its "view of the Potomac, and a distant perspective of Washington city." The Sisters of Notre Dame went so far as to tout their Young Ladies' Literary Institute and Boarding School outside of Cincinnati as "spacious and airy . . . a delightful resort." Protestant and secular schools, such as the Oakland Female Institute of Norristown, Pennsylvania, often marketed themselves similarly; like the St. Joseph's and Ursuline brochure, there is an engraving of the school and grounds. Such descriptions which emphasized the beauty and seclusion of these institutions, as well as the purity and splendor of the natural environment, appealed to the type of antebellum-era fascination with the romantic vistas and panoramic views of the paintings of Thomas Cole and Frederick Church.[44]

Most non-Catholic schools, especially those located within the limits of a city, did not attempt to brag whatsoever about the schools' locations. If anything, they often sought to assuage the fears parents of day-scholars might have felt about exposing their daughters to the temptations and dangers of city life. The Young Ladies' High School of Boston assured parents that the students "are not allowed to go into the street, unless by permission of their parents." Miss D. T. Killbourn's Academy in Baltimore promised that boarders "are always accompanied by one of the Teachers," never leave without permission, and "hold no intercourse with domestics."[45] On the one hand, the placement of Catholic female seminaries and convents reflected Catholic religious aesthetics that emphasized beautiful surroundings and impressive buildings as a way of experiencing spirituality. But in the Catholic brochures, one does not find the same over-assurances of safety or emphasis on rules as in their Protestant counterparts. They did not need to advertise that their female charges would be in a pure, safe, chaste environment, because as the schools were attached to convents, those qualities were assumed to be inherent.

Parents of prospective students, even Protestant ones, may have perceived a convent school education as more elite than similar non-Catholic female seminaries of the day. The accomplishments at the convent schools were more refined, the tuition higher, and the quality of the pupils from just an echelon higher on the social strata. During the early republic there was an unprecedented growth in the number of women attending academies and female seminaries; at least 158 such institutions opened between 1830 and 1860 alone. To have the income available to send a daughter away for secondary education was already a mark of middle-class status.[46] At convent schools like St. Joseph's and Mount Benedict, female scholars learned reading, writing, and arithmetic, as well as history, rhetoric, and science in the upper grades. Parents could also pay extra for lessons in foreign languages, music, and art. Mount Benedict offered classes on such exotic subjects as "Japanning" (lacquer painting), "painting on Velvet, Satin and Wood; and the beautiful style of Mezzotino and Poonah Painting."[47] Because of the presence of many native francophone speakers in the sisterhoods, St. Joseph's offered French lessons free of charge, and the School of the Visitation allowed the most advanced pupils to complete their course of study entirely in French, adding an extra European cache to these institutions. By contrast, the most strictly Protestant schools, such as the Mount Vernon Female School, a rival institution to the Ursuline Academy at Mount Benedict, did not offer anything in the way of traditional female "accomplishments." Their all-male leadership believed such learning frivolous, preferring to give "the best *discipline* to the thinking powers, and secure the most *solid* and *useful* attainments."[48]

Adding the "accomplishments" to a daughter's education did not come cheaply. When music, painting, and foreign languages were tacked onto the cost of room and board (around $150 per year), a family could end up spending as much as $300 on a daughter's education. This was a very hefty sum at a time in which the average laborer earned no more than a dollar a day. To put this in perspective, tuition, room, and board at male colleges such as Dartmouth, Williams, Amherst, and Wesleyan ranged from $100 to $135 per year during the early nineteenth century.[49]

Such fees did not include all of the extra clothing, bedding, and tableware that female scholars were expected to bring in order to be a part of the institution.[50] Parents who wished for the school to provide their daughters with these necessary items were required to pay the school $50 in advance for clothing alone. There were not many families who could afford to outfit a daughter with a Swiss muslin white dress to only be worn once a year—"on Distribution Day," a commencement ceremony that honored the graduates and awarded prizes to the best pupils. Boarders also were required to furnish two silver spoons, one silver fork, one ivory-handled knife, a napkin ring and six napkins, a glass or silver goblet, a soap dish, a toothbrush tray, and a cup for the wash stand.[51] The high material cost and the specificity of the dress and accoutrements necessary to attend an elite institution like St. Joseph's point to an aesthetic valuation and type of gate-keeping that went far beyond learning the three Rs.[52] "Escaped" Ursuline postulant Rebecca Reed, author of notorious best-seller *Six Months in a Convent*, was likely attracted to the Ursulines because their education would have allowed her to transform her class status from that of a servant to a "genteel" well-bred lady. Studying needlework and French among the Ursulines would have elevated her from the cooking and cleaning that characterized the life of a working-class woman.[53] Like postulant Rebecca Reed, well-to-do parents who sent their daughters to convent schools believed such an institution would give them an added aura of refinement and gentility.

In addition to teaching the liberal arts as well as "accomplishments," female academies and seminaries were also expected to impart "moral culture" to students. Having their daughters schooled by nuns may have been attractive to parents because they provided positive examples of purity and virtue at a time when chastity was prized for young women. Many middle-class nineteenth-century women were caught in an unjust sexual double standard. Because the social and economic consequences for unmarried pregnancy were so much steeper for women than men, many women practiced "passionlessness" to their own advantage, to ward off would-be seducers and entice men into proposing marriage.[54] While permanent lifelong celibacy for women was considered unnatural, premarital chastity for middle-class women was a universal requirement—one could not achieve a respectable marriage without it. Sarah Josepha Hale remarked in her own magazine, "The nuns teach by example the gentle and graceful movement and the soft low tone of voice, and in these particulars might be advantageously recommended as models to all instructresses."[55] Nuns and their chaste behaviors were marketed to the public as surely as the facilities and curricula of convent schools. In this sense, education at a convent school may have functioned in the same way as a Shaker cloak or bonnet, metaphorically wrapping up a young woman in chastity and virtue. Emulation, the practice of learning by imitating the mastery of others, played a substantial part in nineteenth-century pedagogy. Who better to teach young girls modesty and virtue than an order of women sworn to lifelong celibacy?[56]

Although the chaste example of nuns may have attracted parents and pupils to these schools, their ambiguous status as women who were neither wives nor mothers may have caused some trepidation. The teaching sisters were very aware that many outside the Catholic community perceived them as cold or even cruel because of their celibacy. Convent schools took pains to explicitly state that the sisters who ran the school were "Ladies." At Mount Benedict in Charlestown, the Ursulines promised, "The Ladies of the establishment provide the students with healthy and wholesome meals" and watch over their charges' morals "with all the solicitude of maternal tenderness." Likewise, at St. Joseph's the Sisters of Charity took their role of in loco parentis very seriously and stated pupils would receive the same "physical care which they would receive under the parental roof."[57]

The unique celibate identity of Catholic nuns also made them ideal candidates for the field of professional nursing. While celibacy, one the one hand, often masculinized nuns in public perception, this gender deviance was a positive quality when it came to performing nursing work in dangerous locations. Throughout the 1830s, poems and articles appeared in both Catholic and secular newspapers lauding the work of the Sisters of Charity during the recent cholera epidemics in New York and Philadelphia.[58] "The Sister of Charity," for example, depicted a nun treating a dying man, being with him in his last moments as he dies of disease. The poem described her as being angelic but also brave, with "fair slight hands" and "large, dark and trembling" eyes. The author sets the unnamed sister's courage as above that of a man: "Men veiled their eyes and fled / Yet *she* stood there / Still sweetly calm and unappalled."[59] Another poem specifically praised the nursing work of the Sisters of Charity as more selfless and heroic than that of contemporary male Protestant missionaries. Protestant preachers founded foreign missions out of a "hollow zeal that loves to climb," neglecting the sick and dying on their own shores. The Sisters of Charity, by contrast, ministered to America's outcasts at great personal cost.[60]

While it is understandable that the audience of a Catholic publication such as the *Catholic Herald* would enjoy reading these positive portrayals of the Sisters, it is remarkable that most of these verses derive from Protestant sources. The cholera epidemics of the 1830s were so destructive and severe, and the lack of institutional welfare so profound, that the Sisters of Charity were able, quite justifiably, to gain the admiration and respect of non-Catholics.[61] In these circumstances the masculine heroism of the sisters was not deviant, but welcome. Their spiritual zeal and willingness to risk illness and death in service to the victims of the epidemics set them apart from married Protestant women doing the work of benevolence. Their celibacy and their renunciation of husbands and children allowed them to venture into these dangerous situations and the public, Protestant and Catholic, recognized this. That sisters died ministering to cholera victims in the nineteenth century is not romantic hyperbole. The letters of Mary Ignatia Greene, an Emmitsburg Sister of Charity, reported four of her fellow sisters had died in just one year and that there had been over 900 deaths from cholera in St. Louis in 1849. Mary Ignatia herself died of cholera in Panama en route to a mission in San Francisco in 1852.[62]

Catholic envy and gender deviance at work in the convent schools and hospitals may have seemed an attractive proposition for some pupils and parents, but to many of the most outspoken anti-Catholic agitators, they were a risky proposition. A cornerstone of many an escaped nun novel (including the best sellers by Rebecca Reed and Josephine Bunkley) was the naïve Protestant girl who entered a convent school only to be "seduced" into becoming a nun. Escaped nun stories traded upon Protestant fears that the trappings of Catholicism—the smells and bells, strange rituals, and bizarre devotions—would be too much for an innocent young girl to resist. Furthermore, in such stories, seemingly pious sisters and kindly priests often turned out to be cruel abusers in disguise. The nameless heroine of aptly named *The Escaped Nun* described it thusly: "After witnessing the imposing ceremonies, the display of ornaments, and all the gorgeous paraphernalia of worship peculiar to the Romish Church, I felt as though I was about to be drawn within the mysterious but attractive pale of that church . . . a fluttering and terrified, but irresistibly attracted bird."[63] Such stories portrayed

Catholicism as something to be feared, preying upon the most vulnerable of society, and young women as its hapless victims. Escaped nun stories were so frightening and believable precisely because Catholic envy was very powerful and very real.

Maine schoolgirl Rebecca Usher's education at the Ursuline Convent at Trois-Rivières, Canada, reveals both antebellum Catholic envy and its darker side. While she was not a real-life Rebecca Reed, many in her own family feared that her two terms of study among the Canadian Ursulines would cause her to succumb to the allure of the convent. The daughter of a wealthy Maine lumber merchant, Usher ended up enrolling at Trois-Rivières while accompanying her father on a business trip to Lower Canada during the fall of 1840. After meeting a priest on the steamboat ride across the St. Lawrence, Rebecca convinced her father to let her stay at the convent for a term while he conducted his business so that she might become fluent in French. She aspired to gain enough proficiency to give lessons herself one day. One term turned into two, much to her family's chagrin. When Rebecca failed to respond to letters in a timely fashion, her family assumed the worst. Her sister Martha wrote to her on New Year's Day 1841, "You must come home with Pa. We shan't consent to your remaining any longer but shall indeed give up if you don't come home this month. You must write us immediately on the reception of this."[64] Somehow, Rebecca was able to convince her family to let her stay until the spring term was finished; she explained to her sister, "I should be sorry to go home now, knowing only a few short and disconnected sentences of a language that I have attempted to learn." To try to study French at home would be "an entire failure" in Rebecca's mind after having been immersed in the culture of the Ursulines.[65]

Rebecca Usher may have convinced her family to let her remain at Trois-Rivières, but that failed to put an end to rampant speculation among her friends and acquaintances that she had entered the nunnery. Ellis Usher wrote to his daughter that "some of the old Ladies say you will never get back again they think the nuns will not part with you. . . . They were amazed if not confounded how came I to be so crazy as to part with a daughter to be imprisoned."[66] Her sister Martha's letters confirmed "the thousand and one reports that are flying about the country" about her sojourn in Canada: "Miss Hays of Bangor received a letter from an Aunt in New Hampshire telling the sad story that 'you were kidnapped from Father when he went to Canada and thrown into a convent and that all his efforts to regain you proved unavailing.'"[67] And while these rumors were referred to in a half-teasing manner, only six years after the burning of the Ursuline convent at

Charlestown and on the heels of the overwhelming sensation of Maria Monk, such fears were perhaps no laughing matter for Rebecca's sister and father. It is telling that in her letters to her sister at the convent, Martha took special pains to mention the names of several young men who had asked after Rebecca, and expressed her excitement over the prospect of a moonlit stroll along the Saco once Rebecca returned home in the summer. A young male acquaintance of Rebecca's, George Woodman, a law clerk recently moved to New York City, also seemed willing to cast Rebecca Usher as the heroine of a picaresque novel. In the potential suitor's mind, Rebecca "had retired, for a time, from that great school of the world in order the better to fit and prepare yourself for its thousand duties, if in fact, you intend to let the light of your countenance be seen again among us."[68]

For her part, Rebecca shrugged off the wild speculation about her life among the nuns with amusement. "I never dreamed of being immortalized, much more of becoming the heroine of a fiction worthy of the lost days of chivalry. . . . Buried alive in a convent what a dreadful thought!!! But then it's romantic. I *did* laugh well over that part of your letter," she responded to Martha. She told her sister to tell the gossips of the neighborhood that "I have seen all the nuns to the number of fifty, I believe, and there is nothing *very terrible* in the appearance of any of them, or very remarkable, except that they dress in black and wear veils." She even suggested to her father that should he really wish to give the old women something to gab about, some of the nuns had playfully threatened not to let her return to America.[69]

Though Rebecca conceded to her father's wishes and returned home with him in April of 1841, she kept in touch with the sisters and seemed to have grown genuinely attached to them and they to her. She admitted she had been something of a "pet" at Trois-Rivières. She sent her father to the convent in the fall of 1841 with many "petits cadeaus" for the sisters, who sent back affectionate letters thanking her. Her former French mistress, Sister St. F. Borgia, wrote back *en français* teasing her that she wished she had sent her new pupils instead of gifts, but "in all seriousness, you know my occupation doesn't give me much leisure, but I must tell you that you are as loved as you always were."[70] Sister Mary Joseph wished she had been able to send back a painting in return for Rebecca's gift and expressed wish for Rebecca to return: "Perhaps you may make a visit to Canada then we could say to our inestimable Miss Usher many things that would not do for a letter."[71] Sister Mary Joseph sent Rebecca's father home with Catholic tracts about the founding of the Ursulines, so it is possible that they hoped their favorite American pupil could be persuaded to become one of them, or at least return for another term of lessons.

Rebecca Usher was never imprisoned in a nunnery. Her law clerk sweetheart was never forced to skate across the St. Lawrence in bitter January to rescue her in a feat of romantic heroism. And yet, perhaps her family's fears were not entirely unfounded. Despite the interests of George Woodman and other young men, Rebecca never married, the only child of Ellis Usher not to do so. It is unclear whether or not she ever succeeded as a teacher of French in Maine, but twenty years later she emerged in the historical record again, this time as a Civil War nurse, recruited by Dorothea Dix herself. As she once went to Canada on her own to study French, so did she serve in battlefield hospitals in Chester, Pennsylvania, and Northern Virginia. In the 1890s, she applied for a veteran's pension under her maiden name. Did Rebecca Usher remain unmarried out of emulation for the nuns who had been her teachers as a girl? Or did her own independent nature cause her to seek them out? Perhaps it was a mixture of both. Later in life Usher became well-acquainted with the nearby Shakers of Alfred, Maine, and considered them "real friends." They were frequent guests at her residence, the "Brick House."[72] Whether it was Catholic envy or a longing for a life outside of marriage, Rebecca Usher treasured her time at Trois-Rivières. According to her niece's family history, her adventures as an Ursuline pupil were among Aunt Rebecca's fondest memories, "a great experience for her and one which she remembered through life with pleasure and satisfaction. In telling of it she always dwelt upon the invariable sweetness and kindness of the sisters to her, an unbeliever."[73] Though she never became either a nun or a Shaker, as a never married woman, Usher seems to have regarded both groups as kindred spirits.

Rebecca Usher was one of many Protestant girls sent to better her "accomplishments" in an antebellum convent school. As part of New England's rising middle class, Rebecca and her family believed her studies in Trois-Rivières would cement her status as a lady of refinement and open the door to future economic opportunities for her as a teacher fluent in French. And yet, because of antebellum prejudices and fears surrounding convents and nuns, the Usher family was forced to weigh these potential advantages against the possibility that convent life would prove irresistible to their young daughter. The Ushers' dilemma over Rebecca's education points to the genuine and pervasive impact escaped nun stories had upon the American psyche as well as the elite cache a convent school represented in the Protestant imagination.

The Graham System as a Religious System

Sylvester Graham's prescriptions for diet and regimen perhaps most clearly form the link between sexuality and "brand." Graham's name itself became synonymous with the system of health he created, from books and lecture series to "Graham bread," "Graham flour," and "Graham boarding houses." Devotees of Graham were commonly called, often mockingly, "Graham-ites," though the followers themselves preferred the term "pure livers." Grahamism, with its rules for sleeping, eating, bathing, and sexual relations, was much more than just a diet—it was an entire way of life.

Grahamites, too, walked a fine line between capitalism and benevolence. As with the *Graham Journal*, Grahamite publications were often not intended to be money-making enterprises. For editors like David Cambell, it was more important to spread the gospel of pure living on the Graham system than it was to turn a profit as a journal editor. Graham himself, often sponsored by a group of citizens for a given lecture series, did not charge for his lectures in Portland, Maine, in 1834. The *Christian Mirror* reported Graham's "*free* lectures are generally thronged and his course is somewhat numerously attended."[74] And yet, Sylvester Graham, William Andrus Alcott, Mary Gove Nichols, and other reformers certainly were entrepreneurial as authors. Despite the philanthropic impulses within Grahamism, Graham's revolutionary system created a demand for products and services that had not previously existed in the marketplace.

Where was one to obtain the "Graham" flour to make "Graham bread" and the potatoes and fresh vegetables that were the staples of the Graham diet? Where could a young Grahamite find an establishment free of forbidden foods and stimulating drinks? Some leading Grahamites such as merchant Nathaniel Perry, publisher Bela Marsh, and boarding-house keepers David Cambell and Asenath Nicholson were only too happy to seize upon these enterprising opportunities. Only a week after Graham began his lecture series in Portland, an enterprising baker, John Pearson, ran an advertisement for "Graham Bread" in the *Daily Evening Advertiser*, encouraging the newly converted to stop by his Casco Street bake house. But it was not always business men and women looking to capitalize on the newest trend; often the demands for these products came from Grahamites themselves. One of Boston's young clerks wrote to Dr. Alcott, suggesting the need for a "Graham Restorator," a restaurant on the Graham system in a central location where the young men of the city could obtain a healthy, cheap meal. Alcott, however, disapproved of "restorators" and "refectories" of any kind, even Graham ones. Such places encouraged young men to mix with strangers of dubious morals. He suggested the young man either purchase bread and milk for his supper or return to his boarding house for dinner rather than indulge himself in the decadent practice of taking meals outside the safety of the home.[75]

The presence of local societies, boarding houses, and businesses that catered to Grahamites created sites and places where Grahamism could be performed and enacted. In this sense, Grahamism functioned in a way that was very similar to a religion. Taking an expansive and anthropological definition of religion, it is easy to see how Grahamism, though ostensibly secular, may have provided a system of beliefs and symbols that endowed its practitioners with certain "transcendent truths."[76] Grahamites certainly understood their larger system as a way of consciously choosing virtue over vice and health over disease. Becoming a Grahamite and rejecting meat, tea, and coffee was to reject the sinful and licentious pleasures such stimulating foods were thought to inspire. This sense of transcendent and moral feeling can be seen in an 1841 article taken from the *Health Journal & Advocate of Physiological Reform*, in which a devotee of the Graham system proposed that instead of calling themselves Grahamites, it would be more apt to call themselves "Millenarians." Grahamites are "Millenarians" because "by strictly observing the physical, moral, and intellectual laws of our being—sinless in every respect—would constitute the Millennium."[77] Like other true believers, Grahamites were compelled to confess their sins in order to prevent backsliding into bad sexual and dietetic habits. In return for their sacrifice of pleasure, they would be reborn into a healthy body in the present moment. They would collect their reward on earth, instead of waiting for heaven.

The quasi-religious aspects of Grahamism can be seen in the testimonies of its ardent followers. Delivered in person at meetings of the American Physiological Society (APS) or in print in various pro-Graham publications, individuals detailed what can best be described as a conversion experience.[78] There is a marked contrast between the life of sin and gluttony, where they ate whatever they wanted and suffered dire consequences in terms of health to a sort of being born-again and regaining health and vigor through the Graham system. Grahamites themselves were actually fairly self-aware of the religious nature of the new regimen. One "new subscriber," having tried and failed at "Thompsonianism, Quackism, Regular-*ism*" and desiring Grahamism to be the last stop asked the journal for some advice: "Must I 'cut' with my old friends, tea and coffee, flesh and all? . . . Please give a *novitiate* a little instruction."[79] George Williams of Russell, Massachusetts, testified to the readers of the *Health Journal* that prior to adopting the Graham system, he suffered "much from severe pain in my side, and felt a direful surety, both physical and mental, that my days were nearly numbered." Worst of all, Williams, like many Grahamites, "was given to low spirits" and experienced "melancholy." He cheerfully concluded, "Living on the Graham system, so termed, has been the death-blow to all my pains and sorrows."[80]

Because of the religious fervor that surrounded conversion to the Graham system, followers of Graham struggled living under the label of "Grahamite." For while on the one hand, Grahamite implied secular medical fads—"Thompsonianism, Quackism, Regular-*ism*"—it also invoked the "antebellum spiritual hothouse" out of which grew new charismatically led religions such as Mormonism and the Kingdom of Matthias.[81] To be a Grahamite was in some ways to be a fanatic, an "ultraist," a misguided soul led astray from conventional wisdom by a charming fraud. In response to these implied accusations, the editors of the *Health Journal* tried to distance themselves from Graham. They assured the public that it was the principles of physiology, not Sylvester Graham himself, that had earned their ardent devotion: "We advocate these views because we believe, with a confidence not to be shaken, that they are immutable, eternal truth. If men choose to call us Grahamites, so be it. . . . We are pledged to principles, not men."[82] To those who embraced the Graham system, it did not matter whether those who opposed them—"bloated wine-bibber(s) and gluttonous flesh-eater(s)"—considered them ultraists or enthusiasts. Though they disclaimed they considered Graham their "master," Grahamites could not help but speak about their faith in pure living in spiritual terms as "immutable, eternal truths." The latter, especially, is reminiscent of Geertz's definition of religion. Grahamites found transcendence and moral value in the sexual and dietetic prescriptions put forward by Graham, Alcott, and Gove. If their testimonies are to be believed, they also found improved health and greater peace of mind.

The same roads that carried Shaker medicines and seeds away from the villages brought word of Graham and Alcott's innovations in sexual reform. Shakers were well aware of Sylvester Graham and his revolutionary system of living. In the 1830s, some Shakers successfully adopted the Graham diet. While Shakers lived separately from the "world's people," they by no means lived in an intellectual vacuum. The *Graham Journal* had an agent in New Lebanon, and arguably the journal could have been easily obtained by an interested Shaker reader.[83] The American Physiological Society in Boston, in turn, was aware of the presence of the Harvard and New Hampshire Shaker villages, and mentioned them in the *Graham Journal*. George Kendall, a Harvard Shaker brother, wrote in to the *Graham Journal* to praise the remarkable recovery he had after adopting the Graham diet at the age of twenty-two and to encourage others to follow Graham's system: "Please to accept my kind and affectionate love with my well wishes for those who may feel disposed to undertake the Graham system of diet." As for the Grahamites, they certainly viewed themselves as allied with Shakers, and proclaimed Grahamism's nonsectarian nature: "We shall with pleasure insert communications from individuals of every sect or denomination," the editor wrote alongside Kendall's letter.[84] Maine Shakers produced the whole wheat Graham flour used to make the infamous Graham bread, ridiculed as "sawdust bread" by critics. It is possible that this was the flour sold in Portland and Boston bakeries and Graham stores.[85]

The mutual interest of both Grahamites and Shakers in promoting sexual restraint might have made Grahamism seem a natural fit for a community that celebrated celibacy as one of its most sacred tenets. George Kendall of Harvard was not alone in his embrace of the Graham diet, and several other Shakers in the Eastern communities also wrote openly of their experiences. Seth Wells, a Watervliet Shaker schoolmaster and theologian, detailed his experiences after four years on the Graham system in manuscript form for circulation among his fellow Shakers. Wells, like many Grahamites, testified to experiencing poor health prior to adopting Graham's recommended diet. In 1834, he "could not walk a mile" and had lost the majority of his teeth and hair, which he attributed to a conventional allopathic doctor's prescription for calomel during an illness in 1806. He was familiar with the works of the foremost health reformers of the day and cited Alcott and Graham for his decision to abstain from coffee and meat in 1835. Now, his health radically improved, Wells believed "what is vulgarly called the Graham system of diet" to be but a natural extension of the self-denial and cross he already bore as part of his Shaker faith. For him, it was such a "small cross" to enjoy improved health and Graham's diet "so far subdued the depravity of my appetite that I feel no more hankering after the various delicacies of the table than if I had never tasted them." A Shaker brother or sister might (and did) talk in the same manner about carnal sexual appetites as Wells did about gustatory ones. For some, the sacrifice of certain decadent food and drink mirrored the sacrifice of the Shaker cross of celibacy.[86]

Ephraim Prentiss, caretaker of the boys' order at Watervliet, applied the Graham diet explicitly to induce sexual restraint among his charges from 1835 to 1837. He also wrote of this experiment in manuscript form for the larger Shaker community. When he was appointed caretaker in 1831, he found the boys a violent, sickly, troublesome, bedwetting lot. Even worse, "their stimulating food evidently excited and brought into action those base propensities which boys of their age ought not to feel—in short, their venereal excitements & filthy indulgences caused me much tribulation." In 1835, the boys were given the liberty to choose for themselves whether or not to embrace the Graham diet, and Prentiss decided to lead by example. Gradually, Prentiss and his young charges gave up first meat and lard drippings, then baked beans and pork, cheese, butter, and milk, embracing a wholly Grahamite diet. Prentiss reported that after only five or six weeks the boys were "less ferocious, more cheerful & simple, and more attentive to business." They no longer fought among each other but transformed into a "playful, harmless and agreeable" bunch. Most importantly, the Graham diet had successfully cured them of the base indulgences alluded to earlier, and even "the most addicted to venereal pollution, had become to all appearance as harmless as babes as to any indulgence of the nature."[87]

Prentiss's application of the Graham diet, though he made it seem consensual, was not well received among his fellow Shakers. As strict and relentless in pursuit of sexual restraint as the Shakers could be, there were some among them who felt that Prentiss had gone too far and was starving his charges, who had been adopted or indentured into the Shakers' care, into submission. Prentiss's own elder, Freegift Wells, believed Prentiss had "restrained his boys altogether beyond the bounds of reason." It is hard not to be suspicious of Prentiss's experiment; withholding food on top of hours of farm labor would probably render any group of boys "teachable and tractable."[88]

Controversy over the Graham diet spilled over into the larger adult Shaker community. While some, like Seth Wells, saw it as a larger expression of the Shaker cross of self-denial, others chafed at the change in diet and disruption to routine. Debates over the Graham diet nearly caused a schism among the Shakers, who prided themselves on being in "union" with one another. Plentiful and delicious food (and most travelers praised Shaker cooking as being very tasty) was one of the few indulgences to be had in a sect that had already sacrificed many pleasures. Unlike the city-dwelling Grahamites who patronized the APS or the clerks and students who subscribed to the *Graham Journal*, Shaker brothers and sisters performed a great deal of physical labor in their farms, kitchens, laundries, and work-shops. In 1835, the ministry ultimately decided against taking a position on whether or not the Shakers as whole should wholly embrace the Graham system and become vegetarians. Notably, Grahamism was twice as popular among Shaker brothers than it was among Shaker sisters. Male members may have been more attracted to Graham's promise of sexual control, while women knew the extra labor involved in cooking separate meals for both vegetarian and nonvegetarian members.[89]

In his history of the Shakers, Brother Isaac Newton Youngs explained that even as late as the 1850s the benefits of the Graham diet were still sub-ject to debate. Youngs recorded that "people have run very wild on this sub-ject, and are of two parties, going to great extremes in opposite directions; the one discarding all indulgence of appetite, all rich or delicious, or high seasoned food, all flesh meat, all grease, butter &c confining themselves to brown bread . . . the other . . . saying, that their own appetite is their best rule and judge of what is best for them." The Graham diet was divisive, he said, not only because people wished to rule their own appetites but because it required "additional labor, especially to the cooks, as it has ren-dered it necessary for themselves to put upon the table, both vegetable and animal food, at one meal." Contrary to Graham and Alcott's promise of easier-to-prepare food and more free time for housewives, preparing two sets of meals made more, not less, work for the kitchen sisters. The end result was such that the church settled more toward the vegetarian "simple diet" out of "a general conviction that plain living is more conducive to health." As a matter of compromise, the ministry banned intoxicating spir-its (except for medicinal purposes), cider, foreign teas, and pork around 1840. Older members were allowed to keep taking tea and coffee if they so wished.[90]

The nineteenth century was not simply an era of increasingly commodi-fied sex but also a time when virtue and purity could be bought and sold. The celibacy surrounding Shaker products and Catholic services helped mark these products as distinctive in a crowded marketplace. The purity of Shaker extracts, the demureness of a Shaker bonnet, and the chaste, lady-like example of an Ursuline sister proved attractive to antebellum consum-ers. Exposure to these minority religious groups through their goods and services helped overcome Protestant prejudice a small bit, especially in the case of Catholic nursing sisters who were willing serve even in the most dangerous of conditions. It is notable and not at all coincidental that goods seemed to arouse less suspicion on the part of consumers than services.

While one can find a great deal of outcry against Protestant girls and orphans being educated by Catholic sisters, it is difficult to find anything but praise for Shaker medicines, seeds, and consumer goods. Because even while one might swallow a spoonful of valerian extract or sarsaparilla syrup, a Protestant consumer never had to worry about it talking back, challenging his religious beliefs, or inducing his daughter to become a nun. The Graham system was certainly a distinctive brand of its own, but its ends and means were rather the opposite of that of Shaker and Catholic products. Shaker and Catholic celibacy marked their goods and services; the Graham system—the diet, the lectures, the boarding houses—was all in the service of attaining sexual restraint. All of the various commercial accoutrements of Grahamism further allowed Grahamites to take something that was ostensibly secular and endow it with the transcendent qualities associated with religion. None of these groups could have successfully marketed their products, educational services, or health reform regimes without the sweeping changes in transportation infrastructure that went hand-in-hand with the market revolution.

The experiences of Rebecca Usher and the Grahamite Shakers also show that antebellum consumers did not accept the premise of these products unthinkingly. To study abroad in a French-Canadian convent and to embark upon a new health regimen were both ambiguous propositions that required individual agency. Neither Usher nor the Shakers were blind followers; each accepted the products offered on their own terms and attempted to use them to suit their own needs and ambitions.

The connection between the sexual restraint of these groups and their ability to succeed in the antebellum marketplace further demonstrates that sexual otherness was in fact a commodity worth buying and selling. More than just a set of behaviors, sexual restraint was an identity and a brand. But antebellum Americans' consumption of sexual restraint did not simply end at purchasing products. As tourists and spectators, they also paid money to see sexual otherness performed and enacted in the emerging tourism and culture industries.

CHAPTER FIVE

Performing Sexual Restraint

In 1850 Eph Horn, J. B. Fellows, and the rest of Fellows's Ethiopian Opera Troupe debuted a routine that soon became a sensation on the minstrel circuit. Horn and his fellow minstrels blacked up to perform a song-and-dance combination that came to be known as "Fi Hi Hi: The Black Shakers Song and Polka" or simply "Black Shakers." The "polka" involved a blackface comic imitation of the dances and ecstatic worship of the Shaker sect (figure 5.1). "Black Shakers" was a hit and was soon adopted by a variety of groups such as the Virginia Serenaders, Christy's, and Bryant's at midcentury. Touring minstrel companies made "Black Shakers" a national sensation, with performances springing up across the country, far beyond the troupe's home in New York City. The enthusiasm for "Black Shakers" was not limited to the Northeast where the Shakers themselves resided; touring troupes performed the act throughout the 1850s–1870s in South Carolina, Louisiana, and even California.[1] And though "The Black Shakers Song" is unfamiliar to twenty-first-century ears, it once shared the bill with such popular tunes as "Camptown Races" and "My Old Kentucky Home." Like these more familiar standards, the song was sold as sheet music, to be played in the parlor or the saloon, long after the troupe had moved on to its next engagement.[2]

"The Black Shakers Song" is more than simply an antebellum cultural curiosity. It offers an ideal lens for viewing nineteenth-century America's fascination with performances of sexual otherness in the form of Shaker celibacy as well as a more familiar fascination with performances of racial otherness. Audiences flocked to see not only the "Black Shakers" minstrel routine but also melodramas such as *The Shaker Lovers* and *The Pet of the Petticoats*, which promised behind-the-scenes glimpses of closed celibate communities. Intrigued by what they had read in pamphlets, books, and newspapers, middle-class Americans went to see the celibate identities of nuns, priests, and Shakers embodied, turning Shaker villages and Catholic convents into some of North America's earliest tourist attractions.

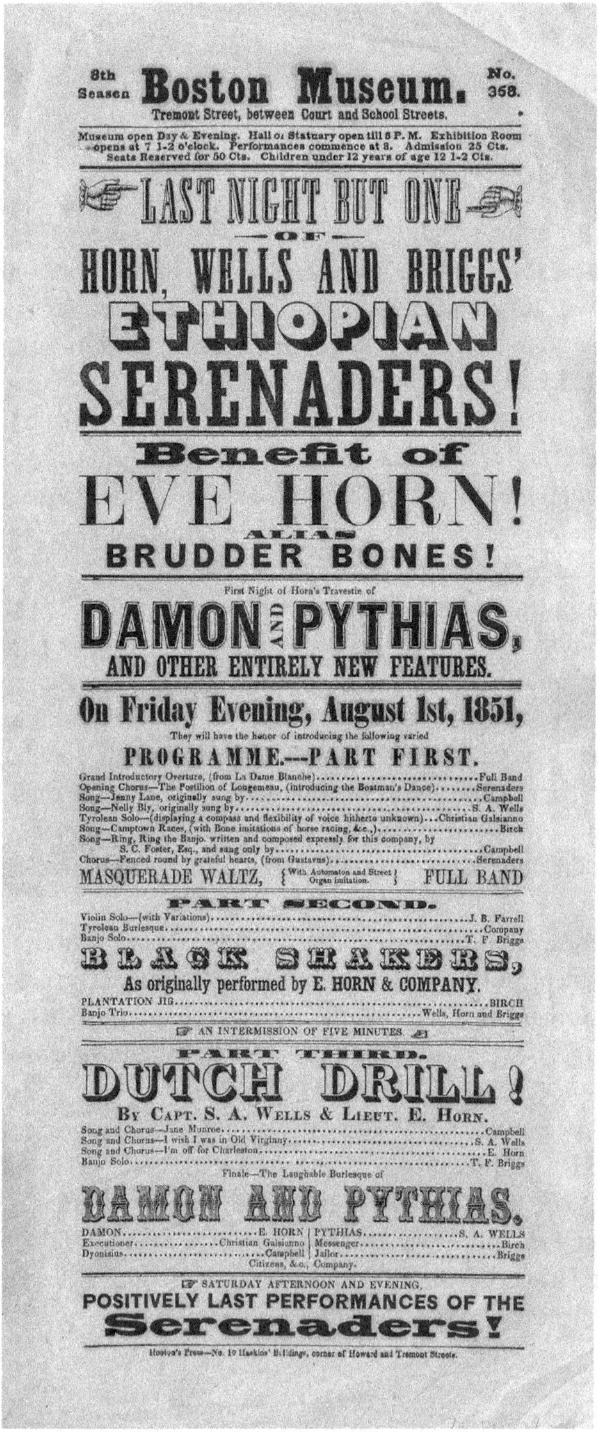

8th Season **Boston Museum.** No. 358.

Tremont Street, between Court and School Streets.

Museum open Day & Evening. Hall of Statuary open till 8 P. M. Exhibition Room opens at 7 1-2 o'clock. Performances commence at 8. Admission 25 Cts. Seats Reserved for 50 Cts. Children under 12 years of age 12 1-2 Cts.

LAST NIGHT BUT ONE

—OF—

HORN, WELLS AND BRIGGS'

ETHIOPIAN

SERENADERS!

Benefit of

EVE HORN!

ALIAS

BRUDDER BONES!

First Night of Horn's Travestie of

DAMON AND PYTHIAS,

AND OTHER ENTIRELY NEW FEATURES.

On Friday Evening, August 1st, 1851,

They will have the honor of introducing the following varied

PROGRAMME.---PART FIRST.

Grand Introductory Overture, (from La Dame Blanche)........Full Band
Opening Chorus—The Postilion of Longemeau, (introducing the Boatman's Dance)........Serenaders
Song—Jenny Lane, originally sung by........Campbell
Song—Nelly Bly, originally sung by........S. A. Wells
Tyrolean Solo—(displaying a compass and flexibility of voice hitherto unknown)...Christian Galsianno
Song—Camptown Races, (with Bone imitations of horse racing, &c.,)........Birch
Song—Ring, Ring the Banjo, written and composed expressly for this company, by S. C. Foster, Esq., and sung only by........Campbell
Chorus—Fenced round by grateful hearts, (from Gustavus)........Serenaders

MASQUERADE WALTZ, {With Automaton and Street Organ imitation.} FULL BAND

PART SECOND.

Violin Solo—(with Variations)........J. B. Farrell
Tyrolean Burlesque........Company
Banjo Solo........T. F. Briggs

BLACK SHAKERS,

As originally performed by E. HORN & COMPANY.

PLANTATION JIG........BIRCH
Banjo Trio........Wells, Horn and Briggs

AN INTERMISSION OF FIVE MINUTES.

PART THIRD.

DUTCH DRILL!

By Capt. S. A. Wells & Lieut. E. Horn.

Song and Chorus—Jane Munroe........Campbell
Song and Chorus—I wish I was in Old Virginny........S. A. Wells
Song and Chorus—I'm off for Charleston........E. Horn
Banjo Solo........T. F. Briggs

Finale—The Laughable Burlesque of

DAMON AND PYTHIAS.

DAMON........E. HORN | PYTHIAS........S. A. WELLS
Executioner........Christian Galsianno | Messenger........Birch
Dyonisius........Campbell | Jailor........Briggs
Citizens, &c., Company.

SATURDAY AFTERNOON AND EVENING,

POSITIVELY LAST PERFORMANCES OF THE

Serenaders!

Hooton's Press—No. 10 Haskins' Buildings, corner of Howard and Tremont Streets.

FIGURE 5.1 Broadside advertising "Black Shakers," August 1, 1851. Courtesy of the American Antiquarian Society.

"Black Shakers" and the Antebellum Stage

Analysis of the "Black Shakers" phenomenon as well as these other performances of sexual restraint can broaden the scope of scholarship on race, sexuality, and performance during this time period. There has been extensive and insightful work on how nineteenth-century white Americans interpreted and consumed racial difference in the form of blackface minstrelsy.[3] Performances of gender identity and sexuality in this era have received considerably less attention. The circulation of these performances, whether by imitators looking to cash in (as with J. B. Fellows & Co.) or in the touristic draw of the genuine article (pilgrimages to Mount Lebanon or the Hotel Dieu in Montreal) also illuminate the confluence of religion and the marketplace during the mid-nineteenth century. Religion, entertainment, and capitalism did not live in separate spheres.[4] In the "The Black Shakers' Song" and other kindred performances, religion, political satire, and discourses of race and sexuality converged, all while turning a sizable profit.

How did Shaker dances find their way from the relative isolation of their utopian community to the urban masses in the minstrel hall? Only the vaguest descriptions of the "Black Shakers" routine can be gleaned from newspaper advertisements and broadsides of the period. Its sheet music indicates that it began as a song (featuring a male soloist) that grew into a larger dance chorus. Minstrel broadsides listed "Black Shakers" as being performed "by the company."[5] "Black Shakers" was routinely performed in the second act, or *olio*, a part of the minstrel show typically devoted to topical issues of the day, such as burlesques of political stump speeches or social reform lectures. Second-act routines were often minimal in terms of spectacle, used as a way to keep the audience engaged as more elaborate scenery and costumes could be readied for the final act.[6] As a form of biting social satire, "Black Shakers" exemplified the *olio* routine. Faux–women's rights' lectures delivered in blackface were also a popular fixture in the second-act *olio*. In July 1851, Fellows Minstrels performed "Burlesque Shakers, with new material" alongside a hornpipe sung in Bloomer drag: "the new style of costume lately introduced and now adopted by some of the most fashionable ladies of our city."[7] Satirical portrayals of middle-class reformers in blackface represented a recent innovation in minstrel performance. The earliest minstrel shows often used a trickster figure to ventriloquize working-class discontent against elites, but actually portraying these characters onstage was a relatively new phenomenon.[8] In this way, "Black

Shakers" would have been understood by audiences to be a modern and innovative minstrel routine.

Like minstrel send-ups of Bloomers and other "ultraist" reformers, "Black Shakers" satirized Shakers for their deviance from antebellum gender and sexual mores. In the song, the lead singer laments that his sweetheart, a "lubbly yallar gal" named Dinah, has rejected him and "gone away to Leb'non state" to become a celibate Shaker sister. The chorus includes the phrase "Massa says it is too late, let her go to Leb'non state." In the second verse, the pining suitor, at a loss for what to do, comically announces, "I'll buy a rope and drown myself: Dat make her mad, I know."[9] An instrumental polka, presumably a Shaker-style dance with the rest of the company, ended the routine.

These lyrics represented a kind of one-two punch, an attempt to satirize religious and sexual outsiders in addition to the minstrel show's usual grotesque portrayal of African Americans. Shakers themselves considered both their dances and ecstatic twirling and shaking as forms of divinely inspired worship.[10] To see them burlesqued by actors upon the stage, especially in the guise of plantation slaves, represented an opportunity to ridicule a dour and prim religious sect. Yet, "Black Shakers" also took aim at black sexuality. For an enslaved woman, whose body and sexuality were the property of her owner, to run away and become a celibate Shaker would have appeared to antebellum audiences as an oxymoron of the highest order. Dinah, the sweetheart-turned-Shaker-sister, provided an interesting twist on a common minstrel archetype of the mulatto woman, or "wench" role. The "wench" was meant to combine the light skin and facial features of a white woman with the assumed sexual promiscuity of a black woman. White minstrel performers as well as their predominantly white working-class audiences projected their own sexual fantasies onto characters like Dinah in the way the "wench" role was hypersexualized. The character was both flirtatious and elusive, and the male character types would spend much of the show attempting to win her favor. In the case of "Black Shakers," the "wench" became not only elusive but impossible to get by joining the Shakers.[11] Turning a character type expected to be overly sexual into a celibate woman was undoubtedly part of the song's punchline.[12] However, the lyrics reveal that Dinah was much more than just a "wench"-turned-Shaker-sister—she was also a runaway, "gone away" from the plantation to the "Leb'non state" and freedom in the Shaker villages of the north. The chorus of "Master says it is too late" implied that a celibate Dinah was a lost cause and a bad investment for the man who enslaved her. As historians of African American women's history have shown, enslaved women were caught between the twin roles of "Jezebel" and "Mammy" in the white imagination. A young enslaved woman like the Dinah of "The Black Shakers Song" was understood to be "governed almost entirely by her libido." Portraying black women as creatures of uncontrollable sexual desire only further served to excuse the sexual abuses perpetrated by white men.[13] Though the song was intended to be a comic piece, played for laughs, its lyrics contained dark undertones of slaveholding men's ownership of enslaved women's bodies.

The routine further mocked the masculinity of the nameless rejected suitor. That the lovely Dinah would choose celibacy over him drives him to contemplate a comic suicide—in true minstrel fashion, he can't even do this properly as he searches for a rope to drown himself. Contrary to the portrayals of aggressive black masculinity that followed in the wake of the Civil War, the minstrel shows of the 1840s and 1850s tended to feature luckless suitors like the singer of "The Black Shakers' Song," who lamented lost loves or expressed nostalgia for their plantation homes.[14] Under the slave regime, enslaved men were denied masculinity and considered to be not fully men. They could not protect their wives and children or themselves from the violence and indignities of slavery.[15] The male singer of "Black Shakers" was thus further unmanned by Dinah's rejection; she chose to become a celibate Shaker rather than accept him as her lover.

To further complicate these representations of race, sexuality, and gender, "wench" roles were played by white men in drag, who would coyly flirt with male performers in front of audiences largely composed of other working-class men. Though "Bloomerizical" bits mocked women's rights reformers' wearing of pants, minstrel performers and their male audience had no such qualms about men appropriating female dress. In the gender politics of early minstrelsy, white male performers laid claim to their right to interpret upon the stage not only blackness but also femaleness. Just as African American performers were not given the right to embody blackness in early minstrelsy, neither were women, white or black, allowed to interpret their own embodied gender.

It is unclear if Eph Horn or other minstrels who performed "Black Shakers" as regular parts of their traveling routines would have been aware of Rebecca Jackson and her "little band" of black Shaker sisters living in Civil War–era Philadelphia or the free black believers in other rural Shaker communities in Canterbury, New Hampshire, New Lebanon, New York, or Pleasant Hill, Kentucky.[16] He may have obtained his inspiration from a lithograph of New Lebanon Shakers dancing, which featured two black male

FIGURE 5.2 "Shakers, Their Mode of Worship." Two black Shaker brothers are visible in the back row. Courtesy of the American Antiquarian Society.

Shakers. This lithograph (figure 5.2), a Currier & Ives print, dates from the 1830s. It is arguably the most famous pictorial representation of Shaker dancing, and was reproduced throughout the nineteenth century in at least eighteen different known variations.[17]

Eph Horn and the rest of the Fellows' Minstrels were not the first to transport Shaker dances from the austerity of the meeting house to the footlights of the stage. The credit for that belongs to the "Shaker Sisters and Brothers" troupe. Here is where fact blends with fiction, and authenticity meets imitation. The Fellows' Minstrels most likely did not derive inspiration from Rebecca Jackson and the actual free women of color who lived in her community of Philadelphia, but from a group of white Shaker impersonators. The "Shaker Sisters and Brothers" troupe consisted of three men and three women, all supposedly apostates from the Canterbury, New Hampshire, Shaker settlement. Two of them, Dr. and Mrs. Tripure, were married, and the others consisted of two unmarried women and two unmarried men. Both J. M. Otis and Dr. Tripure were in fact bona fide Shaker apostates, but it is unclear if the other members of the troupe were as well. In the summer of 1846, the six gave a concert at Brinley Hall in Worcester, Massachusetts, promising "instructive amusements." Though the Shakers themselves had long welcomed "the world" to watch their Sabbath meetings, this concert marked the first time Shaker religion had been consciously packaged as commercial entertainment.[18] The handbill capitalized on curiosity and fascination with the Shakers' strange spiritual practices, especially their dances and trances. Promotional materials promised "visions and conversations with Angels and the Departed Spirits," hymns sung in unknown spirit tongues, songs by Osceola and Pocahontas, "given by inspiration."[19] The highlight of the bill was Miss Julia A. Willard, "the Miraculous Shaker Teetotum," raised in the sect since childhood. A young lady "whose grace and Beauty are of uncommon Fascination," Willard would "whirl round 1500 times," with perfect lighting-like precision. The "Shaker Sisters and Brothers" assured theirs was an entertainment suited to the whole family and that "nothing in their performance can offend refinement or the eye of modesty."[20]

The "Shaker Sisters and Brothers" were not for provincial venues like Worcester's Brinley Hall for long. Only two months after their debut in Worcester, they were playing the Apollo Rooms in New York City in September 1846. Not long after their New York debut, showman P. T. Barnum snapped up the troupe for an extended engagement. Rechristened "The Shaking Quakers," the six Canterbury apostates performed their routine at Barnum's American Museum twice a day, matinees and evenings, through mid-December of 1846. Barnum advertised that in this performance "three beautiful ladies, and three gentlemen from the Society . . . will sing, dance, whirl, and shake in the unique Shaker costume."[21] Later Barnum added a second element to their now familiar routine, in the form of a comic Shaker romance, "A Shaking Courtship," starring comedienne Fanny Wheeler. Like the futile wooing of Dinah in "The Black Shakers Song," "A Shaking Courtship" played on the oxymoronic idea of love and romance within the confines of a celibate Shaker village. As Fellows' Minstrel Hall was located at 444 Broadway in New York City, a little more than half a mile's walk away from Barnum's American Museum, there is a high likelihood that Horn and his company would have seen "The Shaking Quakers" perform at some time during their well-publicized engagement at the American Museum.[22] Interestingly, "Black Shakers" came into being only after the "official" "Shaking Quakers" had left the New York theater scene for good, perhaps as replacement for what had been a theatrical mainstay in the city.

The *Evening Post* claimed that the "Shaking Quakers" had been enjoyed by crowds of thousands, and notably, "their grotesque appearance and interesting performances . . . afford a great deal of rational amusement." "Grotesque" is perhaps the operative word here, as the "Shaking Quakers" shared the bill at Barnum's Museum with other such exotic creatures as an "ourang-outang," a dwarf, and the "twin Caffres" who had white bodies and "ebony faces."[23] Barnum was known for his collection of human oddities and grotesqueries; he made his career showcasing such specimens as Tom Thumb and "the Nondescript" to middle-class audiences. His exhibitions of humans of unusual race, size, and shape are well known—it was the birth of the freak show.[24] With the "Shaking Quakers" concert, Barnum capitalized on American audiences' desires to see sexual deviance and religious eccentricity. The Shaker celibate body—and the erratic dances and trances associated with it—were as unique as Santa Ana's sword and in good company with dwarves and exotic beasts, the latest in a long line of "living curiosities." Whether it was watching the "Shaking Quakers" dance or inspecting Barnum's "Nondescript," the middle class claimed the labels of natural and normal for themselves by contrast.

Performances like the Shaking Quakers at Barnum's museum were part of a larger nineteenth-century fascination with "artful deception." Barnum specialized in providing his predominantly middle-class audience with both "hoaxes" (epitomized by items like the Feejee Mermaid) and the spectacles that featured in his circuses. At a time when middle-class Americans were extremely fearful about deception and inauthenticity in their midst, artful deceptions like Barnum's hoaxes invited them to investigate.[25] Yet illusion and spectacle were not mutually exclusive, and the Shaking Quakers performance provided both. The spectacle aspect is perhaps the most obvious—they sang and danced, and Julia Willard spun round and round with astonishing velocity. And yet the act was also a kind of artful deception which operated on two distinct levels. First, the six-member troupe no longer claimed the status of genuine Shakers, if indeed the majority of them ever were. They themselves straddled the line between stage performers and sanctioned representatives of the religious sect. The second artful deception was a more expansive one, and also applied both to the minstrel dramas and spectatorship at *real* Shaker Sabbath meetings. Audiences, whether at the American Museum, at Fellows' Minstrel Hall, or in the meeting house at Mount Lebanon, flocked to see whether or not the Shakers' ecstatic spirituality—and by extension, their celibacy—was real or, in nineteenth-century parlance, "humbug." Some have argued that antebellum audiences' fascination with humbug resided in its unmasking: "Those who managed to solve the puzzle . . . could rightly consider themselves select and special."[26] The Shaking Quakers, like other Barnum acts, invited audiences to engage, scrutinize, and evaluate. Part of that engagement was a scrutiny of the Shakers' celibacy, their perceived deviance from sexual and gender norms.

The Shaking Quakers and "The Black Shakers' Song" signaled the latest iteration of the anti-Shaker activism that had first emerged in the 1780s in response to Mother Ann's evangelical tour of New England and had manifested itself in outbreaks of mob violence in the 1810s. Though the Shakers continued to fend off lawsuits and prejudicial legislation in the mid- to late nineteenth century, it would be incorrect to paint this as a total transition from impassioned activism to benign satire. Anti-Shaker violence and for-profit Shaker dancing remained interrelated. After the overwhelming success of the Shaking Quakers at Barnum's Museum, a second Shaker performing troupe appeared on the southern circuit, giving a Christmas Eve performance in Washington, D.C., in 1846. It is mostly notable for the fact that lifelong anti-Shaker advocate Mary Marshall Dyer, whose pamphleteering had inspired mob violence against the New Hampshire Shakers nearly thirty years before, shared the bill. Promotional materials prominently advertised a lecture by Dyer as well as traditional dances.[27]

Mary Marshall Dyer was not the sole connection between imitation Shaker dance performances and anti-Shaker politicking in the antebellum era. J. M. Otis, one of the performers prominently featured on the broadsides advertising the Shaking Quaker performances, testified against the Shakers in a hearing before the New Hampshire legislature in 1848. Several damning yet familiar allegations were heard before the New Hampshire legislature, including charges of abuse against women and children, attempts to implicate the Shakers in an untimely death of a child in their care, and tales of children born out of wedlock at the Shaker settlement. Otis, Dyer, and others had gathered close to 500 signatures to petition the legislature for this hearing, on the grounds that the New Hampshire Shakers were guilty of "many gross and inconsistent practices, subversive of the public good" requiring the legislature's intervention.[28] The prosecutor opened his argument by demanding the legislature take action against the Shaker community and "stop these Shakers from creeping about, like the Serpent of old, destroying many a fair Eden of domestic happiness. There is no relation existing in society, of which the law is more jealous and watchful, than that which exists between husband and wife."[29]

Erstwhile Shaker dancer J. M. Otis's performance in the legislative hearing was colorful to the point of lurid. While others talked of abuse, financial swindles, and mysterious deaths, Otis offered up a sexual scandal of the most bizarre variety. Otis had attained the rank of elder, but left the Shakers in 1845. After affirming some of the other allegations of abuse, Otis told the hearing of a strange incident involving a Shaker sister named Catherine Lyon. He related how one sister, Hester Ann Adams, "inspired by the prophet Elisha, or some other prophet or Angel," had claimed before the entire community "that Catherine Lyon had been committing some great sin; something that was abominable in the sight of God." When Lyon denied the accusation, Hester Ann in her role as spirit medium said, "The cleaver, the cleaver . . . Oh, what abomination! What corruption! What filth! Gratifying your lusts with a cleaver!" The offending kitchen implement, which Otis testified measured "about three feet long; handle two feet," was brought before the accused Catherine Lyon, where she was made to repent. Otis claimed this incident happened shortly before his departure in 1843. Catherine Lyon had been a Shaker since the age of ten, and she remained one still, regardless of the scene Otis had described. The validity of Otis's testimony cannot be confirmed. But his words were certainly intended to shock, disgust, and render the Shakers and their spiritual and sexual practices obscene.[30] The defense introduced a handbill for the "Shaking Quakers" troupe into evidence to discredit his testimony. When questioned, Otis replied, "I have performed upon the stage, to represent Shakerism. I was hired to give representations of Shakerism." He denied, however, actively seeking a career as an entertainer and claimed his career as a professional Shaker impersonator was entirely accidental: "The man who hired us, wrote in the bill what he chose to, and we performed as well as we knew."[31] Otis's ambivalent response reflects the marginal status of actors and performers in antebellum America.[32]

For J. M. Otis and Mary Marshall Dyer, there was no disconnect between the politics of the stage and the politics of the courtroom in their campaign against Shakerism. For both of them, any opportunity to keep Shakerism in the forefront of public attention, to win hearts and minds, and to earn a living while doing it, was undoubtedly worthwhile. Otis, like other Shaker apostates, would have left his community with little more than clothes, tools, and a few months' support as a parting gift for his many years as a Shaker. When a man or woman signed the Shaker covenant, he or she renounced rights to back wages upon leaving the community. In return, the believer received room and board while he or she lived and contributed to the sect.

These financial claims on behalf of Otis and the other apostates constituted one part of what the petitioners were trying to get the New Hampshire legislature to address in 1848. To Otis and the five other members of the troupe, who were without a place to live or an established occupation, a steady income in return for a few Shaker dances might have seemed like a good proposition. Like the narratives of escaped slaves, convicts, and prisoners, these performances were often the only thing Shaker apostates had to sell. And by revealing Shaker dances and singing to be works of artifice rather than gifts of the spirit, these apostates further distanced themselves from the strange sect they had once embraced wholeheartedly. Performing Shakerism for profit ironically made them more normal, not less.[33] Ultimately, Otis, Dyer, and the other petitioners were only halfway successful in passing their anti-Shaker bill. Despite an impassioned defense of the Shakers by their counsel and hero of the Mexican-American War, General Franklin Pierce, the bill overwhelmingly passed the New Hampshire State Legislature by a 4-to-1 margin. It failed in the state Senate, the senators recognizing that singling out a religious sect (especially one that paid a large amount of taxes to the state of New Hampshire) was a potential political minefield. Instead the Senate offered up a compromise to the petitioners, loosening the divorce statutes, to better aid women like Mary Marshall Dyer, who had been abandoned by Shaker spouses.[34]

Enthusiasm for performances of celibacy was not just limited to the Shakers. There was never a Catholic equivalent of the "Shaking Quakers" phenomenon, but representations of Catholic celibacy also appeared frequently on the antebellum stage. Most notably was the farce *The Pet of the Petticoats, Or, the Convent*, an operetta performed with regularity in American theaters. *Pet of the Petticoats* was a British import. Like those foreign texts rushed into translation following the burning of the Charlestown convent, *Pet of the Petticoats* made its American debut in 1835, the same year Maria Monk and Rebecca Reed rose to fame. It was performed in repertory consistently into the early twentieth century.[35] The operetta was essentially the escaped nun tale in theatrical form. The essential features were the same: set in a vaguely French locale, the protagonist Paul (the eponymous "pet" and a woman playing a breeches role) reunites two wives being held prisoner in the convent with their dashing soldier husbands. The play even featured a cruel nun named "Sister Vinaigre"; in a comedic twist on the vinegar-faced sister archetype, she is found to be having an affair with the convent-school's dancing master. In the end, all of the couples are reunited, including Sister Vinaigre and her beau. Audiences could watch as heterosexual marriage triumphed over celibacy again and again in every performance. Paul defended his actions in his final monologue: "I have but restored husbands to their wives and wives to their husbands; and those who have been once united in Hymen's bonds we are instructed never to put asunder."[36] On this point that marriage was sacred and inviolate, both the comic actors and the petitioners to the New Hampshire legislature were in complete agreement.

Antebellum audiences thrilled to this comedic farce, and the *New York Herald* called the 1848 production "one of the most amusing pieces that has been performed in some time."[37] *Pet of the Petticoats* was far from obscure; it was a staple of the nineteenth-century theatrical scene and would have been familiar to theatergoing audiences. In its own time, it was regarded as a new and innovative type of theater, and even a bit risqué because it featured a woman showing off her legs in a breeches role. It was also not without controversy—some theatergoers in St. Louis found its satire of women religious offensive, especially in light of the Catholic free schools founded in the city.[38] As a forerunner of the musical comedy genre, escaped nun stories—and by extension, performances of celibacy—occupy a significant place in the history of the American theater.[39] There were other Catholic-themed entertainments in the antebellum era, but none achieved the success or status of *Pet of the Petticoats*.[40] The repeated success of the play and its frequent revival throughout the nineteenth century point to the ways in which antebellum audiences took pleasure in seeing marriage defeat celibacy. Like its close cousin, the escaped nun story, in which the victim-heroine is rescued by her beau from the horrors of the convent, the operetta reinscribed heterosexual norms back onto celibate characters. By having even the dreadful Sister Vinaigre succumb to the charms of romance, the play demonstrated that marriage was inevitable, natural, and inescapable, and celibacy, by contrast, a losing proposition.

Belles, Blues, and Sexual Others: Encounters with the "Fashionable Mob"

Some antebellum Americans were not merely content with secondhand representations of sexual deviance that could be found in an escaped nun story or a newspaper account of a Grahamite lecture. Not even the imitation "Shaking Quakers" or the convent antics of a farce like *Pet of the Petticoats* could compete with the genuine article. Having read *Awful Disclosures* or encounters with Shakers in printed travelogues, Americans embarked to see these identities in the flesh. The burgeoning American tourist industry gave these middle-class white Protestant Americans the opportunity to have encounters with sexual others and to take the "artful deception" gaze they had honed in places like Barnum's Museum on the road.

It is no coincidence that Shaker villages and Catholic convents emerged as North America's first tourist attractions. Though the "fashionable tour," which included the Hudson Valley, Niagara Falls, and Montreal, came into being in the 1820s with the publishing of a guidebook of the same name by Gideon Davison, the convents of Montreal and the Shaker villages at Mount Lebanon and Watervliet appeared in the earliest known American travel guides. As early as 1812, George Temple's *The American Tourist's Pocket Companion* encouraged tourists to include a visit to Lebanon Springs and the nearby Shaker settlement while traveling between Albany and New York City.[41] This early attention is remarkable, showing Americans had an interest in viewing these others, even before the roads, canals, and steamboats created by the "transportation revolution" made the fashionable tour accessible to the middle-class men and women of metropolitan New York and Boston.[42] Because Shaker villages at Mount Lebanon, Watervliet, and Canterbury were located in close proximity to key transportation networks like the steamship lines of the Hudson or the Erie Canal, one wonders if this is "a chicken and the egg" type of situation. Did these places turn into tourist attractions because of their proximity to other tourist attractions? Or were they places of interest and pilgrimage in their own right? That interest predated infrastructure points to the latter. However, location mattered as well. Being part of the "fashionable tour" and proximity to the urban homes of the emergent middle class transformed these places from mere tourist sites to tourist institutions over the course of the nineteenth century.

Scholars of tourism have argued that the emergence of tourism as a behavior went hand in glove with the creation of both middle-class identity and modern concepts of work and leisure in the early 1800s in America and Western Europe.[43] The new middle class had the discretionary income to travel for pleasure as well as a newfound approach to bracketing work from leisure. At this moment, the concept of "holiday time" underwent a transformation from a religiously based calendar to one based on the duality of vacation and work.[44] During this time the ability to visit touristic sites such as Niagara Falls and the White Mountains and to experience leisure culture at Saratoga Springs and other American "first resorts" became markers of middle-class identity.[45] Between 1815 and 1845, tourism became increasingly commodified as the middle class applied the principles of the market revolution to travel. The transportation revolution provided the canals, roads, and railways that allowed tourists to access these sites, but it was "the passenger's consumeristic attitude towards travel that suggested the touristic possibility of the consumption of leisure."[46] It was these middle-class tourists who made Shaker villages and Catholic convents "must-see" sites on the travel itineraries of the antebellum era.

Tourism allowed middle-class Americans to cultivate what has been called "the tourist gaze." The "tourist gaze" in any historical period "is constructed in relationship to its opposite, to nontourist forms of social experience and consciousness. What makes a particular tourist gaze depends upon what it is contrasted with." Theoretically, tourism is predicated on deviance from one's routine, from normal experience — tourists seek out the strange, the exotic, and the grand in their travels.[47] This gaze, rooted in difference and opposites, can be seen in the numerous travel encounters between American tourists and Shakers, Catholics, and even Grahamites in the nineteenth century. Tourists to these sites of sexual deviance validated their own identity as "normal" in contrast with sexual practices they found strange. Visits to convents and Shaker villages constituted a type of "cultural tourism," a practice in which one leaves home "to encounter cultural practices different from whatever you conceive your own to be done by . . . people who are 'different' from you."[48]

Though nineteenth-century tourists doing the fashionable tour may not have crossed national, regional, or even state boundaries, they were consciously seeking out encounters with the different cultural practices of priests, nuns, Shakers, and Grahamites. One can see cultural tourism at work in the various nineteenth-century travel guidebooks (figure 5.3) that advised travelers on how to visit Mount Lebanon or Montreal's Hotel Dieu. Pocket manuals like *The Tourist* (1830) recommended visitors to the resort at Lebanon Springs also visit the nearby Shaker settlement: "In the vicinity of the spring is the Shaker Village, consisting of a considerable number of plain wooden houses, painted and adorned in the most unostentatious manner. The peculiar religious services of this people excite the curiosity of strangers, and access to them is easily obtained."[49] In the large fold-out map that accompanied the pocket-manual, the route to Lebanon Springs from the steamboat landing at Hudson, twenty-five miles to the southwest, was clearly marked. The springs and the Shaker settlement were marketed as a package deal, and were such a popular destination that stages ran between the steamboat landing and Lebanon Springs twice daily, specifically timed to accommodate travelers taking the steamboat up from New York City.[50] *The Fashionable Tour*, which helped to codify American nineteenth-century lei-

A Sketch of

Lebanon Springs.

Its Attractions as a Summer Resort--
A Visit to the Shakers--History
of the Town--Columbia
Hall--Railroad
Guide, &c.

PUBLISHED BY

DANIEL GALE,

Proprietor Columbia Hall.

Chickering & Axtell, Printers, Pittsfield.

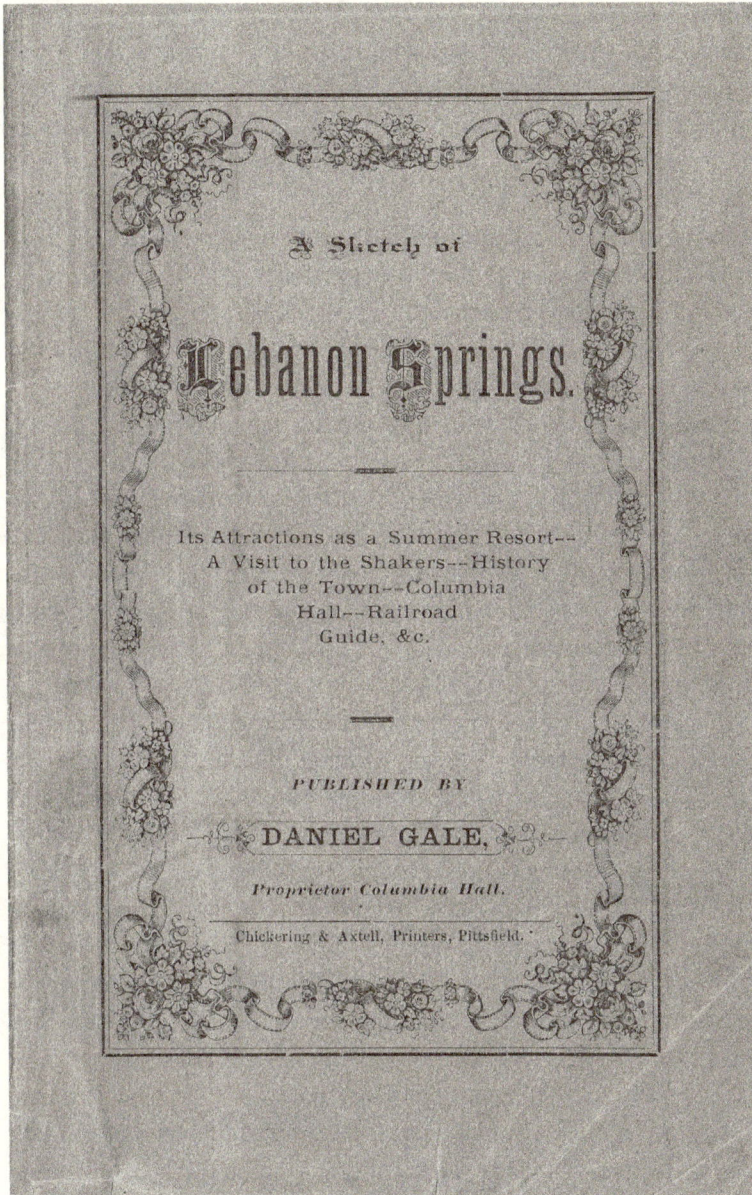

FIGURE 5.3 This guidebook marketed both the water-cure establishments of Lebanon Springs and nearby Mount Lebanon as tourist attractions. Courtesy of the American Antiquarian Society.

sure travel in the antebellum era, similarly took pains to advertise both the Shaker villages of America and the convents and seminaries of Quebec as tourist attractions. In this 1821 guide, the three convents of Montreal along with the Jesuit and Ursuline institutions at Trois-Rivières are described in detail, down to the number of nuns living there and the color of their habits.[51]

Travel journals and guidebooks not only contained factual descriptions of convents and Shaker villages, they also proffered judgment on the religious, sexual, and gender deviance of the people who inhabited these spaces. Published travel guides were more than just how to get from A to B, tips on where to stay, and the names of stagecoach companies; they were mini-ethnographies. Dean MacCannell in his pioneering study of tourism has argued that this criticism and distancing are also intrinsic to the touristic experience. Any attendee of "a cultural production" either accepts its "moral and aesthetic conclusion" or uses this experience to reject it, "trash" it, or call it a "fraud."[52] And yet, it is important to recognize that these touristic evaluations were as complex as the individuals who made them. So, the pseudonymous author of *Taghkonic*, Godfrey Greylock, could within the span of scarcely two pages denounce the Shakers' "strange distortions of the social system" while praising their great circular stone barn at Hancock, Massachusetts, as "the noblest looking agricultural structure I ever saw." For Greylock (whose name was itself a touristic pun on the tallest mountain in Western Massachusetts), a trip to Mount Lebanon was nearly the equivalent of a trip to Europe, for Mount Lebanon was "the capital of the Shaker world—the rural Vatican which claims a more despotic sway over the minds of men than ever Roman Pontiff assumed."[53] Greylock was far from the only traveler to hold this view; he gives a thorough description of the collection of antebellum urbanites come out to witness the Shakers' Sabbath meeting: "Portly citizens in the glossiest of broadcloths and most rubicund of faces, with massive watch seals and heavy gold headed canes, hirsute exquisites, redolent of Broadway and *eau de vie*; ladies, radiant in smiles and diamonds; men, eminent in politics, science and literature; belles, blues, and heiresses; in short they were a fashionable mob."[54]

Though Godfrey Greylock's 1853 travelogue has faded into obscurity, cultural tourism to Shaker communities also made appearances in the most well-known travel literature of the antebellum era. Charles Dickens, Harriet Martineau, Alexis De Tocqueville, Nathaniel Hawthorne, and even the actress Charlotte Cushman made sure to see the Shakers while doing the "fashionable tour."[55] And all of them took the opportunity to observe and critique the sect and their sexual behaviors, and share their critiques with a national and often international audience. Harriet Martineau remarked upon her visit to Mount Lebanon in the 1830s, "I have never witnessed more visible absurdity than in the way of life of the Shakers." Martineau found the Shakers' fields, orchards, and gardens "flourishing," and their homes spacious and well kept. But she could not separate their sexual practices from their religiosity: "Their thoughts are full of the one subject of celibacy. . . . Their religious exercises are disgustingly full of it."[56] Dickens, in his *American Notes*, also stopped by the Shakers at Lebanon on the final leg of his journey through the United States and Canada. The novelist's visit coincided with the Shakers' spiritual revival, the "Era of Manifestations." During the Era of Manifestations, the Shakers closed their meetings to the public for the first time in their history out of fear that spectators would drive away their honored guests from the spirit world.[57] Even after having been denied the right to see the Shakers at their worship, Dickens nevertheless felt comfortable passing judgment on them all the same from the little he was able to glimpse from roadways of New Lebanon. Based on his impressions from a "print in my possession" (most likely the Currier & Ives print in figure 5.2), Dickens described the Shaker meeting he was not allowed to attend. He concluded based on the visuals of the print and secondhand accounts from friends who had seen the Shakers at worship that it was "infinitely grotesque." Dickens had a visceral dislike of the Shakers and what he thought they represented. To him they embodied all "which would strip life of its healthful graces, rob youth of its innocent pleasures, pluck from maturity and age their pleasant ornaments, and make existence but a narrow path towards the grave."[58]

Dickens was annoyed to have been refused admittance to the Shakers' Sabbath meeting. The tone of his account smacked of entitlement denied. To Dickens the Shakers were a touristic attraction, where one went after taking the stage from Albany but before embarking on a steamboat down the Hudson. For the Shakers to be forbidden to visitors was to him as absurd and inconvenient as Niagara Falls ceasing its flow. For Dickens and other visitors, the Shakers were not simply a religious organization with a Sunday worship service but specifically a touristic site. There is the unspoken assumption that like the "Shaking Quakers" at Barnum's museum, actual Shakers should also be able to present their religious exercises at regularly appointed times for any visitor who wished to see them.

Less famous travel diaries and letters reflected similar degrees of the voyeurism expressed by Harriet Martineau and Charles Dickens. These travelers were not renowned published authors, but the "tourist gaze" empowered them to critique the Shakers, priests, and nuns they encountered. Professional critics and ordinary tourists alike sought out these moments of "staged authenticity" in their touristic encounters, to gain access to what sociologist Erving Goffman has called "the back region" or "backstage." In contrast to the "front region," the official location where outsiders observe a performance, the back region reveals the performance to be an "illusion" or fabrication by showing the mechanics of the performance, similar to the actual backstage of a working theater where props and costumes are stored and actors drop the masks of their characters.[59] One can observe tourists pursuing access to the truest and most authentic "back stage" experience, the final stage that is "the social space that motivates touristic consciousness."[60] It was never simply enough to view the Shaker village or Montreal's Hotel Dieu from the outside; nineteenth-century tourists were forever trying to gain access to *real* Shakers dancing, *real* nuns at prayer. Like Dickens, they became frustrated when their voyeuristic desires were denied.

One can see these same sentiments in the travel diary of Mira Sharpless Townsend. A Philadelphia Quaker, she journeyed with her husband from Philadelphia to Montreal via Niagara Falls in 1839. Townsend was disappointed to find that though she was allowed to view the "grey nuns" at Montreal's Recollet convent at prayer, "their own private apartments we could not get to see. . . . At the Hotel Dieu (Maria Monks convent) we were particularly curious of course, but we were told that since her disclosures, they keep themselves much more secluded & the public are not admitted to even guess at the hidden mysteries of the place." Townsend was yet again frustrated when denied entrance to the Ursuline Convent at Trois Rivières. Such secrecy only confirmed her worst suspicions about the lives of nuns and priests; "so much privacy is a bad design." Even though Townsend had no more interaction with the Canadian Ursulines than Charles Dickens did with the Lebanon Shakers, she felt comfortable proclaiming them birds in cages, "chartered by sorrow . . . heart broken exiles."[61] Maria Fay, who did the "fashionable tour" with her parents in the 1830s, similarly expressed her disappointment at being turned away from the nuns' private quarters at the Hotel Dieu in Montreal. Fay's disappointment is especially ironic, as she was the daughter of a wealthy Boston judge and herself a pupil at the Ursuline convent at Charlestown when it burned in 1834. Even though she was quite familiar with nuns and life at a convent school, she sought out the touristic sites of Catholicism with the same zeal as she did Niagara Falls or Auburn Prison.[62] Mary Clark, a native of Concord, New Hampshire, was inspired to take a weekend jaunt to the Shaker village at Canterbury with a gentleman friend after reading Mary Marshall Dyer's pamphlet. Clark's 1823 visit only served to confirm what she already believed—that the Shakers were "deluded" and that Dyer's narrative was the truth. Her visit inspired her to purchase a copy of Dyer's book and send it to her cousin along with the letter describing her trip to Canterbury.[63]

To a much lesser extent, Graham boarding houses were also sites of tourism and voyeurism. Between 1832 and 1845, approximately sixteen boarding houses were founded in the northeastern and midwestern United States, run entirely on the Graham system. A Graham house was, in a way, its own kind of closed community. Asenath Nicholson's New York Graham house, in addition to banning spirits, tobacco, and all stimulating foods, also adhered to a strict regime of cold-water baths and early rising, Graham's additional prescriptions for controlling the libido and staving off solitary vice.[64] On a few occasions, journalists conducted a bit of investigative reporting on Graham houses. One Mr. Murdock, an actor, reported of his encounters at David Cambell's Brattle Street Graham boarding house for the *New York Herald*. When Cambell said they'd be happy to have the actor and his family as long as they lived on the Graham principle, Murdock told him, "That fact, with your appearance to corroborate it, is amply sufficient to induce me to look further. I wish you a very good morning, sir, and an appetite for your dinner. You should have that sauce at least, for it seems you get no other." In his rebuttal, Cambell offered that he was of average height and weight and that there was "nothing remarkable" about his appearance.[65] Boarding houses in nineteenth-century America were semipublic spaces that mixed the private sphere of domesticity with the commercial needs of the marketplace. Like convents and Shaker villages, they were places the public felt they had a "right" to enter.[66] Graham houses were destinations for not only Grahamites but also abolitionists, and were at times some of the only spaces black reformers could reliably count upon to find lodgings during crowded antislavery conventions. Graham housekeepers like Asenath Nicholson may have intentionally played up her house's unhospitable reputation for hard beds and plain water as a kind of camouflage to discourage lodgers hostile to antislavery causes and interracial cohabitation.[67]

The connection between Grahamite principles and tourism can be seen more clearly in the flourishing of water-cure resorts in the 1850s and beyond. Even after Graham's death, his dietetic and sexual restraint principles were adopted by many practitioners of hydropathy, or water cure. In addition to the soakings and wet sheet wrappings that were the staples of hydropathy, water-cure resorts ran on the Grahamite vegetarian diet. Like Grahamism, water cure associated sexual vice, both solitary and social, with disease. Hydropathy promised the human body could be perfected through diet and the judicious application of water treatments. Moreover, water-cure practitioners, too, sought to empower female patients over a male medical establishment and especially promised miracle cures for feminine ailments relating to menstruation, menopause, and postpartum care. Furthering the connection, Grahamites Mary Gove Nichols and David Cambell helped to run water-cure establishments in the 1840s and 1850s.[68] Notably, Cambell served as general-manager of the Lebanon Springs resort established by Joel Shew, the leading hydropathic physician in America at the time. The close proximity between the Lebanon Springs resort and the Shakers' Mount Lebanon community further enhanced the resort's association with sexual restraint. Patrons at Lebanon Springs were certainly encouraged by guidebooks to visit the Shakers.[69]

Tourists, from Charles Dickens with his lithograph of Shakers dancing to Mira Sharpless Townsend with her familiarity with Maria Monk's *Awful Disclosures*, came to sites having already preexperienced through print what they were about to experience in person. This kind of "mechanical reproduction" led Townsend to specifically seek out Maria Monk's convent, in the same way others traveled to Niagara Falls or Mammoth Cave after encountering these through engravings or published travelogues.[70] With mechanical reproduction, tourism to Shaker villages and Catholic convents became part of a cyclical and self-perpetuating process. Tourists like Townsend and Dickens read about the Shakers at Lebanon or the Hotel Dieu in Montreal, leading them to visit these places. They in turn wrote about their experiences, reproducing their accounts for another generation of tourists, leading more to come and experience these sites, beginning the cycle again.[71] The end result was a product even further removed from authenticity. This cyclical process is how a cultural phenomenon like "The Black Shakers' Song" came to be, a minstrel version of a Shaker performance concocted by P. T. Barnum and a group of Shaker apostates. The performance became further removed from real Shaker worship every time a new minstrel troupe performed the routine.

A desire to access the authentic "back region" of a Catholic convent or to replicate the touristic encounters of others may not have been the sole motivation that drove tourists to these sites. Nineteenth-century tourists were complex and sometimes contradictory people. They were drawn to encounters with strange sexual and religious others, yet they also regarded convents and Shaker villages as places of industrial innovation. Contrary to what might motivate someone to visit a reconstructed "living museum" like Hancock Shaker Village or Pleasant Hill, Kentucky, today, nineteenth-century tourism to such sites was often driven by the desire to see cutting-edge modernity, not nostalgia for an agrarian past. Many of the "fashionable mob" that came to Sabbath worship at Mount Lebanon were urban dwellers. In their eyes, the Shakers with their vacuum-operated herb distillery, steam-powered workshops, and giant kitchens that could feed upwards of hundreds were not markers of a quaint rural existence, but the very latest science and technology had to offer.[72] Large buildings like the Great Stone Dwelling at Enfield Shaker Village and the convents in Montreal were in and of themselves impressive architectural wonders at a time when such structures were far from commonplace in North America. In this regard, tourism to convents and Shaker villages resembled another brand of antebellum tourism: visits to prisons and asylums. Maria Fay and her family also visited Auburn Prison on their tour through upstate New York and Canada.[73] Tourists flocked to see prisons and asylums not merely for their architectural uniqueness, but because of the radical social reorganizations they housed. For foreign visitors especially, prisons like Auburn, Ossining (Sing Sing), and Pennsylvania's Eastern State Penitentiary were to America what cathedrals were to Europe.[74]

Shaker villages, Catholic convents, and to a certain extent Graham houses also represented a radical social reorganization. Just as penitentiaries and asylums attempted to revolutionize society's treatment of the criminal and the insane, these spaces proposed a radically new sex-gender system, one in which sexual intercourse was either absent or severely limited. In touring these locations of sexual otherness, nineteenth-century tourists participated in the systematic branding and exile Foucault deemed an integral part of the modern age. Tourism operated as yet another disciplinary mechanism in the nineteenth-century society.[75] Like prisons and madhouses, convents and Shaker villages were undoubtedly "institutions," physically bounded spaces set apart from the normal world. However, unlike inmates of the prison and the madhouse, Shaker, Catholic and Grahamite "inmates" were there by choice, not by the disciplinary power of the state.[76] The invisible line between tourist and actual nun, priest, or Shaker was a sexual one that kept the sexually normal separate from the sexually abnormal.

Yet Shakers and Catholics were not passive victims to the tourist gaze. They were remarkably self-aware of their status as tourist attractions and the curiosity they incited. Records from the time reveal a careful negotiation on the part of these sexual others between how much they were willing to allow outsiders access to the types of "back room" experiences that were typically members-only. It was a delicate balance; if they appeared too standoffish, they were accused of secrecy; too open, they risked desecrating private rituals by opening them up to the public gaze.[77]

This kind of shrewd negotiation can also be seen in the experiences of travelers Maria Fay and Mira Sharpless Townsend in their travels to the Canadian convents. The nuns allowed Townsend and her companions to see their patients in the hospital and the orphaned children in their care at Montreal's Hotel Dieu. They encouraged the travelers to buy trinkets made by the nuns to help support their good works, "but nothing very pretty & everything very dear," Townsend complained. Townsend still found what she had read about in the pages of Maria Monk's scandalous tale more plausible than what she saw with her own eyes. She had a hard time believing that the sacrament of confession was not often sealed with a kiss when the penitent was a young woman. And as far as the nuns' care for the sick and orphaned went, "charity covers a multitude of sins."[78] Young Maria Fay, herself a former pupil at the Ursuline convent school in Boston, expressed a more favorable opinion of the Hotel Dieu. Though she could not see the nuns' private apartments, Fay remarked of the nursing sisters, "I almost think their dress becoming." It was the sort of offhand romantic observation that struck fear into the heart of every staunch anti-Catholic who worried about young, impressionable Protestant women like Fay being "seduced" into convents.[79] Significantly, Fay desired only the superficial outward trappings of the life of nun—she desired their dress, not their life of celibacy and service. Despite her long-standing familiarity with the Ursuline sisters who tutored her as a student at Mount Benedict, in the end Fay evaluated them only on whether or not their dress was "becoming."

Shakers were at times willing participants in their own commodification. It was a very difficult line to walk, as they were torn between the prospect of gaining new converts through public exposure and their own desire to keep themselves apart from "the world." When the Shakers made the conscious decision not to engage in missionary activity after the first decades of the nineteenth century, they became more dependent than ever on recruiting new converts through open worship services at their existing villages. For every twenty or thirty spectators who came merely to gawk at the Shakers' worship, there was always the possibility that one or two would open their hearts and minds to the Shaker gospel. One such person was young Octavia Fitton, who stopped at one of the Maine Shaker communities while en route to visit her grandfather in New Hampshire. Fitton extended her visit longer than her father thought prudent. He wrote an angry letter to the Shaker elders, telling them young Octavia was there without his permission and had better be on her way. Should she disobey him, he promised to be "troublesome" to both Octavia and the Shakers.[80]

Unfortunately for the Shakers, the gawking spectators who clogged up the drive at Mount Lebanon with their coaches far outnumbered potential future believers like Octavia Fitton. In 1849, the Shakers at Watervliet attempted to set some boundaries on their interactions with visitors: "In consequence of the frequent intrusions and annoyances from many of the multitude who visit this Society for recreation, we are constrained by a sense of duty and propriety to give the following NOTICE: Hereafter, we shall not admit people to walk around and among our buildings, and in our gardens as frequently as we have done." The Watervliet Shakers found that interest in their community, located near the junction of the Hudson River and the Erie Canal, was more than they could reasonably handle without interrupting the rhythm of their daily routine. "We consider it unreasonable to wait upon every coach load, or company who resort here and ask to be admitted to the Church. . . . We shall sometimes have more than twenty such applications from different companies in one day. This is a heavier tax on our time and duties, than we feel able, or consider reasonable to meet." The second half of the Shakers' "Notice" was targeted specifically at those spectators who came to attend Sunday worship. Reminding visitors that they had built their new meetinghouse entirely of their own expense without one penny of outside or public assistance, they were happy to admit the public to worship with them—"All the recompense we ask or desire . . . is good behavior." The Shakers defined "good behavior" as the public taking their seats on time, using the spitting boxes provided instead of spitting on the floor, wiping their feet before entering the meetinghouse, and finally, "to show no approbation with anything like mockery, or uncivil deportment."[81] They were hardly unreasonable requests to make of visitors.

Shakers also required their overnight guests to abide by the requirements of Shakerism while within the confines of their village; if a married couple stayed the night, husbands and wives were required to sleep separately. As one Shaker told a Boston doctor visiting Hancock, "It'll do 'em good to sleep separate now & then, they ought to have a little cross once in a while." But some visitors felt that the Shakers should accommodate them, rather than the other way around. The Hancock Shakers reported, "A man came here one time to stop, & they told him what the regulation was, 'what

I can't sleep with my wife?' & he called for his carriage right off." The Shakers said that if on the steamboat men and women could endure having separate cabins, why should it be any more onerous for a night's stay in their village?[82]

"Social reproduction" where "groups, cities, and regions begin to name themselves after famous attractions" is regarded as the final and most established stage of touristic phenomena. Both the "Shaking Quakers" troupe and the "Black Shakers" minstrel routine can be considered examples of this phase of "social reproduction" of Shaker tourism.[83] They were not authentic performances of Shakerism by real Shakers, but audiences sought out these encounters all the same. Viewing these artificial performances might have even motivated a few to seek out that truer back region experience by joining the "fashionable mob" at Mount Lebanon. Artful deception and the "tourist gaze" were linked, both part of the critiquing investigative process that helped these middle-class tourists and spectators differentiate themselves from those they found abnormal. Citizens of the middle class sought out these encounters with sexual others to discover for themselves whether a Shaker or a nun's sexual restraint was real or just "humbug." And being able to judge celibacy as performed by the Shakers at Mount Lebanon or the nuns at Montreal gave them all the more power to reject it and walk away from their travels secure in the supremacy of married heterosexuality. On the surface, there was no danger of them being swayed into staying behind at the Shaker Village or the Hotel Dieu because they were protected by the veneer of the touristic encounters. The point of tourism is that it is a temporary departure from "normal" ordinary life. If one were to stay, he or she would no longer be a tourist but would become a convert instead. One can see this anxiety in the experience of Octavia Fitton, whose father thought she had overstayed what was supposed to be only a temporary sojourn to the Shakers' settlement.

The development of tourism and performance surrounding these groups was not apolitical, but merely a subtler, newer iteration of the politics of violence that surrounded the mob attacks earlier in the century. Performance as a political tool could be quite effective, if the near-passage of an anti-Shaker bill in the New Hampshire legislature in 1849 was any indication. By the 1850s, the violent mobs of the 1810s and 1830s that terrorized Shaker villages, Catholic convents, and Grahamite lectures had transformed themselves into fashionable ones. Yet the same suspicion, abhorrence, and odd fascination with sexual restraint endured.

Conclusion

On the morning of July 5, 1863, sixteen Charity sisters and their director, Father Francis Burlando, left the comfort of their motherhouse in Emmitsburg to tend the hundreds wounded at the Battle of Gettysburg. The large white cornettes of the sisters' headdresses flapped in the breeze, providing an unlikely flag of truce that granted them safe passage through the pickets. The carriage wheels of their omnibus, heavy with medical supplies, rolled through mud and blood as the sisters passed mass graves of Union and Confederate dead on their way into town. Union officers who had previously quartered at St. Joseph's House were "very glad" to see the sisters, and gave them the town's hotel for their private use. Gettysburg's Catholic church had been converted to a makeshift hospital and was filled to capacity with soldiers with missing limbs and infected wounds. The grounds of Gettysburg College held over 600 sick and wounded prisoners of war who needed tending as well.[1] Sister Camilla O'Keefe remarked, "The services of the sister were much needed and appreciated too by the government."[2]

The Charity sisters slept on the floor without mattresses or bedding their first night in Gettysburg. They cared for the soldiers, the men's bodies covered with "filth" and "vermin" to an extent the sisters could scarcely stand or believe. Already experienced in the cholera, yellow fever, and typhus epidemics that had plagued American cities during the antebellum era, the Charity sisters and other women religious possessed nursing skills that were in high demand during the Civil War. More than a dozen religious orders of women, some of whom had no prior nursing experience, mobilized to serve.[3] The sisters at Gettysburg knew they could expect few reinforcements, as members of the order had already been dispatched to nurse soldiers in Washington, D.C., Philadelphia, and Point Lookout, leaving St. Joseph's motherhouse to run on a skeleton crew.[4] That first night, the sisters were the only women in a town full of dead and dying men: "We didn't see a woman in the whole place that evening." When a group of ladies from Baltimore arrived a few days later offering their services, the Union officers "refused them saying the Sisters of Charity were caring for them." The Union army thought the Charity sisters more trustworthy, suspecting the society belles of being rebel spies. The sisters' bravery, selflessness, and expertise won them the admiration of many who had previously viewed them with suspicion. One Gettysburg gentleman was to have said, "Can it be that these are the persons that I have almost hated, and are now serving our poor men with so much care—with motherly kindness?" The sisters themselves had expected to encounter "some pain" surrounded by so many non-Catholic men. In the aftermath of battle, however, "bitterness had lost its edge."[5] Official histories of the Daughters of Charity regard the Civil War as a turning point in American Protestant-Catholic relations, the sisters' service to soldiers on both sides of the conflict helping to diminish decades of anti-Catholic prejudice.[6]

While the Sisters of Charity and other men and women religious were serving the nation during wartime using their unique skills and status, the Shakers' commitment to nonmilitarist masculinity put them at odds with the Union war effort. Despite nearly a century of vocal pacifism and noninterference in political affairs—no Shaker man had ever voted or held an elected office higher than postmaster—Shaker men were still being forced by local authorities to comply with the draft. One young Shaker brother from the Shirley, Massachusetts, community had been shackled with irons and taken to a Union training camp, where a sergeant threatened to shoot him for failing to participate in military drills before ultimately releasing him. The Shakers did not believe it was possible "to love a man and shoot him at the same time," nor could they afford to pay for substitutes, spiritually or financially.[7]

Concerned for the safety of their male members and unwilling to compromise their pacifist principles, elders Benjamin Gates and F. W. Evans set out on a journey from Mount Lebanon to Washington, where they petitioned President Lincoln and Secretary of War Edward Stanton.[8] The two Shaker elders presented Lincoln with a "memorial" in which they humbly asked Shaker brothers to be exempted from the draft. According to their careful calculations, when accounting for age and infirmity, only about seventy Shaker men would be fit for military service, costing the Union roughly $21,000 to exempt them. This was not a small amount, the Shakers knew. They then reminded the president that it was minuscule in proportion to the over $600,000 in principal and interest the U.S. Treasury owed in unclaimed veterans pensions belonging to Shaker brothers who had fought in the War of Independence and War of 1812. Impressed by the Shakers' shrewdness and unwavering commitment to their faith, Lincoln granted them their exemption, saying, "You *ought* to be made to fight! We need regiments of men such as you." The Shakers reassured the president of their loyalty and promised to pray for the "Continuance of this Free Government" even if their pacifist beliefs prevented them from fighting for it.[9]

After this "pleasant interview" with the president, the Shakers regarded Lincoln with a special fondness. They sent him one of their famed ladder-backed chairs as a token of thanks and friendship. Lincoln pronounced it "a very comfortable chair" and expressed his appreciation.[10] A month before his assassination, the Shakers wrote to Lincoln again, inviting him to spend some time in rest and relaxation in the hills at Mount Lebanon, assuring that he would be received by "sympathizing friends, brothers and sisters in Christ."[11] Lincoln did not live long enough to take the Shakers up on their invitation. But soon after the war in 1867, Secretary of War Stanton did, bringing his wife and child to the Shakers' central ministry. He reminisced with the Shakers about the late president, and told them that the time spent at Mount Lebanon "I count as being among the happiest moments of my life. . . . From my earliest recollection, you Shakers had always been talked of in my father's house, and I always felt a desire to visit you." He called Benjamin Gates "a brother of my heart" and told them how he had worked hard to persuade the president of the rightness of their cause. As he was leaving, Eldress Antoinette Doolittle, who had once fought so ardently to make her parents understand her Shaker conversion, expressed her wish that God would bless Stanton with new prosperity in the postwar years. Eyes filled with tears, Stanton said that during the darkest hours of the war, when his "heart was heavy," the prayers of "righteous" men and women like the Shakers were his only "solace."[12]

These anecdotes reveal how Catholic men and women religious and their Shaker counterparts positioned themselves at an incredibly tense and transformational moment in American history, when the loyalties of many were being tested and questioned. Rather than experiencing the violence of convent burnings or the harsh legal repressions that some had called for during the Know-Nothings' rise to power, celibate women like the Daughters of Charity were welcomed openly by officers, soldiers, and civilians. Their labor in the war effort was considered more desirable than that of Protestant civilian women. It would be easy to see this episode as one in which an outsider group somehow gains inclusion through patriotic service. But to do that would be an oversimplification that minimizes their unique status as celibate women. This was a moment in which their sexual restraint and ability to transcend traditional femininity made them especially desirable. As Dorothea Dix and her nursing corps worried about having young single

Protestant women away from home caring for soldiers, the celibacy of the Catholic sisters made their virtue unimpeachable.[13] What had previously made the sisters seem odd, suspect, and strange had been transformed by the necessities of war into a virtue.

The Shakers' case is less straightforward but perhaps no less extraordinary. The Shakers' negotiations with Lincoln and Stanton are all the more revealing of the change in their regard by the American public when compared with how Shakers were treated during previous conflicts. Their welcome at the White House could not be further than the imprisonment on charges of treason experienced by Ann Lee during the Revolution and the suspicion and hostility directed toward male Shaker converts who refused to participate in militias and musters around the time of the 1810 Turtle Creek riot. The Shakers won the respect of Lincoln and his war department not by compromising their values but by sticking to them. They presented Lincoln with the kind of straightforward bargain they had gained a reputation for in their business dealings. It is notable that they gifted him one of their chairs, one of the products they had become most associated with in the nineteenth century and the one made iconic by collectors in the centuries to come.

The self-conscious branding and in the Shaker case, commercialization, around certain goods and services that both groups had undertaken allowed those who were against sex to occupy a place that was both inside and outside the nation by midcentury. Their celibate sexual values were still opposed to middle-class family-centered mores that exalted marriage, but they had shown Americans that their distinctness could be tolerated and even valuable. In the case of Sylvester Graham, his legacy would almost entirely be a commercial one. The number of people calling themselves "Grahamites" shrank after Sylvester Graham died in 1851. Though Graham himself was gone, his ideas linking health to diet and sexuality lived on, most of all in fellow health reformer John Harvey Kellogg. Kellogg, who had been a sickly child, absorbed Graham's ideas about vegetarian diet at a young age. As a medical student doing his residency at New York's Bellevue hospital, Kellogg ate no more than an apple and seven "Graham crackers" for breakfast every day. When he was appointed superintendent of the Battle Creek Sanitarium in 1876, Kellogg imposed a regimen inspired by the Graham system for all his patients. Kellogg was also known to speak out against alcohol and sexual "self-abuse" as leading causes of disease, preaching Graham's ideas into the late nineteenth century.[14] Kellogg's promotion of cereal grains at his sanitarium has made Grahamite principles a staple of the American breakfast table into the present day. When the National Biscuit Company (subsequently renamed Nabisco) began to mass-produce thin crackers made from wheat flour in 1898, they called their product the "Graham Cracker," because of the association between Graham's name and healthy living. Now made with sugar and preservatives, the Graham cracker is a far cry from the Graham bread popularized in the 1830s and even farther from Sylvester Graham's promotion of sexual restraint.[15]

Shaker chairs, Catholic hospitals, the Graham cracker. It would be easy to view the lasting legacy of Shakers, Catholic celibates, and Grahamites as one of products and services, instead of people, given the sharp decline in numbers all three have experienced since the nineteenth century. The number of priests in the United States has decreased by roughly 38 percent since 1970, while the number of women choosing a religious vocation has declined nearly 75 percent.[16] The fate of the Shakers is even starker. Only one Shaker settlement, the village at Sabbathday Lake, Maine, is currently active. There are at present only two Shakers left in the world. Even in the face of what might be an inevitable extinction, the Shakers have refused to compromise their beliefs on celibacy.[17] Neither has the Vatican heeded calls to reform the celibate priesthood.

Perhaps like the nineteenth-century American middle class, we in the present find the simplicity of Shaker furniture or a slice of whole-grain Graham bread easier to swallow than extremes of sexual abstinence. The legacy of Shakers, Catholic celibates, and Grahamites should be more than simply a material one. The deliberate and consciously constructed nature of these groups' sexual restraint is something that stands apart in relationship to both their nineteenth-century contemporaries and modern-day sexual identities. Shakers, Catholic priests and sisters, and sexual reformers like the Grahamites formed alternative family structures outside of the biological family, and in the case of the Grahamites, also sought to reform marriage from within. The presence of these groups also teases apart how for many Americans, normative gender was inextricably linked to a normative sexuality and a normative body, provoking attacks that their celibacy caused sickness and monstrosity. And while those who were against sex resisted gender norms of both passive femininity and aggressive masculinity, they never completely transcended them either. Catholic sisters and Grahamite wives still found themselves deferential to a larger patriarchal culture. Shaker sisters and brothers saw each other as spiritual equals but could not envision a utopia in which men cooked or women made furniture.

Shakers, Catholic men and women religious, and Grahamites had remarkably different trajectories during the latter half of the nineteenth century, but the questions they raised were of real and lasting importance. They challenged the assumed naturalness of sexual activity and the centrality of marriage to the human experience. In doing so they radically posited that the positive value accorded to sex within marriage was a matter of perspective. Long before the idea of sexuality being a socially constructed phenomenon was discussed in academic and activist circles, advocates of sexual restraint saw prevailing sexual norms as a matter of custom, rather than an inevitable fate. They also successfully navigated the print, consumer, and performance cultures of their time as active participants, not hapless victims.

How much sex should a person have? With whom? What sexual activities are "normal"? These were the questions being asked during the first eighty years of the history of the United States. We are still asking them today. A century and a half later, American society has its own assumptions about the "naturalness" of sex, which vary according to religious identity, gender, class, race, and ethnicity among other factors. But similarly to our nineteenth-century forebears, many would probably consider a life without sex to be unnatural or oppressive. Celibacy still remains a suspect sexual behavior. In the wake of recent sexual abuse scandals in the Catholic Church, concerns have been raised about celibacy's place in the modern priesthood. Some critics have argued that celibacy encourages sexual abuse. In a recent opinion piece for the *New York Times*, columnist Frank Bruni wrote that "the pledge of celibacy that the church requires of its servants is an often cruel and corrosive thing. It runs counter to human nature. It asks too much."[18] The late Richard Sipe, himself a former priest, has argued that celibacy is a "charism" or gift, one that cannot be made mandatory.[19] In all of these debates about the place of celibacy for the Catholic priesthood, few question whether or not celibacy is good for Catholic nuns or sisters. Assumed ideas about women's "passionlessness" and the male libido which turns monstrous when repressed have persisted into the twenty-first century.

Challenges to the assumed naturalness of sexual activity also echo in the voice of the growing asexuality movement. Asexuals, according to David Jay, founder of AVEN, the Asexuality Visibility and Education Network, are people who do not experience sexual attraction. Jay and other asexuals work very hard to differentiate themselves from celibates. They believe that celibacy is a choice, whereas their asexuality is a biologically determined identity. Asexuals often discuss their sexual identity and struggles in a way that utilizes language from the gay and lesbian civil rights movement. They speak of the need to "come out" as asexual and to resist those who would pathologize them as mentally ill.[20] Members of AVEN see radical potential in having a culture-wide conversation on sexuality that includes asexuality. David Jay and other asexuals find the current sexual dialogue "inauthentic," one "that fetishizes and celebrates sexuality, and equates it with the sum of our value and relationships."[21]

Asexuality, as an orientation, challenges feminist and queer understandings of sex positivity which have long dominated third-wave feminist thought. For asexuals, a refusal to engage in compulsory sexuality is liberating. Pleasure may be found in "queerplatonic" relationships that do not feature sex; danger comes in the form of sometimes well-meaning friends and professionals who dismiss asexuality as "a phase" or who see lack of sexual attraction as either symptomatic of illness or an illness in itself. Asexual advocates inside and outside of the academy are critical of the "erotic chauvinism" they see as inherent in our society, which uses words like "repressed" and "dysfunctional" to shame people who are not having some idealized norm of sexual activity.[22]

Those in the asexuality movement who would wish to reclaim Shakers, Catholic celibates, or the Grahamites as part of a usable past would be wise to remember that these groups and individuals by and large did not consider their sexual identities to be something that came naturally, easily, or biologically.[23] Their decision to be against sex was a deliberate choice, one that set them at odds with their communities and families, often at great personal cost. Determining what sexual practices were "natural" and "normal" was as much of an issue in 1830 as it is today. In the context of these recent debates, a history of sexuality that includes sexual restraint appears very relevant. Studying sexual restraint gives us a broader picture of the sexual landscape of early America as well as the sexual landscape of our own present moment.

Notes

Abbreviations in the Notes

ASC   Edward Deming Andrews Memorial Shaker Collection, Winterthur Museum & Library, Greenville, Delaware

CM   Congregation of the Mission of the Western Province Records, De Andreis-Rosati Memorial Archives, DePaul University, Chicago, Illinois

HSV   Hancock Shaker Village Library, Hancock, Massachusetts

JDC   Joseph Downs Collection of Advertising Ephemera, Winterthur Museum & Library, Greenville, Delaware

LC   Shaker Collection, Library of Congress, Washington, D.C.

MEHS   Maine Historical Society, Portland, Maine

MHS   Massachusetts Historical Society, Boston, Massachusetts

NAZ   Sisters of Charity of Nazareth Archives, Special Collections, University of Notre Dame Archives, Notre Dame, Indiana

SL   Schlesinger Library, Harvard University, Cambridge, Massachusetts

SMB   St. Mary's of the Barrens Seminary Records, De Andreis-Rosati Memorial Archives, DePaul University, Chicago, Illinois

WML   Winterthur Museum & Library, Greenville, Delaware

WRHS   Western Reserve Historical Society, Cleveland, Ohio

Introduction

1. Youngs, "Transactions of the Ohio Mob," Cathcart Collection, Western Reserve Historical Society, Cleveland, OH, hereafter abbreviated as WRHS; "Expedition against the Shakers," *The Review* (Nashville), October 26, 1810.

2. Youngs, "Transactions of the Ohio Mob," WRHS.

3. Colonel Smith was also a grandfather seeking custody of his grandchildren from their Shaker father, Smith's son, James Smith Jr. Smith, *Remarkable Occurrences*.

4. "Dreadful Conflagration!," *Eastern Argus* (Portland, ME), August 13, 1834.

5. On newspaper accounts of the Charlestown riot, see "Disgraceful and Unprecedented Outrage," *Baltimore Patriot and Mercantile Advertiser*, August 15, 1834; "Meeting in Charlestown," *New Bedford Mercury* (MA), August 15, 1834. A descriptive account of the Charlestown riot can also be found in Schultz, *Fire and Roses*, 1–7.

6. Reed, *Six Months in a Convent*.

7. Schultz, *Fire and Roses*, 223–28, 273.

8. *New Hampshire Sentinel* (Keene), July 31, 1834; "Anti-Graham Riot," *Barre Gazette* (MA), March 10, 1837; "Mob Law," *The Liberator* (Boston, MA), March 24, 1837.

9. "Anti Graham Riot." On Grahamism's empowerment of white and black female reformers, see Haynes, *Riotous Flesh*.

10. The myriad motivations behind the Charlestown convent burning have been well examined, especially in Schultz's *Fire and Roses*. It is important to note that the 1830s and 1840s in the Northeast saw a great number of riots, directed not just at religious or sexual outsiders but also at abolitionists and free black businesses and institutions. See Gilje, *Rioting in America*; Tager, *Boston Riots*; Richards, *"Gentlemen of Property and Standing."*

11. Youngs, *Testimony of Christ's Second Appearing*, 22–23. The life of Mother Ann Lee is also described in Andrews, *People Called Shakers*, and Francis, *Ann the Word*.

12. Youngs, *Testimony of Christ's Second Appearing*, 26.

13. Youngs, 26.

14. *Testimonies of . . . Mother Ann Lee*, 71–73. The 1816 *Testimonies* were a kind of collective biography of Ann Lee, composed from the reminiscences of her surviving followers in 1816. Lee died in 1784, and there are no spiritual writings or records from her lifetime. Lee and her first followers mistrusted the written word and were reluctant to put their beliefs down in writing, because they favored the immediacy of prophecy and spiritual revelation to doctrine. Though it must be acknowledged that using the *Testimonies* as a source comes with a caveat, they are perhaps the best record of the lives of the earliest Shakers.

15. *Testimonies of . . . Mother Ann Lee*, 70.

16. Youngs, *Testimonies of Christ's Second Appearing*, 26–28.

17. *Testimonies of . . . Mother Ann Lee*, 81.

18. The Shakers were actually able to absorb many of these religious dissenters, such as the followers of Shadrach Ireland, during Mother Ann's preaching tour of New England. Winiarski, *Darkness Falls*, 19, 407, 432–33.

19. On the early experiences of Ann Lee in America, see Brewer, *Shaker Communities, Shaker Lives*, 1–5; Stein, *Shaker Experience in America*, 61. The most outspoken Shaker apostates in the late eighteenth century were Daniel and Reuben Rathbun/ Rathbone. Several members of the Rathbun family joined the Shakers later to quit them. See Rathbone, *Reasons Offered for Leaving the Shakers*, 3, 7, 24–28.

20. The Cane Ridge Revival began in Bourbon County, Kentucky, in 1801 and is widely considered to be one of the landmark events of the Second Great Awakening in the United States. Hatch, *Democratization of American Christianity*, 13, 70 and McNemar, *Kentucky Revival*.

21. Shaker demographics are discussed in Stein, *Shaker Experience in America*, 87–89, 114, 115, 229. For evaluating the "success" of different communitarian groups, see Kanter, "Commitment and Social Organization." Early Mormonism had communitarian elements, but Kanter's study of longevity did not include Mormons, as they did not retain these elements in the long term.

22. Statistics on the growth of the American Catholic Church in the nineteenth century are taken from Wittberg, *Rise and Decline of Catholic Religious Orders*, 39, and McGuinness, *Called to Serve*, 5, 8–10.

23. On Seton and her order, see O'Donnell, *Elizabeth Seton*.

24. The majority of women who joined were married women who joined along with their husbands; only seventeen of the initial forty-one charter members were unmarried. Male members paid $1 a year to join or $15 for a lifetime membership;

ladies could become members at half price. *Graham Journal of Health and Longevity*, April 4, 1837; Alcott, *Address*, 4; *Constitution of the American Physiological Society* 4, 5, 17–19, 124–41.

25. The innuendos around Grahamism often played on the dual nature of appetite, hunger for sex and hunger for food. In one encounter with a Graham boardinghouse keeper, a well-known actor wished him a good appetite for his dinner, saying, "You should have that sauce at least, for it seems you get no other." "Murdock the Actor," *Graham Journal of Health and Longevity*, November 28, 1837.

26. Talvacchia, Pettinger, and Larrimore, *Queer Christianities*, 5, 11.

27. Evans, "White Cross Celibacy." When Shakers did reference historical antecedents as arguments in favor of celibacy, they cited the early Christians, the Vestal Virgins of Rome, and other sects from antiquity like the Essenes rather than Catholic monastics. See Fraser, "Is Celibacy Contrary to Natural and Received Law?" I have not been able to find any Catholic critiques of Shakers in the nineteenth century, but it is very likely they would have viewed them as upstart Protestant sectarians, the most extreme outgrowth of the fracturing that had begun with the Reformation, similar to how they viewed other new religious movements like Mormonism. See Noll, Von Reisach, and Cramer, "Jesuit Interpretation of Mid-Nineteenth-Century America."

28. On the origins of Catholic celibacy, see Abbott, *History of Celibacy*, 63–88. On the development of Shakerism in England, see Garrett, *Spirit Possession and Popular Religion*, 46, 56.

29. Greylock, *Taghconic*, 121.

30. Geertz, *Interpretation of Cultures*, 90.

31. Haynes, *Riotous Flesh*, 47–49; Nissenbaum, *Sex, Diet, and Debility*; Greylock, *Taghconic*, 129–30.

32. Graham's medical advice about the dangers of masturbation and linking a high libido to a rich diet might hardly seem like science in the twenty-first century, but the fact was, his regimen was seen as scientific by medical practitioners of the day as well as ordinary men and women.

33. Durkheim, "Elementary Forms of the Religious Life," 107–25. Ann Taves expands upon Durkheim's understanding of the sacred, arguing that things set apart be understood as possessing a kind of "specialness." Taves, *Religious Experience Reconsidered*, 16–17, 26, 36.

34. Paden, "Before 'the Sacred' Became Theological"; Taves, *Religious Experience Reconsidered*, 16.

35. Robert Orsi says of "lived religion," "There is no religion apart from this, no religion that people have not taken up in their hands. . . . Religion is always religion-in-action." Orsi, "Is the Study," 172, and Orsi, *Between Heaven and Earth*, 1–18.

36. Talvacchia, Pettinger, and Larrimore, *Queer Christianities*, 5.

37. Lofton, "Everything Queer?," 96.

38. Talvacchia, Pettinger, and Larrimore, *Queer Christianities*, 5. The ex-gay movement promoted by some evangelical churches can channel same-sex-oriented believers into a kind of "queerish celibacy" by promoting heterosexual marriages. See Gerber, "'Queerish' Celibacy."

39. Anthony M. Petro in a contemporary sense still views gay sex as a more radical challenge to heteronormativity than gay celibacy. See Petro, "Celibate Politics."

40. Stuart, "Sacramental Flesh," 69–70. These challenges to heteronormativity are also discussed in Cheng, *Radical Love*.

41. Major efforts to preserve the material culture of the Shakers began with Edward Deming Andrews and Faith Andrews. Andrews, *People Called Shakers*; Brewer, *Shaker Communities, Shaker Lives*; Foster, *Religion and Sexuality* and *Women, Family, Utopia*. Feminist appraisals of Shaker sexuality can be found in Kitch, *Chaste Liberation*; Campbell, "Women's Life in Utopia"; and Procter-Smith, *Shakerism and Feminism*.

42. Billington, "Maria Monk and Her Influence"; Billington, *Protestant Crusade*.

43. Sokolow, *Eros and Modernization* and Nissenbaum, *Sex, Diet, Debility*.

44. A prime example of this is April Haynes's recent *Riotous Flesh*. Haynes's explicitly intersectional framework allows the agency of female reformers, white and black, to take center stage in what had previously been considered to be a male-dominated movement. Their anti-masturbation activism emerges as a quest for female self-determination and bodily autonomy, rather than simple prudery.

45. On comparative studies of the Shakers, Mormons, and Oneida Perfectionists, see Foster, *Women, Family, Utopia*; Foster, *Religion and Sexuality*; Kern, *Ordered Love*.

46. Nissenbaum, *Sex, Diet, and Debility*, 1–11.

47. Rosenberg, *Cholera Years*.

48. I am inspired by Eve Kosofsky Sedgwick's reading of the coming out narrative and how she describes the disclosure of private and unseen information that cannot be immediately visible. Sedgwick, *Epistemology of the Closet*, 75.

49. Bloch, *Gender and Morality in Anglo-American Culture*, 148.

50. *Aristotle's Masterpiece*, 34.

51. Kanter, *Commitment and Community*; Fogleman, *Jesus Is Female*.

52. Heyrman, *Southern Cross*, 129–32.

53. Bach, *Voices of the Turtledoves*.

54. Butler, *Awash in a Sea of Faith*, 137–41; Juster, *Disorderly Women*, 140.

55. An 1807 Ohio bill attempted to render Shaker men "civilly dead" before the law, and would have prevented any male Shaker convert from deeding his land to the sect. It ultimately did not pass. See Tiffin and Kirker, "Providing for the Relief and Support of Women Who May Be Abandoned by Their Husbands, and for Other Purposes," 1807, WRHS. Know-Nothing legislators did manage to get "nunnery committees" approved for a brief time in the 1850s, but they were quickly disbanded after they turned up no evidence of convent wrongdoings. Mannard, "Maternity . . . of the Spirit."

56. Halttunen, *Confidence Men and Painted Women*; Johnson, *Shopkeeper's Millennium*.

57. Halttunen, *Confidence Men and Painted Women*, 29.

58. These topics have been well documented in Hessinger, *Seduced, Abandoned, and Reborn*; Ryan, *Cradle of the Middle Class*; Cohen, *Murder of Helen Jewett*; Fuhlman, "Peculiar People"; Givens, *Viper on the Hearth*; Eckhart, *Fanny Wright*; Sears, *Sex Radicals*; Cohen, "'Anti-Marriage Theory,'" among others.

59. Johnson, *Shopkeeper's Millennium*, 11.

60. On libertine republican newspaper editors' antagonism toward Graham, see Haynes, *Riotous Flesh*, 81–130.

61. This is discussed in Godbeer, *Sexual Revolution in Early America*, 127–30, 228–33 and Ryan, *Regulating Passion*.

62. Clare Lyons argues that during the 1780s and 1790s, a transatlantic "pleasure culture" that tolerated adultery, prostitution, and children born out of wedlock flourished in Philadelphia. See Lyons, *Sex among the Rabble*.

63. On female moral reform, see Ryan, *Cradle of the Middle Class* and Haynes, *Riotous Flesh*. Abolitionists attacking the sexual abuses inflicted on enslaved women as evidence of the immorality of slaveholding men has been critically examined in Paton, *No Bond but the Law* and "Decency, Dependence, and the Lash"; Fuentes, *Dispossessed Lives*; Walters, "Erotic South"; Sanchez-Eppler, *Touching Liberty*. On anti-polygamy reform's role in Anti-Mormonism, see Fuhlman, *"Peculiar People"*; Givens, *Viper on the Hearth*; Gordon, "Liberty of Self-Degradation"; Davis, "Some Themes of Counter-Subversion"; Talbot, *Foreign Kingdom*.

64. Jonathan Ned Katz defines heterosexuality as a "different-sex erotic ideal" that has its roots in late nineteenth-century sexology. By rejecting sex itself as a site of pleasure, those who engaged in sexual abstinence existed outside and in opposition to this heterosexual matrix. Katz, *Invention of Heterosexuality*, 14. The transition toward a homogenizing heteronormativity is also discussed in LaFleur, *Natural History of Sexuality*.

65. Rubin, "Thinking Sex." When it comes to sexual abstinence, Rubin herself appears to have fallen victim to her own critique. Though she catalogues society's acceptance and distaste of all manner of sexual behavior from married heterosexuality to sadomasochism and pedophilia, celibacy is entirely absent from her anthropological understanding of sexual behavior.

66. Godbeer, *Sexual Revolution*, 11–12; D'Emilio and Freedman, *Intimate Matters*, 31; Rubin, "Thinking Sex"; Godbeer, *Overflowing of Friendship*, 3.

67. Manion, "Language, Acts, and Identity in LGBTQ Histories."

68. Halperin, "Forgetting Foucault."

69. Dorsey, "'Making Men What They Should Be'"; Cleves, *Charity and Sylvia*. Ruth Mazo Karras has also seen evidence that medieval female prostitutes may have taken on a sexual identity unrelated to the gender of their sexual partners; see Karras, "Prostitution."

70. Foster, *Long before Stonewall*, 8.

71. Myles, "Border Crossing." Some seventeenth-century New England Quakers were married couples who chose to mark their conversion to Quakerism by being openly celibate while still remaining married as a conscious display of their new faith. Scholars of sexuality who work in the Early Modern period like Carla Freccero have likewise questioned the Foucauldian "acts versus identities" pronouncement. Freccero points out that this might be biased, as it is based almost entirely on legal and juridical sources and that using cultural and literary sources to discuss sexuality yields more complexity. See Freccero, *Queer/Early/Modern*, 42.

72. Clark, "Introduction," in *Desire*.

73. Anna Clark uses the metaphor of "twilight moments" to describe "sexual acts and relationships that take place without ever being acknowledged or named—as if barely perceived in the murky twilight." See Clark, "Introduction," and "Twilight Moments" in *Desire*.

74. This recasting of celibate desire can be found in Gustafson, "Celibate Passion," 277; Petro, "Celibate Politics," 45; and Cheng, *Radical Love*, 56–57.

75. Boydston, "Gender."

Chapter One

1. Greylock was writing under a pseudonym. Mount Greylock is a peak in Western Massachusetts, close to the Shaker settlement at Mount Lebanon. Greylock, *Taghconic*, 121, 123, 129–30.

2. Lucius Sargent Diary, August 11, 1860, MEHS.

3. *Escaped Nun*, 153.

4. *Escaped Nun*, 152–54.

5. By "gender trouble" I mean the incomplete performances of gender as defined in Judith Butler, *Gender Trouble*.

6. I understand "gender" to be, in the words of Joan Scott, "a way of referring to the social organization of the relationship between the sexes." Furthermore, masculinity and femininity are not just whatever men and women do but historically contingent and culturally constructed processes, subject to change over time. See Scott, "Gender," 28; Scott, "Evidence of Experience," 777; Boydston, "Gender."

7. Ryan, *Mysteries of Sex*, 80.

8. Cott, "Passionlessness," 233.

9. Klepp, *Revolutionary Conceptions*, 244, 207–8. Klepp argues that though many men in the nineteenth century supported family planning and desired smaller families in the industrializing era, overall, family limitation—of which abstinence was the only foolproof method—made most men resentful.

10. *Graham Journal of Health and Longevity*, February 2, 1839, 44. Critics of the Graham diet often accused the whole wheat bread eaten by Grahamites of being made with sawdust.

11. The increased regulation of prostitution and the creation of "vice districts" in the nineteenth century are discussed in LaFleur, *Natural History of Sexuality*, 164–88.

12. On the "reverend rake" archetype, see Gedge, *Without Benefit of Clergy*. David Reynolds also terms this type of literature "dark reform" or "immoral didactism." Reynolds, *Beneath the American Renaissance*, 55–60. On the print revolution, see Loughran, *Republic in Print*.

13. Wittig, "One Is Not Born a Woman," 11–12.

14. Butler, *Gender Trouble*, xi–xii. Butler gives a specific example in this passage of how homosexual identity ("becoming gay") can trigger feelings of anxiety and alienation from one's gender identity. I believe her thinking about the interconnectedness of sexuality and gender can still be applicable in a historical context, before the emergence of "modern" sexual identity. Gayle Rubin has also posited that gender identity exists within a heterosexual matrix, and that to step outside that matrix is to lose one's gender identity. See Rubin, "Traffic in Women"; Rich, "Compulsory Heterosexuality."

15. Changes in print technology such as stereotyping and the rise of publishing houses contributed to an explosion of print in the early nineteenth century. The "transportation revolution" that created an expansion in canals, roads, and eventually rail-

roads also made the shipping of books cheaper and allowed publishers to reach readers faster. See Gross, "Introduction," and Casper, "Case Study"; Michael Winship, "Manufacturing and Book Production," in *History of the Book in America Vol. 3*. The transportation and communication and revolutions of the early republic are described in Howe, *What Hath God Wrought*, 203–42.

16. The myriad motivations behind the Charlestown Riot have been explored in Schultz, *Fire and Roses* as well as Gilje, *Rioting in America*; Tager, *Boston Riots*.

17. Griffin, "Awful Disclosures."

18. Yacovazzi, *Escaped Nuns*, 105–23.

19. Fabian, *Unvarnished Truth*, 4–7.

20. Dhu, *Stanhope Burleigh*, 345. The Sisters of the Sacred Heart (or *Religieuses de Sacré Coeur de Jesus*) were an order of nuns who sometimes associated with the Jesuits and shared their commitment to education. As there was specifically a strain of anti-Jesuit sentiment within a more general anticlerical and anti-Catholic sentiment, they were singled out for their affiliations with the Jesuit order. See Carreel, Osiek, and Gimber, *Philippine Duchesne*.

21. *Escaped Nun*, 28.

22. Andie Tucher has traced these archetypes through the seduction novels of the late eighteenth century through the penny press and female moral reform literature of the 1820s and 1830s. She also argues that James Gordon Bennett cast Helen Jewett as a siren, contrary to his rivals in the penny press, who preferred to depict her as an innocent seduced into a tragic life of dissipation, ending in her untimely death. Tucher, *Froth and Scum*, 67, 63. The life and death of Helen Jewett is examined in P. Cohen, *Murder of Helen Jewett*.

23. Though homosocial relationships were common for both men and women during this period, flash newspapers point to the fact that many sporting men found the idea of two women in sexual relationship more than a little titillating. One such short story, appearing in the *Boston Satirist and Blade*, involved a woman named "Billy," impersonating a man, who attends an "underworld" ball and gets propositioned by one of the city's most prominent courtesans. "Dissipation: A Tale of Charlestown," *Boston Satirist and Blade*, February 19, 1848.

24. The Know-Nothing movement, while anti-Catholic in general, targeted Jesuits specifically. Jesuits had been singled out for persecution from within and without since their inception and were sometimes regarded as being a secret society within the Catholic Church, charged with ultramontanism and highly loyal to the pope. Increasing Jesuit emigration to the United States in the wake of the 1848 revolutions only exacerbated anti-Jesuit prejudice. See Schroth, *American Jesuits*, 73; McGreevy, *American Jesuits and the World*, 8–25.

25. Luke, *Female Jesuit*, vii–ix.

26. *Escaped Nun*, 244.

27. Schultz, *Fire and Roses*, 57–60;

28. Hazel, *Nun of St. Ursula*, 1, 49.

29. This image appeared twice as "The Sacrifice" first in the *Cabinet of Modern Art* (1852), 63 and in *Missionary Manual* (1855), 366. It also appeared as "Taking the Veil," *Friendship's Offering* (1849), "The Bride of Heaven" in *Affection's Gift* (1855). It was crafted

by the noted engraver Sartain. Based on marginalia present in the American Antiquarian Society's editions of these books, one (*Cabinet of Modern Art*) was presented as a Christmas gift from a mother to her daughter; another (*Friendship's Offering*) from a family to their music teacher, Mr. Kimball, who in turn re-gifted it to his second wife.

30. Halttunen, *Confidence Men and Painted Women*, 139. Hair was not only made into jewelry but embroidered into artwork and fashioned into wreaths, rings, and watch chains. Wearing an object made from a deceased loved one's hair showed the wearer to be a person of sincerity and feeling. Sheumaker, *Love Entwined*.

31. Cooper, *Hair, Sex, Society, Symbolism*. The connection between a woman's hair and sexual power can be seen in Victorian literature as well as paintings, exemplified by the art of Dante Rosetti. See Gitter, "Power of Women's Hair." The religious tonsure of a nun's hair had its roots in Benedictine monasticism and played an important role in the hagiography of saints like Clare of Assisi, who demonstrated her commitment to religious life by revealing her shorn head to her family. See Mooney, *Clare of Assisi*, 15–29; Berger, "Of Clare and Clairol."

32. Kelso, *Danger in the Dark*, 80–81.

33. Dhu, *Stanhope Burleigh*, 399.

34. Bloch, "Untangling the Roots of Modern Sex Roles," in *Gender and Morality in Anglo-American Culture*, 43–45.

35. Halttunen, *Confidence Men and Painted Women*, 71.

36. Halttunen, "Pornography of Pain," 320–24. I agree with Karen Halttunen that pornography in the nineteenth century goes beyond mere depictions of genital contact and bleeds over into areas that included the "eroticization of pain." Bruce Dorsey has argued that anti-Catholicism was indeed an antebellum reform movement, and includes it along with antislavery, women's rights, and temperance in his study. Dorsey, *Reforming Men and Women*.

37. Larned, *American Nun*, 126.

38. Hazel, *Nun of St. Ursula*, 63.

39. Cross, *Priests' Prisons for Women*, 5.

40. "Stanhope Burleigh," *Frederick Douglass' Paper*, February 23, 1855; February 2, 1855.

41. Though Brownson later converted to Catholicism and repented his reform beliefs in the 1840s, during the years he was editor of the *Quarterly Review*, he was still largely allied with reform and antislavery causes. Brownson, "Review of *The Mother*," *The Boston Quarterly Review*, July 1838.

42. The LPI would have the last laugh in all of this; it survived for over a hundred years, and when it finally disbanded in the 1970s, it was the oldest continually operating women's club in New England. "Eunice Cobb, Universalist Pioneer," *The Bulletin*, 24; Ladies' Physiological Institute Handbook (1948), SL.

43. "Mrs. Gove's Extraordinary Anatomical Lectures," *Morning Herald*, April 20, 1839.

44. "Abby Kelly, the New Prophetess," *Morning Herald*, May 29, 1840; "The Case of Mrs. Restell," *Morning Herald*, August 21, 1839; "Mysterious," *Morning Herald*, Tuesday, May 7, 1839. Bennett noted that Kelley and Gove were both natives of Lynn, Massachusetts, and therefore "possess all the peculiar and distinctive parts of character that are common to the females of certain parts of New England."

45. "Mrs Gove's Lectures on Female Anatomy," *Morning Herald*, April 3, 1839.

46. *Graham Journal of Health and Longevity*, February 2, 1839, 44.

47. Bloch, *Gender and Morality in Anglo-American Culture*, 136–54; Godbeer, *Sexual Revolution in Early America*, 263–67.

48. Stott, *Jolly Fellows*, 77, 98. Clare Lyons's *Sex among the Rabble* also argues that prior to the nineteenth century, a transatlantic "pleasure culture" flourished in port cities in Philadelphia, and that there was a greater toleration of sexual promiscuity even within genteel circles. See Lyons, *Sex among the Rabble*, 1, 60–61, 114.

49. Antebellum "manliness" based on restraint contrasted with masculinity based on physical prowess and power that emerged in the late nineteenth century has been thoroughly examined in Bederman's *Manliness and Civilization*, 11, 13.

50. Greenberg, *Manifest Manhood*, 11–12.

51. Reprinted from the *New York Review* in the *Graham Journal of Health and Longevity*, November 21, 1837, 257. Reprinted from the *New York Review* in the *Graham Journal of Health and Longevity*, November 28, 1837, 268–69.

52. *Boston Medical and Surgical Journal*, April 20, 1836 and February 10, 1836.

53. "The Clockmaker: Chapter XVIII: The Grahamite and the Irish Pilot," *Brown's Literary Omnibus*, January 12, 1838, 3–32. "Anti-Graham Riot," *Barre Gazette*, March 10, 1837.

54. Rathbone, *Reasons Offered for Leaving the Shakers*, 3, 7, 24–28. Several members of the Rathbun/bone family joined the Shakers and later apostatized. Reuben lasted longer than the rest of his family. Reuben also spelled his name differently, which is not atypical for the late eighteenth century. Rathbone actually had attained the position of elder at the Hancock Massachusetts Shaker family. They took his apostasy very hard. See Daniel Goodrich's history of the early Shaker church at Hancock, "The Rise and Progress of the Church," HSV.

55. McNemar, *Kentucky Revival*, 94–95.

56. The story of Jeremiah Minter has been well documented in both Heyrman, *Southern Cross*, 132, 152, and Lyerly, "Tale of Two Patriarchs."

57. Minter, *A Brief Account of the Religious Experience . . . of Jeremiah Minter*, 11.

58. Edward Tiffin and Sherman Kirker, "Providing for the Relief and Support of Women Who May be Abandoned by Their Husbands, and for Other Purposes," 1807, WRHS; Chapman, *Being an Additional Account*, 75, 79.

59. Smith, *Shakerism Detected*, 20–22. On Shaker veterans and their benefits, see Sanchez, *Mr. Lincoln's Chair*.

60. Smith, *Remarkable Occurances*, 9; Chapman, *Being an Additional Account*, 11; McNemar, *Kentucky Revival*, 101; Goodrich, *Rise and Progress of the Church*, HSV. On yeoman farmers, see Opal, *Beyond the Farm*, 46.

61. Writings about the Shakers frequently compared them to "despotic" Catholics, and called Shaker villages "convents." Both Ann Lee and the Turtle Creek Shakers faced accusations that they were secretly on the side of the British. See Greylock, *Taghconic*, 121 and Stone, *Lo Here*, iii–iv, 60.

62. Smith, *Remarkable Occurrences*, 17; McNemar, *Kentucky Revival*, 117–19.

63. Smith, *Shakerism Detected*, 5, 37–43. On Tecumseh's revival, see Dowd, *Spirited Resistance*.

64. Schultz, "Introduction," in *Veil of Fear*, xvii.

65. Monk, *Awful Disclosures*, 24, 6.

66. Stone's investigation revealed very quickly that Monk's description of the Hotel Dieu did not match the actual convent in any way. Monk's own mother affirmed Monk had never been a nun and had in fact been a resident of an asylum, the Charitable Institution for Female Penitents, and had suffered a head injury as a child. Stone, *Maria Monk and the Nunnery of the Hotel Dieu*; Billington, *Maria Monk and Her Influence*; "Maria Monk," *Dictionary of Canadian Biography*.

67. Reed, *Six Months in a Convent*, 139–40.

68. Morse, *Confessions of a French Catholic Priest*, 109–10, 131. He also claimed that priests took married women as their mistresses, then abused the power of the confessional to grant forgiveness for the sin of adultery.

69. This discovery was brought to light relatively recently in Beaghton, "Hugo and Sand," 21–24.

70. Recent revelations of clerical abuse survivors and especially the release of sealed church records identify the confessional as a place where priests sexually abused and harassed those in their pastoral care, sometimes in the very same manner described by Reed. The past needs to be taken on its own terms, and there are certainly limits to what archival research can tell us about this type of sexual abuse. The pattern of abusing the powers of the confessional in the present suggests that some of Reed's allegations should not be entirely dismissed. See Pettinati, *Hand of God*. The website BishopAccountability.org maintains an extensive record of priestly abuse in the United States and all relevant documents.

71. Thompson, "Shaker Lovers," 259. A similarly melodramatic tale of doomed Shaker love was found in Shaker apostate Harvey Elkins's autobiography. See Elkins, *Fifteen Years*, 102–19. The Shaker lovers were named Urbino and Ellina; they seem more suited to an Italian opera than to a Shaker village and appear very fictionalized.

72. On nineteenth-century moral reform movements, see Ryan, *Cradle of the Middle Class*; Hill, *Their Sisters' Keepers*.

73. Mary Seraphina Wickham to John Timon, July 1, 1840, CM. The Congregation of the Mission encompassed those orders following the rule of St. Vincent de Paul. They were a missionary order headquartered in France but spread about the globe. The provincial was the leader of that division of the mission.

74. Clark, *Masterless Mistresses*.

75. Stein, *Shaker Experience in America*, 151–53.

76. Marjorie Procter-Smith was among the first to question just how "feminist" Shakerism actually was; see *Shakerism and Feminism*.

77. Stein, *Shaker Experience in America*, 160.

78. *The Shakers' Manual*, Shaker advertising ephemera, ASC.

The contact person for all of the Shaker seeds and medicines was always male during the early to mid-nineteenth century. Later in the century as female believers began to dramatically outnumber male ones, Shaker sisters' names would appear in print, especially in regard to more feminine industries like cloak-making or foodstuffs.

79. Most notably, John Dunlavy's 1818 *The Manifesto* contained not one single mention of Ann Lee. Dunlavy was a former minister who read Hebrew, Latin, and Greek

and is considered one of the most theologically rigorous thinkers the Shakers ever had. On women's loss of spiritual power in developing religions, see Juster, *Disorderly Women*.

80. The Sisters of Charity of Nazareth followed a similar rule. NAZ, 49; Schultz, *Fire and Roses*, 97.

81. Clark, *Masterless Mistresses*, 4–5.

82. Trouble began when the Emmitsburg motherhouse sent a circular letter to bishops in those dioceses in which Sisters of Charity taught, notifying them it was against modesty for the sisters to be teaching and caring for young boys. In a plan that seemed to have been in the works for at least two years, Hughes suggested that the Sisters of Charity in his diocese swear their vow of obedience to him, rather than to the motherhouse in Emmitsburg. Many within the Sisters of Charity suspected Hughes's true motives were nothing but a grab for power. In the end, thirty-one Sisters of Charity chose to remain in New York City and carry out their work under the auspices of the city's bishop unaffiliated with their original order. See *Mother Etienne Hall*, 6, 15–16, 18, 28–30.

83. The Sisters of Charity of Nazareth were separate from the similarly named order founded by Elizabeth Seton, yet they both followed the rules set out by St. Vincent de Paul and remained within the same "family" of Catholic orders. "Sketch of the History of the Sisters of Charity of Nazareth," NAZ.

84. "Sketch of the History of the Sisters of Charity of Nazareth," NAZ.

85. Mary Seraphina Wickham to John Timon, July 1, 1840, CM; Mary Edmond St. George Moffat to James T. Austin, November 15, 1834. Ursuline Convent Records, Catholic University of America, Washington, DC.

86. "Man Should Have a Help-meet for Him," *Graham Journal of Health and Longevity*, February 16, 1839.

87. *Graham Journal of Health and Longevity*, August 18, 1838, 266–67.

88. "What Shall We Have for Dinner" and "How Shall We Treat Our Friends" in *Graham Journal of Health and Longevity*, June 22, 1839. 215.

89. Ginzburg, *Women and the Work of Benevolence*.

Chapter Two

1. Webster, "celibacy," *An American Dictionary of the English Language* (italics are Webster's).

2. "Celibacy," *Merriam-Webster Online*; Bernard, *Webster's New World Dictionary*, 228.

3. Webster, s.v. "chastity."

4. Of experience, Joan Scott writes, "Subjects are constituted discursively and experience is a linguistic event (it doesn't happen outside established meanings), but neither is it confined to a fixed order of meaning. Since discourse is by definition shared, experience is collective as well as individual." Scott, "Evidence of Experience." The identities of sexual restraint I discuss and Shaker, Catholic, and Grahamite experiences of practicing sexual abstinence are not ahistorical; they are a product of the social and cultural milieu of the early nineteenth century. I am not making any

claims to a universal shared experience of sexual restraint; rather, I am interested in how practicing sexual restraint created a sense of sexual identity in this specific historical context.

5. Foucault, *History of Sexuality*, Vol. 1, 43. Foucault cites 1870 and the medicalization of homosexuality as the birth of the homosexual as a "species." Such classifications of individuals dovetail with the rise of modern science, social Darwinism, and the disciplines of psychology and sexology. Prior to the late nineteenth century, Foucault argues that homosexuality was a sin to be punished by the church, not an identity to be studied.

6. Gayle Rubin describes certain sexual behaviors as existing within a "charmed circle," while other nonnormative behaviors are confined to the "outer limits" of sexual respectability. Rubin, "Thinking Sex."

7. The rhetoric of the modern lesbian and gay rights movement, especially organizations like the Human Rights Campaign, has advocated for equal rights and protections for lesbians and gays on the basis that sexual orientation is something one is "born with" and cannot be changed, an inherited biological characteristic like skin or eye color. Queer theorists question the validity of arguing for civil rights on biological grounds; even if sexuality is a "choice" like religious identity, one should not be discriminated against for that choice. Some argue that the biological argument privileges gay male experience over that of lesbians, who when surveyed are more likely to not identify as being gay from birth. See Phelan, *Sexual Strangers*; Whisman, *Queer by Choice*.

8. Nancy Cott has argued that nineteenth-century middle-class white women self-consciously utilized "passionlessness" as a strategy to gain familial and social advantages. Cott, "Passionlessness."

9. The demographic decline of Shakerism in the late nineteenth and twentieth centuries is charted in Stein, *Shaker Experience in America*, 337–53.

10. On leadership in the early Shaker community, see Stein, 1–57.

11. Bates, "Sketch of the Life and Experience of ife of Issachar Bates," ASC, 11.

12. Doolittle, *Autobiography of Mary Antoinette Doolittle*, 45.

13. "The Direct Road to Happiness" in Dewitt, "A Collection of Hymns and Spiritual Songs, Improved in Our Worship," ASC.

14. "Solemn Work," in DeWitt, "A Collection of Hymns and Spiritual Songs Improved in Our Worship," ASC.

15. "The New Tongue" in "A Collection of Hymns and Spiritual Songs Compiled by the Millennial Church Copied by Mary Hazard," ASC.

16. Garrett, *Spirit Possession and Popular Religion*, 5, 194.

17. *The Testimony of Christ's Second Appearing*. On how biblical time and quotidian experience merged in early America, see Juster, *Doomsayers*, 4.

18. Kanter, *Commitment and Community*, 75–78.

19. Kanter, 139–43.

20. Wergland, *One Shaker Life*, ix, 18–20.

21. Wergland, xi, 23–24.

22. Graham, "New Lebanon Shaker Children's Order," 216–18; Stein, *Shaker Experience in America*, 134; Wergland, *One Shaker Life*, 24.

23. Youngs, "Autobiography in Verse," quoted in Wergland, 33–34.

24. Youngs, *Family and Meeting Journal*, undated entries, ca. 1817, LC.

25. Wergland, *One Shaker Life*, 34.

26. Youngs, *Family and Meeting Journal*, May 1 and December 18, 1817; Wergland, *One Shaker Life*, 36.

27. Youngs, *Family and Meeting Journal*, July 19 1816, July 24 1816, February 29, 1820.

28. On histories of Grahamite reform, see Sokolow, *Eros and Modernization* and Nissenbaum, *Sex, Diet, Debility*.

29. Nissenbaum, *Sex, Diet, Debility*, 140.

30. Haynes, *Riotous Flesh*. See *Graham Journal of Health and Longevity*, June 6, 1837, May 3, 1839.

31. Jacques, "George Jacques Diary," Vol. 1, 1841–1845, Vol. 2, 1852–1856, WML.

32. The Washingtonians were unique among Temperance societies for their secular rather than religiously oriented nature. Tyrrell, *Sobering Up*; Zimmerman, "Dethroning King Alcohol."

33. Jacques referenced Samuel B. Woodward, the superintendent of the Worcester, Massachusetts, state lunatic asylum. His study drew a link between masturbation and insanity. See Woodward, *Hints for the Young*.

34. An educated man, Jacques was fond of sprinkling his diary with French expressions. Jacques, "George Jacques Diary," January 4, 1844, June 5, 1843, September 4, 1843, WML.

35. Jacques, "George Jacques Diary," April 8, 1841, WML.

36. Jacques, "George Jacques Diary," February 23, 1843, December 18, 1843, WML. Jacques at times seemed to indicate that he might have been living with his parents upon his return to Worcester, which might explain why he took such pains to camouflage his diary entries.

37. Jacques, "George Jacques Diary," December 3, 1845, WML.

38. "Records of the Proceedings of the Ladies Physiological Society," April 7, 1837, Rebecca Codman Butterfield Papers, MHS.

39. "Records of the Proceedings of the Ladies Physiological Society," April 10, 1837.

40. Brooks, "A Truthful Testimony from Woman," *Health Journal, & Advocate of Physiological Reform*, March 26, 1842, 83–84.

41. "Letter from P. D. Hathaway," *Health Journal, & Advocate of Physiological Reform*, August 28, 1841, 300–302.

42. Dougherty, *Life of Mother Elizabeth Boyle*, x.

43. Dougherty, 58.

44. Collegium Urbanum De Propaganda Fide, *Pontificium*.

45. Callahan, "Preface," in *Diary of Richard L. Burtsell*, iii.

46. Callahan, *Diary of Richard L. Burtsell*, 41.

47. Callahan, 288–89.

48. Callahan, 286–87.

49. Flash papers frequently made fun of bachelors as objects of pity, simultaneously licentious and too cold hearted to wish upon any woman. See *Boston Satirist*, April 14, 1843; *Monthly Cosmopolite*, July 1, 1850; *New York Whip*, March 19, 1842.

50. Callahan, *Diary of Richard L. Burtsell*, 289.

51. Burtsell was thoroughly committed to antislavery and also spreading the Catholic faith among African Americans. He later helped found St. Benedict the Moor, the first African American Catholic Church north of the Mason-Dixon Line in 1883. His radicalism continued into his later years when he would defend his friend Dr. McSweeny participation in the controversial Anti-Poverty Society. McSweeny might have been traditional about celibacy, but he was willing to risk excommunication for socialist economic reform. See Shelley, *Greenwich Village Catholics*, 127–28; McKenna, *Battle for Rights*, 86–99.

52. Callahan, *Diary of Richard L. Burtsell*, 290.

53. Callahan, 96–102.

54. Bridget Brophy became Sister Mary Ida on February 24, 1855 and served as a sister for forty years until her death. Father H. de Luynes to Sisters of Charity of Nazareth, June 26, 1854, NAZ.

55. H. de Luynes to Father Haseltine, April 11, 1859, NAZ.

56. H. de Luynes to Mother Frances, September 15, 1859, NAZ.

57. Surviving records from the Sisters of Charity of Nazareth collection do not confirm or deny whether or not Theresa Eberle ever took her vows. Father Haseltine to Father J A Elet S.J., October 16, 1841, NAZ.

58. Father de Luynes to Father Haseltine, January 25, 1861, NAZ.

59. "A Sketch of St. Mary's Seminary as an Educational Institution," SMB. St. Mary's of the Barrens was a seminary run by the Vincentian order, with the objective of training priests who would serve in a missionary capacity. The seminary also taught male lay scholars and non-Catholics. When St. Mary's was founded in 1818, it was the third seminary established for the training of priests on American soil.

60. "Domestic Councils Minutes," April 18, 1857, February 4, 1858, SMB.

61. "Domestic Councils Minutes," February 4, 1858, SMB. The council was fearful of his intellectual vanity and an obedience that came from the head and not from the heart. The keeper of the minutes recorded that vanity was especially dangerous and considered an "occasion of losing one's vocation."

62. "Domestic Councils Minutes," March 12, 1858, July 28, 1857, SMB.

63. Fitzgerald, *Habits of Compassion*, 32. Oral histories with nuns who entered convent life in the early twentieth century remember being taught a jingle, "Never one, seldom two, always three or more," as novices as a device for steering clear of particular friendships. While most seem to have interpreted it as a prohibition against being "exclusive" with any one sister, others wondered if "it was something about chastity." Sylvester, I.H.M., "PFs, Persistent Friendships," and Gilsky, "Official IHM Stance."

64. "Rules of the Seminarians of the St. Mary's Preparatory Seminary," 1844, SMB.

65. References to homosexuality did appear in these sexually explicit publications, but the amount is minuscule in comparison to the many mentions of heterosexual debauchery. See Cohen, Gilfoyle, and Horowitz, *Flash Press*, 192–98.

66. "A Sketch of St. Mary's Seminary as an Educational Institution," SMB. The Parisian Vicentians tried to ban lay scholars from the institution altogether from 1835 to 1850, and the Missouri Vincentians protested this decision. This historical record is unclear as to what degree the Missouri seminary defied their orders.

67. "Rules of the Seminarians," SMB. Such rules were apparently received directly from St. Vincent de Paul himself, who charged his followers "to fly as the plague of communities, all kind of private connexions, partialities and friendships" and "not to seek to gain the affection of anyone." Relationships outside the traditional family will be discussed in greater detail in chapter 3.

68. Humez, *Gifts of Power*, 21–22.

69. Watervliet Family Writings, quoted in Humez, *Gifts of Power*, 28; Pleasant Hill, Kentucky, and other southern Shaker communities had originally owned slaves, but manumitted them early in the nineteenth century; several formerly enslaved Shakers decided to remain on as full members of their communities after manumission.

70. The Shakers underwent a spiritual revival, called the Era of Manifestations, during the 1830s and 1840s, during which time attention was focused internally on Shaker communities and less on an outward public ministry. Though the Shakers welcomed "spectators" to their meetings and printed many pamphlets during this era, the central ministry at Mount Lebanon decided against sending out missionaries. Stein, *Shaker Experience in America*, 112.

71. Humez, *Gifts of Power*, 40–41; Williams, *Called and Chosen*, 109–11. The Philadelphia community was tiny in comparison to Shaker villages in the Northeast and Midwest, which at the time boasted hundreds of members living in several smaller groupings, or families, spread across hundreds of acres of farmland. Stein, *Shaker Experience in America*, 88–89.

72. Humez, *Gifts of Power*, 41.

73. On white stereotypes of black womanhood, see White, *Ar'n't I a Woman?*, 27–30 and M. Jones, *All Bound Up Together*.

74. Dunbar, *Fragile Freedom*, 68, 117.

75. Passionlessness is described in Cott, "Passionlessness," 219–36.

76. The circumstances of escaped nun Olivia Neale are described in Mannard, "'What Has Become of Olivia Neal?'"

77. Morrow, *Persons of Color*, 150–53.

78. Cohen, "Respectability of Rebecca Reed."

79. Morrow, *Persons of Color*, 117–19.

80. Haynes, *Riotous Flesh*, 11.

81. Haynes, 59, 62–64.

82. Haynes, 156–57. Cassey is described in Dunbar, *Fragile Freedom*, 126.

83. Describing the sexual violence women experienced under slavery and the licentiousness of white masters was a prominent fixture of antislavery literature, especially in the 1840s and 1850s. Such lurid and near-pornographic descriptions were accepted as suitable middle-class reading material as long as they were in the service of reform. Halttunen, "Pornography of Pain."

Chapter Three

1. Maupin, *Logical Family*.

2. On "families of choice," see Weeks, *Same Sex Intimacies*; Weston, *Families We Choose*; Stacey, "Families of Man."

3. Lawrence, *One Family under God*, 72–95. Mormons, too, used familial designations in their polygamous family units, such as the designation of "sister wives." Talbot, *Foreign Kingdom*, 42.

4. Sasha Roseneil, "Living and Loving beyond the Boundaries of the Heteronorm," 244, 241.

5. Berlant and Warner, "Sex in Public," 554. Berlant and Warner argue that by making sexual intimacy private, heteronormativity creates a privatized sexual culture where only its own practices can be rendered legitimate in public.

6. "Mrs. Gove's Extraordinary Anatomical Lectures," *Morning Herald*, April 20, 1839.

7. This method of attack can be seen most obviously in the treatment of John McDowell, founder of the Female Benevolent Society. Reynolds, *Beneath the American Renaissance*, 61–64.

8. Warner, *Publics and Counterpublics*, 22–23.

9. On the type of "marking" that happens when one "comes out" and makes visible an otherwise hidden sexual identity, see Sedgwick, *Epistemology of the Closet*, 75.

10. A 1636 Massachusetts law actually forbade single people—male and female—from living alone. In the second half of the seventeenth century, lawmakers felt that married men were unduly burdened and thus shifted a greater tax burden and more civic obligations onto single men. Over the course of the eighteenth century, the majority of these taxes were either repealed or allowed to expire. McCurdy, *Citizen Bachelors*, 3–4, 207–11.

11. Lee Virginia Chambers-Schiller has argued that the same pattern emerged in the South and West later in the century, especially for the age cohort of women born in the 1840s and 1850s and who would have reached marriageable age around the time of the Civil War. Marriage data for the United States are hard to obtain, as marital status was not recorded in the census until 1850. Chambers-Schiller, *Liberty, a Better Husband*, 5.

12. "Life of Issachar Bates," ASC, 11, 22–23, 29.

13. "Life of Issachar Bates," ASC, 31–33.

14. "Life of Issachar Bates," ASC, 37.

15. "Life of Issachar Bates," ASC, 38–39.

16. "Life of Issachar Bates," ASC, 42.

17. "Life of Issachar Bates," ASC, 43–44.

18. De Wolfe, *Shaking the Faith*, 130–31.

19. Doolittle, *Autobiography of Mary Antoinette Doolittle*, 9, 21, 22.

20. Doolittle, 23–25.

21. Doolittle, 28.

22. Doolittle, 28–29.

23. Doolittle, 30–31. It is not strange that Doolittle kept in touch with her family after becoming a Shaker, as they lived within the same town. The sect allowed for periodic visits between Shakers and non-Believing family members. It was advantageous to keep on good terms with non-Believing members, as cousins, nephews, and distant relatives could be a source of new members as well as powerful allies within the world.

24. During the 1820s and 1830s, children under the age of sixteen accounted for 20 to 30 percent of a given Shaker village's population. Though some might have been brought by Shaker parents, most were probably indentures. These data are taken from Shaker records and U.S. Census schedules. See Stein, *Shaker Experience in America*, 87–89.

25. Wealthy Storer Diary, April 6, 1851, April 9, 1851, ASC.

26. Wealthy Storer Diary, May 18, 1849, ASC.

27. For information on Cornelia Connelly's early life and marriage, see Flaxman, *Woman Styled Bold*, 1–34.

28. Quoted in Flaxman, 78.

29. Cornelia Connelly quoted in Flaxman, 77–78.

30. Flaxman, 93, 80.

31. England was selected to appease some influential English Catholics who desired convent schools like those run by the RSCJs on English soil. Flaxman, 106.

32. Flaxman, 105.

33. Flaxman, 98–100.

34. Bishop Wiseman quoted in Mother Maria Thèrése, SHCJ, *Cornelia Connelly*, 93.

35. Cornelia was eventually reconciled with her daughter, Adeline, toward the end of her life, but not with her sons, who blamed her for the dissolution of their family. Cornelia Connelly quoted in Maria Thèrése, *Cornelia Connelly*, 93.

36. Pierce Connelly quoted in Maria Thèrése, 94.

37. Flaxman, *Woman Styled Bold*, 135.

38. Pierce Connelly quoted in Flaxman, 145; Maria Thèrése, *Cornelia Connelly*, 102.

39. Flaxman, *Woman Styled Bold*, 146.

40. Flaxman, 153.

41. *Supplement to the Case of Rev. Pierce Connelly*, 8.

42. Maria Thèrése, *Cornelia Connelly*, 107.

43. Maria Thèrése, 104.

44. Flaxman, *Woman Styled Bold*, 161.

45. Flaxman, 162.

46. Flaxman, 245–46.

47. The Sisters of the Holy Child currently minister in North and South America, Europe, and Africa. Their specific areas of focus are the education of women and underprivileged children and currently operate fifteen grade schools as well as Rosemont College in Pennsylvania. They also work for justice for immigrants and migrants. For more details about their contemporary ministry, see https://www.shcj.org/how-we-serve/ministries/.

48. *Form of Ceremony for . . . Our Lady of Mercy*, 11, 22.

49. Father Moranvillé to Elizabeth Boyle, April 4, 1810, repr. Dougherty, *Life of Mother Elizabeth Boyle*, 21.

50. Catholic Tract Society of Baltimore, No. 14, *Nuns and Monastic Institutes*, 3.

51. Catholic Tract Society of Baltimore, Nos. *15 & 16 Nuns and Monastic Institutes* 4–5.

52. Clara Bowen to Mother Catherine Spaulding, November 7, 1852, NAZ.

53. Clara Bowen to Mother Catherine Spaulding, November 7, 1852, NAZ.

54. Sister Eulalia Kelly to John Timon, July 4, 1840, Provincial Files of John Timon, CM.

55. Carroll Smith-Rosenberg first coined the term "female world of love and ritual" to describe the intimate friendships between women in the nineteenth century. Close male friendships were also common, and were not necessarily viewed as abnormal or homosexual in nature. Jonathan Ned Katz describes the physically and emotionally intimate relationship experienced by Abraham Lincoln and Joshua Speed during Lincoln's days as a young lawyer in Springfield. The two shared the same bed for more than eight months, and Speed declared "no two men were ever more intimate." See Katz, *Love Stories*, 3–7. Richard Godbeer has also examined the normalcy of same-sex male friendship during the early republic in *Overflowing of Friendship*.

56. *Sketch of the Life and Experience of Issachar Bates Sr*, ASC, 49, 71–72.

57. *Sketch of the Life and Experience of Issachar Bates Sr*, ASC, 121.

58. William Sharp and Andrew Houston to the Ministry at New Lebanon, September 29, 1834, ASC.

59. Youngs, *Concise View of the Church*, ASC.

60. Youngs, *Concise View of the Church*, ASC.

61. Unfortunately, these union meetings (however platonic they were intended to be) provided the basis for allegations of "spiritual wifery" by apostates such as Mary M. Dyer—the assumption being that where there was smoke, there must be fire in these platonic pseudo-marriages.

62. Quoted in Wergland, *Sisters in the Faith*, 105.

63. Andrews and Andrews, *Religion in Wood*, xiii.

64. Graham targeted the newly emergent middle class engaged in "white-collar" managerial work as those whose bodies might be overstimulated. Presumably, laborers and farmers who engaged in regular physical activity had bodies more adept at handling the stimulations caused by sex and orgasm. Graham, *A Lecture to Young Men on Chastity*, 79–81. Fellow physiologist William Andrus Alcott also continued to promote the idea that the frequency of sexual intercourse for married couples should be limited to "the number of lunar months." See Alcott, *Physiology of Marriage*, 116.

65. Hunt, "Sickness and Death of Sylvester Graham," *New York Daily Tribune*, September 24, 1851; Nissenbaum, *Sex, Diet, and Debility*, 146.

66. "An Appropriate Bridal Present," *The Liberator*, June 29, 1855; "Selections Marriage and Parentage," *The Liberator*, May 26, 1854.

67. Wright, *Marriage and Parentage*, 11, 69.

68. Wright, 74.

69. Wright, 245.

70. For a thorough history of the marital rape clause in U.S. law, see Hasday, "Contest and Consent." Even though marital rape is criminalized in all fifty states, in many states there is still a higher burden of proof for the prosecution of marital rape, such as the need to prove force or the threat of force.

71. Wright, *Marriage and Parentage*, 245–46.

72. Wright, 248.

73. Margaret Sanger's relationship with eugenicist ideology has been amply documented by historians of reproduction. See Gordon, *Moral Property of Women*; Ordover, "Margaret Sanger and the Eugenic Compact," in *American Eugenics*.

74. Wright, *Marriage and Parentage*, 16.

75. Wright, 77.

76. Wright, 69, 72.

77. Perry, *Childhood, Marriage, and Reform*, 173–75.

78. Perry, 181.

79. Perry, 194–96, 200.

Chapter Four

1. Beadie, *Education and the Creation of Capital*, 4–5; Howe, *What Hath God Wrought*, 525–26.

2. Sellers, *Market Revolution*; Stokes and Conway, *Market Revolution in America*. Some scholars have questioned whether the term "market revolution" has been used too capaciously, as a kind of shorthand for describing all of the social upheaval of Jacksonian America. I understand it more narrowly to describe the rise of the urban middle class and the increased access to consumer goods from the 1820s onward. See Feller, "Market Revolution"; M. Ryan, "Narratives of Democracy."

3. The ubiquitous nature of commercial sex in nineteenth-century urban America is discussed prominently in Cohen, *Murder of Helen Jewett*; Guilfoyle, *City of Eros*; and LaFleur, *Natural History of Sexuality*.

4. Hemphill, "Selling Sex and Intimacy," 179–82.

5. Cronon, *Nature's Metropolis*, 149–52.

6. Moore, *Selling God*, 11. Moore further argues that secularization should not be thought of as the withdrawal of religion from the public sphere but the commodification of it.

7. Newspapers from this period advertised that similar Shaker patent medicines could be found in Boston, Concord, New Ipswich, New Boston, and St. Albans, Vermont. See *Barre Patriot*, November 23, 1849; *Barre Patriot*, February 15, 1850; *Constitution*, January 9, 1850; *Constitution*, May 22, 1850.

8. References to Shaker-made apparel often appeared in short fiction, indicating the commonplace nature of such objects. See "A Dangerous Woman," *Harper's New Monthly Magazine*, April 1860.

9. A. Miller, *Shaker Herbs*, 9; Andrews, *Shaker Herbs and Herbalists*, 3

10. A. Miller, *Shaker Herbs*, 9; *Newburyport Herald*, February 11, 1831, 4; *Providence Patriot & Columbian Phoenix*, May 11, 1831, 4.

11. A. Miller, *Shaker Herbs*, 11–13, 17.

12. Andrews, *Shaker Herbs and Herbalists*, 3, 8–9.

13. Elisha Myrick, *Diary Kept for the Convenience of the Herb Department* (ca. 1853), ASC.

14. On the Shakers' use of consignment, see Kreiser and Dare, "Shaker Accounting Records at Pleasant Hill." On the history of consignment in general, see Baker, "History of the Book Trade"; Price, "Last Phase."

15. "Account Book of Shaker Travelling Seed Salesman 1834–1843" (ca. 1834), ASC; Stein, *Shaker Experience in America*, 138.

16. *Providence Patriot*, November 6, 1824; *Salem Gazette*, July 15, 1828, 4; *Providence Patriot Columbian Phoenix*; May 11, 1831; *The Jeffersonian*, February 5, 1846, 3.

17. Color lithography provided more detailed illustrations than letterpress or copper engravings, as it allowed an image to be painted or inked directly onto the stone from which the impression was made by an artist; Hudson, *Design and Printing of Ephemera*, 25, 43, 48–49. In the late nineteenth century, Shakers did appear alongside advertisements for their products as a popular colored advertisement for "Shaker Family Pills."

18. *Shakers' Manual*, 7, 1.

19. Advertisements, ca. 1740- ca.1940, Col. 214, JDC.

20. *Life in Boston*, April 11, 1857. The etymology of the word "gay" indicates that from the seventeenth century onward, it was used to refer to a life of indulgence and sexual dissipation or to outrageous and flamboyant style, both associated with prostitution. Not until the early twentieth century did "gay" emerge as slang for homosexuality. See Chauncey, *Gay New York*, 19, 379.

21. Collections of Trade Catalogues and Ephemera, JDC.

22. Quoted in *Shakers' Manual*. More information about the syrup operation at Canterbury can be found in "A Short Sketch of Our Journey to the East" (ca. 1850), ASC. The unnamed Shaker sister who kept this travel journal made a special visit to see the aforementioned *Shakers' Manual* being packaged alongside the sarsaparilla syrup.

23. In 1841, the Shakers processed twenty-five pounds of pennyroyal. See *Journal of Domestic Events Kept by Benjamin Lyon*, ASC. Though the Shakers never directly marketed their herbs as abortifacients or "female pills," Janet Farrell Brodie suspects that the Shakers' booming medicinal extract business could not have stemmed from simple middle-class demand alone and was driven by those needing to prevent or end pregnancies. Brodie, *Conception and Abortion in 19th-Century America*, 42–44, 166.

24. Lears, *Fables of Abundance*, 43.

25. Howe, *What Hath God Wrought*, 470–72.

26. The Shakers even developed a pill-drying rack that could dry as many as 120 coated pills at a time. Sprugg, *By Shaker Hands*; "The Shakers," *Harper's New Monthly Magazine*, June 1857, 172–74.

27. *Shakers' Manual*, 7. The Shakers did own printing presses but did not make their own labels. Diaries from various herb departments reveal that the Shakers sent to printers in Boston and Albany for their labels and catalogues.

28. Elisha Myrick, *A Diary Kept for the Convenience of the Herb Dept 1853-57*, January 5, 1853; May 10, 1853, ASC.

29. "Shaker Papers," in Rickards, *Encyclopedia of Ephemera*, 290.

30. Young, *Toadstool Millionaires*, 14–15, 21.

31. Miller, *Shaker Herbs*, 11. *Catalogue of Medicinal Plants and Extracts*. Later catalogues would modify this to "Why send to the Atlantic shores / For plants that grow at our own doors?"

32. De Courtais, *Women's Hats*, 114–16. The "Dorothy" cloak was named after Dorothy Durgin, the Canterbury Shaker sister who designed the pattern. Famously, the Mount Lebanon Shakers made two cloaks for Mrs. Cleveland. The first one was found to have an imperfection, so they gladly sent her a new one. Miller, *From Shaker Lands and Shaker Hands*, 161–62.

33. "To Correspondents," *Godey's Lady's Book*, October 1853.

34. Mary W. Janvrin, "Mrs. Vining's Help," *Godey's Lady's Book*, November 1863.

35. Wergland, *Sisters in the Faith*, 73–84.

36. The *Shaker Manual* was printed at the Boston Stereotype Foundry. Stereotype plates were expensive to manufacture, though they allowed for larger print jobs and were usually only undertaken in cases where the printed material was expected to have a large circulation. The fact that this pamphlet was stereotype printed indicates that the Shakers expected it to be widely distributed along with their medicines.

37. *Shaker Manual*.

38. The decline in the numbers of Shakers is attributable to a number of factors. The industrial revolution opened up new opportunities for men and women outside of agriculture. The Shakers' own spiritual revival, the Era of Manifestations, in the 1830s and 1840s, also turned off many believers. See Stein, *Shaker Experience in America*, 236–37.

39. On studies of white audiences and minstrelsy, see Lott, *Love and Theft* and Roediger, *Wages of Whiteness*. The antebellum phenomenon of white actors in "Indian" roles is well documented by Deloria's *Playing Indian*.

40. *Fourth Annual Catalogue of the Teachers and Scholars in the Young Ladies' High School; First Annual Catalogue of the Mount Vernon Female School 1829–1830*. The Young Ladies' High School of Boston was one such institution in the 1830s. All of the major teachers, especially the language and dancing "masters," were male, while female teachers served as "assistants." The Mount Vernon Female School had female teachers but an exclusively male executive board of trustees, including the Rev. Lyman Beecher.

41. *Catholic Herald*, September 25, 1834.

42. Smith, *Gothic Arches*.

43. John Davis, "Catholic Envy," in Morgan and Promey, *Visual Culture of American Religions*, 107–9.

44. *Catalogue of the Pupils of Saint Joseph's Academy; Catalogue of the Students . . . of the Boarding School of the Sisters of Notre Dame; Catalogue of Pupils of the Georgetown Academy of the Visitation*.

45. *Curricular and Catalogue of the Oakland Female Institute; Catalogue of the Teachers and Scholars in the Young Ladies' High School; Miss D. T. Kilbourn's Academy Baltimore*.

46. Kelley, *Learning to Stand and Speak*, 28, 67.

47. Mount Benedict Pamphlet, ca. 1830. John Gilmary Shea Collection, Georgetown University.

48. *Catalogue of the Pupils of Saint Joseph's Academy*, 3; *Catalogue of Pupils of the Georgetown Academy of the Visitation, B.V.M.*, 4; *Catalogue of the Mount Vernon Female School*, 9–10.

49. The cost of $150 per year was definitely at the higher end of tuition for a female academy; the Greenfield High School for Young Ladies charged the same. Yet, there were also schools in the $100–$130 per year range. See Kelley, *Learning to Stand and Speak*, 81–82.

50. *Catalogue of the Pupils of St. Joseph's Academy*.

51. *Catalogue of the Pupils of St. Joseph's Academy*.

52. In the post-Revolutionary years, a daughter who had "accomplishments" in the visual and musical arts was a marker of elite social standing. Even as female academies began to mirror the academic curriculum of male colleges, the most elite schools still offered the "accomplishments" at an additional charge. See Kelley, *Learning to Stand and Speak*, 69–71.

53. Cohen, "Respectability of Rebecca Reed."

54. Cott, "Passionlessness," 233.

55. Excerpt from *Mrs. Hale's Magazine* in *Catholic Herald*, September 25, 1834.

56. On emulation as a pedagogical practice, see Opal, "Exciting Emulation."

57. *Catalogue of the Pupils of Saint Joseph's Academy near Emmitsburg*.

58. Though these items were reprinted in a premiere Catholic periodical, the *Catholic Herald*, they initially debuted in non-Catholic papers, the *Commercial Advertiser* and *Mrs. Hale's Magazine*.

59. "The Sister of Charity," *Catholic Herald*, August 21, 1834.

60. Watts, "The Sister of Charity . . . Written after Meeting a Sister of Charity in the Hotel Dieu," *Catholic Herald*, March 13, 1834.

61. Charles Rosenberg has argued that the cholera epidemics of the 1830s fundamentally shook Americans' faith in their own progress, especially at a time when disease was often associated with a lack of virtue and immoral behavior. Though tuberculosis and malaria claimed more victims between 1832 and 1866, cholera was especially frightening to Americans, as it was both a novel and a terrifying way to die. Rosenberg, *Cholera Years*, 1–17.

62. Greene, *Letters from Sister Mary Ignatia to Her Own Mother*, 18, 44–46.

63. *The Escaped Nun* was actually what DeWitt & Davenport published after Josephine Bunkley obtained her injunction and bears little resemblance to Bunkley's story or experience, other than that it takes place in the middle states. *Escaped Nun*, 19–20.

64. Martha Usher to Rebecca Usher, January 1, 1841, Rebecca Usher Papers, MEHS.

65. Rebecca Usher to Martha Usher, January 14, 1841, Rebecca Usher Papers, MEHS.

66. Ellis Usher to Rebecca Usher, March 13, 1841, Rebecca Usher Papers, MEHS

67. Martha Usher to Rebecca Usher, March 13, 1841, Rebecca Usher Papers, MEHS.

68. George Woodman to Rebecca Usher, March 27, 1841, Rebecca Usher Papers, MEHS.

69. Rebecca Usher to Martha Usher, March 26, 1841, Rebecca Usher Papers, MEHS.

70. Sister St. F. Borgia to Rebecca Usher, October 28, 1841, Rebecca Usher Papers, MEHS.

71. Sister Mary Joseph to Rebecca Usher, October 27, 1841, Rebecca Usher Papers, MEHS.

72. Hobbs, *Brick House and Its People*, 13.

73. Hobbs, 19–20.

74. "Graham's Lectures," *Christian Mirror*, June 26, 1834.

75. "City Restorators," *Library of Health*, 33–35.

76. Geertz, *Interpretation of Cultures*, 90.

77. "Grahamism alias Millennialism," *Health Journal, & Advocate of Physiological Reform*, February 10, 1841.

78. Christine Heyrman in describing conversion experiences among Methodists and Baptists in the early nineteenth-century American South has written of the way that such moments of spiritual epiphany were often preceded by intense feelings of despair and worthlessness. Many Grahamites felt the same helplessness regarding their physical and emotional health before accepting the Graham system. Heyrman, *Southern Cross*, 33–36. Conversion has also been described as a liminal experience, the transition between an "old" and a "new" self; Juster, *Disorderly Women*, 15; Shea, *Spiritual Autobiography in Early America*.

79. *Graham Journal of Health and Longevity*, January 5, 1839.

80. "Testimony of George Williams, Russell, June 1, 1840," *Health Journal, & Advocate of Physiological Reform*, June 17, 1840.

81. Butler, *Awash in a Sea of Faith*, 226; Johnson and Wilentz, *Kingdom of Matthias*.

82. "To Our Friends and the Public," *Health Journal, & Advocate of Physiological Reform*, May 6, 1840.

83. Although there was a resort at Lebanon Springs that certainly catered to the health-seeking crowd as well as tourists, the Shaker community would have certainly provided a more abundant and permanent set of readers. See *Graham Journal of Health and Longevity* 3, no. 2 (1839): 40.

84. "Grahamism Not Sectarian," *Graham Journal of Health and Longevity*, May 2, 1837; *Graham Journal of Health and Longevity*, May 26, 1838. The *Graham Journal* recommended Shaker mattresses made from hickory shavings, for Grahamites looking to eschew the decadent feather mattresses believed to promote ill health and licentiousness. David Cambell furnished his own Brattle Street Graham boarding house with such mattresses, purchased from the Shakers.

85. Alfred, Maine, Shaker Community flour sack, ca. 1850, ASC.

86. Wells, *Experience and Testimony in Favor of Plain and Simple Diet* (Watervliet, NY: ca. 1838), ASC.

87. Prentiss, *Report of Interesting Experiences with the Boys of Whom He Was Caretaker* (Watervliet, NY: ca.1837), ASC.

88. Freegift Wells, *Notebook #4* (Watervliet, NY: ca. 1835), 11 WRHS.

89. The aforementioned spat between Wells and Prentiss radiated out among other Shaker communities, causing much partisan feeling. Both men eventually ended up being transferred away from Watervliet. Brewer argues that the ministry's failure to take a position on Grahamism paved the way toward further indecision and poor leadership, especially in dealing with the Era of Manifestations, the Shaker spiritual revival of the late 1830s–1840s. Brewer, *Shaker Communities, Shaker Lives*, 109–12.

90. Youngs, *A Concise View of the Church of God and of Christ on Earth New Lebanon*, 282–302, ASC.

Chapter Five

1. *Charleston Courier*, February 12, 1851; "Brooklyn Letter," *Times-Picayune*, September 20, 1851; *Daily Ohio Statesman*, November 3, 1851. The song debuted in April 1850 when the troupe was still working under the name of Pierce's Minstrels. J. B. Fellows

took over management in September of that year and renamed the troupe after himself. See Lawrence and Strong, *Strong on Music*, 125.

2. On performances of the "Black Shakers" routine, see "Local Intelligence Deacon Foster's Concert," *Daily Atlas*, February 2, 1850; *Salem Observer*, December 21, 1850. On the advertisement of "Fi Hi Hi: The Black Shakers' Song" as sheet music, see "New Music," *Times-Picayune*, March 15, 1850; *Charleston Courier*, February 21, 1851.

3. Lott, *Love and Theft*; Lhamon, *Raising Cain*; Cockrell, *Demons of Disorder*; Toll, *Blacking Up*.

4. Nord, *Faith in Reading*; Gac, *Singing for Freedom*, 202–5.

5. "Home again! Second week! Music and mirth! at the Horticultural Hall, School St. 1851.," American Broadsides and Ephemera Series 1.

6. Toll, *Blacking Up*, 161.

7. Odell, *Annals of the New York Stage*, 6:76.

8. Toll, *Blacking Up*, 162–63.

9. "Fi, Hi, Hi: The Black Shakers Song & Polka," Lester S. Levy Sheet Music Library, Johns Hopkins University, https://jscholarship.library.jhu.edu/handle/1774.2/5802.

10. On the meaning of dance in Shaker worship, see Brewer, *Shaker Communities, Shaker Lives*, 124; Stein, *Shaker Experience in America*, 101–2.

11. Some of the most popular minstrel songs, such as "Lucy Long" and "Juliana Phebiana Constantina Brown," described the sexuality of black women in graphic detail. Roediger, *Wages of Whiteness*, 121.

12. Toll, *Blacking Up*, 140, 144. On portrayals of black men as sexually aggressive in the late nineteenth and early twentieth centuries, see Bederman, *Manliness and Civilization*, 8–9.

13. White, *Ar'n't I a Woman?*, 27–30.

14. Roediger, *Wages of Whiteness*, 121.

15. Enslaved men were themselves victims of sexualized violence under slavery, often forced to strip naked and endure public beatings or ordered to put their bodies on display in the slave market. See Orelus, *Agony of Masculinity*, 67–70; Scully, "Masculinity, Citizenship," 37–55.

16. Stein, *Shaker Experience in America*, 201.

17. Emlen, "Shaker Dance Prints," 14–26.

18. Anti-Shaker activists like Mary Marshall Dyer had given lecture and lyceum tours since the beginning of the century as well, but did not offer song-and-dance routines. See De Wolfe, *Shaking the Faith*.

19. Conversations with native spirits were a hallmark of the Shakers' Era of Manifestations. Elizabeth Freeman argues that the "queerness" of Shaker dance as well as the Shakers' strange celibate practices made white observers perceive them as racially as well as sexually suspect. Freeman, *Beside You in Time*, 27–51.

20. "Concert at Brinley Hall, Worcester, on Monday Evening, July 27th, 1846," American Broadsides and Ephemera Series.

21. Odell, *Annals of the New York Stage*, 5:305; *New York Evening Post*, October 7, 1846.

22. Odell, *Annals of the New York Stage*, 6:75.

23. Odell, 6:305, 228–229.

24. Cook, *Arts of Deception*, 121.

25. Cook, 14–16; Cook, *Colossal P. T. Barnum Reader*, 4.

26. Tucher, *Froth and Scum*, 58–59.

27. *Daily National Intelligencer*, December 24, 1846; *Richmond Whig*, January 19, 1847. During June of 1847, one troupe of Shaking Quakers performed in Columbus, Ohio, while the original troupe returned for an engagement at Barnum's Museum in New York City. Since it could not have been in two places at once, the Ohio troupe must have been the imitator, possibly related to the second troupe Mary Marshall Dyer toured with in Washington, D.C. and Virginia. "Novel Concert and Lecture," *Ohio Statesman*, June 28, 1847; *Commercial Advertiser*, June 29, 1847.

28. *Report of the Examination of the Shakers*, 5.

29. *Report of the Examination of the Shakers*, 6.

30. *Report of the Examination of the Shakers*, 23–24.

31. *Report of the Examination of the Shakers*, 26.

32. Grimsted, *Melodrama Unveiled*, 86. Grimsted has argued that nineteenth-century actors could be respected as individuals and accepted into polite society, but as a profession they were regarded with mistrust.

33. Fabian, *Unvarnished Truth*, 4–7. Fabian argues that people sold captivity narratives (or in the case of the Shaking Quakers, a captivity "performance") "to demonstrate life among the 'aliens' had not altered them beyond recognition" to "rejoin the society of family and friends" or "gain compensation for property lost." The performances of J. M. Otis and company fit all three criteria.

34. Untitled, *Daily National Intelligencer*, January 8, 1849; "The Shaker Case," *New Hampshire Patriot*, January 11, 1849; Untitled, *New Hampshire Patriot*, January 18, 1849.

35. "Amusements," *Times-Picayune*, August 27, 1911; "March Stage History," *Philadelphia Inquirer*, February 25, 1912.

36. Buckstone, *Pet of the Petticoats*, 44.

37. "Theatrical and Musical," *New York Herald*, September 10, 1848.

38. Lampert, "Thy First Temple," 41–44.

39. Laird, *Cambridge Companion to the Musical*, 18. *Pet of the Petticoats* debuted in the 1830s; however, it did not have the distinction of having the appellation "musical comedy" appended to it until the 1860s. It remains one of the earliest pieces ever to have been termed a "musical comedy." Like a modern "musical," *Pet of the Petticoats* featured dialogue along with songs and dancing.

40. Wilson, *History of the Philadelphia Theater 1835–1855*, 59, 64, 596, 694. Other such amusements included *Sisters of Charity*, which had two performances at Philadelphia's Arch St. Theater in March of 1850; *The Jesuit's Colony or the Indian's Doom*, a "new national drama written by a gentleman of Philadelphia" in 1838; and *The Convent Ruins or Father and Sons*, a melodrama by Mrs. H. Siddons which ran for two performances in 1837. They were not revived to the same extent as *Pet of the Petticoats*.

41. Davison, *Fashionable Tour*; Temple, *American Tourist's Pocket Companion*, 72.

42. Taylor, *Transportation Revolution, 1815–1860*, 132. On the rise of the "fashionable tour" and the influence of the market revolution on tourism, see Mackintosh, "'Ticketed Through.'"

43. MacCannell, *Tourist*; Urry, *Tourist Gaze*.

44. This duality in the organization of time and how it maps onto modernity is discussed in Graburn, "Tourism," 28.

45. On middle-class leisure culture at mineral springs, see Sterngass, *First Resorts* and Chambers, *Drinking the Waters*.

46. Mackintosh, "'Ticketed Through,'" 67. See also Mackintosh, *Selling the Sights*, 86.

47. Urry, *Tourist Gaze*, 1–2.

48. Jane Desmond examines what she calls "people tourism," the cultural tourism of American and Western European encounters across racial and ethnic boundaries in Hawaii and "animal tourism" of zoos, theme parks, and safaris. Desmond sees both types of tourism as being rooted in a kind of bodily difference between the tourist and the people and animals that are the objects of tourism. Desmond, *Staging Tourism*, xv.

49. *Tourist or Pocket Manual for Travelers*, 58–59.

50. *Tourist or Pocket Manual for Travelers*, 25–26.

51. Davison also described "the Shaker's village" in his guide, and included details such as the color of the buildings and how many acres of cultivated land the Shakers had at the time. Davison, *Fashionable Tour*, 128–34, 149.

52. MacCannell, *Tourist*, 31.

53. Greylock, *Taghconic*, 118–21.

54. Greylock, 118–21.

55. Charles Dickens, *American Notes*, vol. 2; Martineau, *Society in America*, vol. 1; de Tocqueville, Harry Reeve, tr. *Democracy in America*; Hawthorne, *American Notebooks*; Cushman, *Some Lines in Verse about Shakers*.

56. Martineau, *Society in America*, 310–16.

57. Stein, *Shaker Experience in America*, 216–17.

58. Dickens, *American Notes*, 218–22.

59. Goffman, *Presentation of Self in Everyday Life*, 144–45. Goffman explains that a "back region or backstage may be defined as a place relative to a given performance, where the impression fostered by the performance is knowingly contradicted," a place where "suppressed facts make an appearance." It is these "suppressed facts" that make the "back region" more authentic and elusive for the tourist or audience. Goffman used "backstage" and "back region" interchangeably in his work, to contrast with his notion of the "front region," the bounded space where the performance takes place. See Goffman, 112–13.

60. MacCannell, *Tourist*, 102.

61. Mira Sharpless Townsend Diary, 1839, SL.

62. Maria Fay Diary, 1835, SL.

63. Mary Clark to Francis and Eliza Jackson, July 16, 1823, Francis Jackson Papers, Massachusetts Historical Society.

64. Nicholson wrote a "how-to" instructional manual for setting up a boarding house (and housekeeping in general) on the Graham system. She was a frequent contributor to Grahamite journals and publications during the 1830s and 1840s. Nicholson, *Nature's Own Book*.

65. "Murdock the Actor" reprinted in *Graham Journal of Health and Longevity*, November 28, 1837.

66. Gamber, *Boardinghouse in Nineteenth-Century America*, 58.

67. Haynes, "Radical Hospitality."

68. On the development of water cure and its association with reform movements, see Cayleff, *Wash and Be Healed*; Sklar, "All Hail to Pure, Cold Water!," 64–69, 100–101. Mary Gove merged Grahamite principles with new doctrines of free love at her water-cure establishment; see P. Cohen, "'Anti-Marriage Theory.'"

69. Nissenbaum, *Sex, Diet, Debility*, 149–51.

70. MacCannell has four criteria or processes for how a given locale becomes a touristic site: sacralization, enshrinement, and mechanical and social reproduction. MacCannell has argued that anticipation of sites is part of the touristic experience. Shaker villages and Catholic convents meet these other criteria as well. MacCannell, *Tourist*, 44–45.

71. MacCannell, 44–45.

72. The Shakers and their technological innovations graced the pages of *Scientific American* and *Harper's*. "The Shakers," *Harper's Magazine*, July 1857; "The Shaker Washing Machine," *Scientific American*, March 1860.

73. Maria Fay Diary, SL.

74. J. Sears, *Sacred Places*, 87–89.

75. Foucault, *Discipline and Punish*, 199. Foucault argues that the nineteenth century saw the rise of bifurcations and dichotomies in the service of creating a perfect society whereby symbolic lepers (the mad, the abnormal, the criminal) were excluded from society in "disciplinary partitioning." Authority comes from the ability to enforce the binary brand of abnormal/normal, mad/sane, dangerous/harmless. I would argue that there is a similar type of disciplinary partitioning at work in this type of tourism, even if it is not directly related to state power.

76. It was actually fairly commonplace to refer to nuns and Shakers as "inmates" of their respective institutions. Such references are found even in Catholic newspaper sources. The word may have had a more neutral connotation than it does today, when it is usually associated with prisoners. See "Disgraceful Outrage," *Catholic Herald*, August 21, 1834.

77. Schultz, *Fire and Roses*, 57–60.

78. Mira Sharpless Townsend Diary, SL.

79. Maria Fay Diary, SL.

80. N. Fitton to Isaac Brackett, October 16, 1827, MHS.

81. "Notice to Visitors," Watervliet Shaker Community, 1849, ASC.

82. "Lucius Sargent Diary," MEHS.

83. MacCannell, *Tourist*, 45.

Conclusion

1. McNeil, *Charity Afire*, 1–3, 7, 10.

2. McNeil, 3.

3. McNeil, iv–v.

4. McNeil, 3.

5. McNeil, 14, 5–7.

6. McNeil, vi. See also Barton, *Angels of the Battlefield*, Libster and MacNeil, *Enlightened Charity*.

7. A. White, *Shakerism*, 197, 181–82.

8. The Shakers' trip to Washington likely happened in the spring of 1863, after conscription was put into effect throughout the Union. For other accounts of the meeting with Lincoln, see Stein, *Shaker Experience in America*, 201–3 and Sanchez, *Mr. Lincoln's Chair*.

9. A. White, *Shakerism*, 182–83.

10. Abraham Lincoln, "To the Shakers," in *Collected Works of Abraham Lincoln*, vol. 7, 485.

11. Quoted in Stein, *Shaker Experience in America*, 203.

12. A. White, *Shakerism*, 203–4.

13. Dix initially only wanted "plain-looking" women over thirty to serve in her nursing corps. Eggleston, *Women in the Civil War*, 184.

14. Schwarz, *John Harvey Kellogg*, 32–35, 46; Engs, *Clean Living Movements*, 114–15.

15. Smith, *Food and Drink in American History*, vol. 1, 408–10. Recipes for "Graham Crackers" appeared in cookbooks in the decades between Graham's death and Nabisco's decision to trademark and mass-produce them.

16. Statistics on the number of priests and sisters in the United States obtained from Center for Applied Research in the Apostolate at Georgetown University, "Frequently Requested Church Statistics."

17. Sabbathday Lake Shaker Village, "Our Beliefs." The Sabbathday Lake Shakers welcome vocations according to their website, but converts must undergo a novitiate period before becoming full members.

18. Frank Bruni, "The Wages of Celibacy," *New York Times*, February 25, 2013.

19. A. W. Richard Sipe, "Frequently Asked Questions."

20. For general information on the asexuality movement and AVEN, see Rachel Hills, "Life without Sex: The Third Phase of the Asexuality Movement," *The Atlantic*, April 2, 2012 and AVEN's website, www.asexuality.org. AVEN in cooperation with researchers from the Kinsey Institute at Indiana University lobbied for the removal of "hypoactive sexual desire disorder" as a condition in the DSM-V but were unsuccessful. Asexual activists believe that their identity is being pathologized as an illness, similar to the way homosexuality was treated by the psychiatric community prior to 1974. See Prause and Graham, "Asexuality"; Cerankowski and Milks, "New Orientations."

21. David Jay, quoted in Hills, "Life without Sex."

22. Cerankowski and Milks, "New Orientations," 657.

23. These references to an "asexual past" can often be found on AVEN's online message forum. See, for example, June 14, 2014 (5:02 P.M.), "Is There Any Asexual History?" and September 28, 2014, comment on "Nuns the First Asexuals?," Asexual Visibility and Education Network Forum.

Bibliography

Primary Sources

Archives and Collections

American Antiquarian Society, Worcester, Massachusetts
    Draper-Rice Family Papers
    Schools and Colleges Collection
    Sylvester Graham Papers
Catholic University of America University Archives, Washington, DC
    Ursuline Convent Records
Countway Medical Library, Harvard University, Boston, Massachusetts
De Andreis-Rosati Memorial Archives, DePaul University, Chicago, Illinois
    John Timon Papers, Provincial Files, Congregation of the Mission–Western
        Province
    St. Mary's of the Barrens Seminary Records
Georgetown University Special Collections, Washington, DC
    John Gilmary Shay Collection
Hancock Shaker Village Library, Hancock, Massachusetts
Houghton Library, Harvard University, Cambridge, Massachusetts
    Amos Bronson Alcott Papers
Library of Congress, Washington, DC
    Shaker Collection
Maine Historical Society
    Lucius Sergeant Diary
    Rebecca Usher Papers
Massachusetts Historical Society
    Francis Jackson Papers
    Rebecca Codman Butterfield Papers
New Hampshire Historical Society
    Franklin Pierce Papers
New York State Archives
    Shaker Collection
Schlesinger Library, Radcliffe Institute, Harvard University,
        Cambridge, Massachusetts
    James C. Whitten Ephemera Collection
    Ladies' Physiological Institute of Boston Records
    Maria Fay Diary
    Mira Sharpless Townsend Diary

University of Notre Dame Special Collections Library, Notre Dame, Indiana
     Archives of the Sisters of Charity of Nazareth, Kentucky
Western Reserve Historical Society, Cleveland, Ohio
     Cathcart Shaker Collection
Winterthur Museum and Library, Greenville, Delaware
     Edward Deming Andrews Memorial Shaker Collection
     George Jacques Diary
     Joseph Downs Collection of Manuscripts and Printed Ephemera

Digital Archives and Databases

American Broadsides & Ephemera Series
Center for Applied Research in the Apostolate at Georgetown University
Cornelia Connelly Papers
Hamilton College Library Digital Collections
Levy Sheet Music Collection, Johns Hopkins University

Newspapers and Periodicals

*The American Catholic
     Historical Researches*
American Watchman
The Atlantic
*Baltimore Patriot and
     Mercantile Advertiser*
Barre Gazette
Barre Patriot
Boston Daily Advertiser
*The Boston Medical and
     Surgical Journal*
*The Boston Quarterly
     Review*
Boston Satirist
Boston Satirist and Blade
The Broadway Belle
Brown's Literary Omnibus
The Bulletin
Catholic Herald
Charleston Courier
Chicago Times
Christian Mirror
Commercial Advertiser
Concord Gazette
Connecticut Journal
Constitution

Daily Atlas
*Daily National
     Intelligencer*
Daily Ohio Statesman
Eastern Argus
Essex Gazette
Frederick Douglass' Paper
Godey's Lady's Book
*The Graham Journal of
     Health and Longevity*
*Harper's New Monthly
     Magazine*
*Health Journal, & Advocate
     of Physiological Reform*
The Jeffersonian
The Liberator
The Library of Health
Life in Boston
*Life in Boston and
     New York*
The Monthly Cosmopolite
Morning Herald
National Aegis
*National Messenger
     [Washington, DC]*
New Bedford Mercury

*The New Hampshire
     Patriot*
*New Hampshire Patriot
     and State Gazette*
New Hampshire Sentinel
New York Daily Tribune
New York Evening Post
New York Herald
The New York Times
The New York Whip
Newburyport Herald
New-England Chronicle
Ohio Statesman
Pennsylvania Evening Post
Philadelphia Inquirer
Plain Dealer (Ohio)
Providence Patriot
*Providence Patriot
     Columbian Phoenix*
Public Advertiser
*Religion and Ethics
     Newsweekly*
Repertory
The Review
     (Nashville, TN)
Salem Gazette

Salem Observer Spirit of Seventy-Six Times-Picayune
Scientific American   (Washington, DC)
Sentinel of Freedom The Sun

Searchable Online Databases, Newspapers, and Periodicals

19th-Century U.S. Newspapers, Gale Cenage
AAS Historical Periodicals Collection, 1691–1876
America's Historical Imprints (Evans & Shaw-Shoemaker)
Early American Newspapers (America's Historical Newspapers), Readex

Published Primary Sources

Affection's Gift. Philadelphia: E. H. Butler, 1855.
Alcott, William A. *An Address Delivered before the American Physiological Society March 7 1837*. Boston: Light, 1837.
———. *An Address Delivered before the American Physiological Society at Their First Annual Meeting*. Boston: Marsh, Capen & Lyon, 1837.
———. *Confessions of a Schoolmaster*. Andover: Gould, Newman and Saxton, 1839.
———. *Forty Years in the Wilderness of Pills and Powders or the Cogitations and Confessions of an Aged Physician*. Boston: John P. Jewett, 1859.
———. *The Physiology of Marriage*. Boston: John P. Jewett & Company, 1856.
———. *The Young Man's Guide*. Boston: Perkins and Marvin, 1836.
Aristotle's Masterpiece. New-York: Printed for the United Company of Flying Stationers, 1788.
Buckstone, J. B. *The Pet of the Petticoats: An Opera in Three Acts*. New York: O. A. Roorbach, 1856.
Bunkley, Josephine. *Miss Bunkley's Book: The Testimony of an Escaped Novice from the Sisterhood of St. Joseph*. New York: Harper & Brothers, 1855.
Cabinet of Modern Art. Philadelphia: E. H. Butler, 1852.
Callahan, Nelson, ed. *The Diary of Richard L. Burtsell, Priest of New York: The Early Years, 1865–1868*. New York: Arno, 1978.
Catalogue of Medicinal Plants and Extracts. Ohio: Day Star Print, 1847.
Catalogue of Pupils of the Georgetown Academy of the Visitation, B.V.M. 1860–61. Baltimore, 1861.
Catalogue of the Pupils of Saint Joseph's Academy Near Emmitsburg Maryland for the Academic Year 1856–57. Baltimore: John Murphy, 1857.
Catalogue of the Students, and Award of Premiums of the Young Ladies' Literary Institute and Boarding School of the Sisters of Notre Dame. Cincinnati: AG Sparhawk, 1846.
Catalogue of the Teachers and Scholars in the Young Ladies' High School. Boston: WW Clapp, 1831.
Catholic Tract Society of Baltimore. *No. 1, Address of the Editorial Committee of the Catholic Tract Society of Baltimore to the Public*. Baltimore, 1839.

———. No. 2 *The Excellence and Dignity of Religion*. Baltimore, 1840.

———. Nos. 14–16 *Nuns and Monastic Institutes*. Baltimore, 1841.

Chapman, Eunice. *Being an Additional Account on the Conduct of the Shakers*. Albany, 1817.

Constitution of the American Physiological Society with a Catalogue of Its Members and Officers. Boston: Marsh, Capen & Lyon, 1837.

Cross, Andrew B. *Priests' Prisons for Women, or, A consideration of the question, whether unmarried foreign priests ought to be permitted to erect prisons into which, under pretense of religion, to seduce or entrap, or by force compel young women to enter, and after they have secured their property, keep them in confinement and compel them, as their slaves, to submit themselves to their will, under the penalty of flogging or the dungeon? : in twelve letters to T. Parkin Scott, Esq., member of the Baltimore Bar, and Vice Consul of the Pope*. Baltimore: Sherwood, 1854.

Curricular and Catalogue of the Oakland Female Institute. Philadelphia: Young & Deross, 1853.

Cushman, Charlotte. *Some Lines in Verse about Shakers*. New York: William Taylor, 1846.

Davison, Gideon. *The Fashionable Tour: Or a Trip to the Springs, Niagara, Quebeck, and Boston in the Summer of 1821*. Saratoga Springs: G. M. Davison, 1822.

De Tocqueville, Alexis. *Democracy in America*. Translated by Harry Reeve. New York: G. Adalard, 1838.

Dhu, Helen. *Stanhope Burleigh or the Jesuits in Our Homes*. New York: Stringer & Townsend, 1855.

Dickens, Charles. *American Notes*. Vol. 2. London: Chapman and Hall, 1842.

Doolittle, Mary Antoinette. *Autobiography of Mary Antoinette Doolittle: Containing a Brief History of Early Life . . . Among the Shakers*. Mount Lebanon, NY: n.p., 1880.

Dougherty, James ed. *Life of Mother Elizabeth Boyle*. Staten Island, NY: Press of the Immaculate Virgin, 1893.

Dunlavy, John. *The Manifesto: Or A Declaration of the Doctrines and Practices of the Church of Christ*. Pleasant Hill, KY: P. Bertrand, 1818.

Dyer, Mary Marshall. *A Brief Statement of the Sufferings of Mary Dyer Occasioned by the Society Called Shakers*. Concord: Joseph C. Spear, 1818.

Elkins, Harvey. *Fifteen Years in the Senior Order of the Shakers*. Hanover, NH: Dartmouth Press, 1853.

The Escaped Nun, Or, Disclosures of Convent Life. New York: De Witt & Davenport, 1855.

Evans, F. W. "White Cross Celibacy." Mount Lebanon, NY: n.p., 1888.

First Annual Catalogue of the Mount Vernon Female School 1829–1830. Boston: TR Marvin Printer, 1829.

Form of Ceremony for the Reception and Profession of the Sisters of Our Lady of Mercy. Boston: Patrick Donahoe, 1854.

Fourth Annual Catalogue of the Teachers and Scholars in the Young Ladies' High School. Boston: WW Clapp, 1831.

Fraser, Daniel. "Is Celibacy Contrary to Natural and Revealed Law." In *The Celibate Shaker Life*, 3–5. New Lebanon, NY: n.p., 1889.

Friendship's Offering. Boston: Phillips & Sampson, 1849.

Graham, Sylvester. *A Lecture to Young Men, on Chastity: Intended Also for the Serious Consideration of Parents and Guardians*. New York: Light & Stearns, 1837.

Greene, Susan Batchelder, ed. *Letters from Sister Mary Ignatia to Her Own Mother*. Boston: Damrell & Moore, 1853.

Greylock, Godfrey. *Taghconic; Or Letters and Legends about Our Summer Home*. Boston: Redding, 1852.

Goodwillie, Christian, ed. *Writings of Shaker Apostates and Anti-Shakers, 1782–1850*. Vol. 2. London: Taylor & Francis, 2017.

Guralnik, David, ed. *Webster's New World Dictionary of the American Language*. New York: World, 1970.

Hawthorne, Nathaniel. *The American Notebooks*. Edited by Randall Steward. New Haven, CT: Yale University Press, 1932.

Hazel, Henry. *The Nun of St. Ursula or the Burning of the Convent, a Romance of Mt. Benedict*. Boston: F. Gleason, 1845.

Hobbs, Janet Webb. *The Brick House and Its People* (ca. 1930).

Kelso, Isaac. *Danger in the Dark: A Tale of Intrigue and Priestcraft*. Cincinnati, OH: Queen City Publishing House, 1855.

Larned, Mrs. L. *The American Nun or the Affects of Romance*. Boston: Otis, Broaders, 1836.

Lincoln, Abraham. "To the Shakers." In *Jay*, edited by Roy P. Basler, 485–86. Vol. 7. New Brunswick, NJ: Rutgers University Press, 1953.

Luke, Jemima Thompson. *The Female Jesuit: Or, The Spy in the Family*. New York: M. W. Dodd, 1851.

Martineau, Harriet. *Society in America*. Vol. 1. New York: Sunders and Otley, 1837.

McNeil, Betty Ann, DC, ed. *Charity Afire: Pennsylvania 1862–1865*. Hanover, PA: Sheridan, 2011.

McNemar, Richard. *The Kentucky Revival*. Cincinnati: Browne, 1807.

Meacham, Joseph. *A Concise Statement of the Principles of the Only True Church . . . at New-Lebanon*. Bennington, VT: Haswell and Russell, 1790.

Minter, Jeremiah. *A Brief Account of the Religious Experience . . . of Jeremiah Minter*. Washington, DC: 1817.

Miss DT Kilbourn's Academy Baltimore. *Third Annual Circular 1854–1855*. Baltimore: John W. Woods, Printer, 1854.

Missionary Manual. Philadelphia: Cuthburt Montgomery, 1855.

Monk, Maria. *Awful Disclosures of the Hotel Dieu Nunnery*. New York: n.p., 1836.

Morse, Samuel, ed. *Confessions of a French Catholic Priest*. New York: John S. Taylor, 1837.

Mother Etienne Hall. Emmitsburg, MD: Published by the Daughters of Charity, 1939.

Nicholson, Asentath. *Nature's Own Book*. New York: Wilbur & Whipple, 1835.

Marie-France Carreel et al., ed. *Philippine Duchesne, Pioneer on the American Frontier (1769–1852)*. Vol. 1. Society of the Sacred Heart, 2019.

Rathbone, Reuben. *Reasons Offered for Leaving the Shakers*. Pittsfield, MA: Chester Smith, 1800.

Rathbun, Valentine. *Some Brief Hints of a Religious Scheme*. Norwich, CT: John Trumbull, 1781.

Reed, Rebecca. *Six Months in a Convent*. Boston: Russell, Odiorne & Metcalf, 1835.

Report of the Examination of the Shakers of Canterbury and Enfield before the New-Hampshire Legislature November Session 1848. Concord, NH: Ervin B. Tripp, 1849.

Roscoe, Thomas, ed. *Female Convents, Secrets of Nunneries Disclosed*. New York: D. Appleton, 1834.

Sabbathday Lake Shaker Village. "Our Beliefs." Accessed June 30, 2020. https://www.maineshakers.com/beliefs/.

The Shakers' Manual. Boston: Boston Stereotype Foundry, 1852.

Smith, James. *Remarkable Occurrences Lately Discovered among the People Called Shakers of a Treasonous and Barbarous Nature*. Carthage, TN: Moore, 1810.

———. *Shakerism Detected*. Paris, KY: n.p., 1810.

Stone, Horatio. *Lo Here and Lo There or The Grave of the Heart*. New York: Burgess, Stringer, 1846.

Stone, W. L. *Maria Monk and the Nunnery of the Hotel Dieu*. New York: Howe and Bates, 1836.

Supplement to the Case of the Rev. Pierce Connelly. London: Hatchard and Bosworth, 1853.

Temple, George. *The American Tourist's Pocket Companion, or, A Guide to the Springs and Trip to the Lakes*. New York: D. Longworth, 1812.

Testimonies of the Life, Character, Revelations and Doctrines of Our Ever Blessed Mother Ann Lee. Hancock, MA: J. Tallcott & J. Deming, Jr., 1816.

Thompson, Daniel. "The Shaker Lovers." In *May Martin and other Tales of the Green Mountains*, 253–306. Boston: Sanborn, Carter, Bazin, ca. 1852.

Tiffin, Edward, and Sherman Kirker. "Providing for the Relief and Support of Women Who May Be Abandoned by their Husbands, and for Other Purposes." N.p., 1807.

The Tourist or Pocket Manual for Travelers. New York: J & J Harper, 1830.

Webster, Noah. *An American Dictionary of the English Language*. New York: S. Converse, 1828.

White, Anna. *Shakerism, Its Meaning and Message*. Columbus, OH: F. J. Heer, 1904.

Woodward, Samuel B. *Hints for the Young in Relation to the Health of Body and Mind*. Boston: Light, 1840.

Wright, Henry C. *Marriage and Parentage or the Reproductive Element of Man as a Means to His Elevation and Happiness*. Boston: Bela Marsh, 1855.

Wright, Julia McNair. *Almost a Nun*. Philadelphia: Presbyterian Publication Committee, 1868.

———. *Almost a Priest*. Philadelphia: McKinney and Martin, 1870.

———. *Priest and Nun*. Philadelphia: Crittenden & McKinney, 1869.

Youngs, Benjamin. *The Testimony of Christ's Second Appearing . . . in This Latter-day*. Lebanon, OH: John M'Clean, 1808.

Secondary Sources

Abbott, Elizabeth. *A History of Celibacy*. Cambridge, MA: Da Capo, 2000.

Abzug, Robert. *Cosmos Crumbling: American Reform and the Religious Imagination*. New York: Oxford University Press, 1994.

Andrews, Edward Deming. *The People Called Shakers; A Search for the Perfect Society*. New York: Oxford University Press, 1953.

———. *Shaker Herbs and Herbalists*. Stockbridge, MA: Berkshire Garden Center, 1959.

Andrews, Edward Deming, and Faith Andrews. *Religion in Wood: A Book of Shaker Furniture*. Bloomington: Indiana University Press, 1966.

Bach, Jeff. *Voices of the Turtledoves: The Sacred World of Ephrata*. Harrisburg: Pennsylvania State University Press, 2005.

Baker, Hugh Sanford Cheney. "A History of the Book Trade in California, 1849–1859." *California Historical Society Quarterly* 30, no. 3 (1951): 97–115.

Bannet, Eve Tavor. *Transatlantic Stories and the History of Reading, 1720–1810: Migrant Fictions*. New York: Cambridge University Press, 2011.

Barton, George. *Angels of the Battlefield: A History of the Labors of the Catholic Sisterhoods in the Late Civil War*. Philadelphia: Catholic Art Publishing Company, 1898.

Beadie, Nancy. *Education and the Creation of Capital in the Early American Republic*. New York: Cambridge University Press, 2010.

Beaghton, Andrea. "Hugo and Sand in Morse Code." *French Studies Bulletin* 31 (2010): 21–24.

Bederman, Gail. *Manliness and Civilization: A Cultural History of Gender and Race in the United States, 1880–1917*. Chicago: University of Chicago Press, 1997.

Berger, Teresa. "Of Clare and Clairol: Imaging Radiance and Resistance." *Journal of Feminist Studies in Religion* 18, no. 1 (2002): 53–69.

Berlant, Lauren, and Michael Warner. "Sex in Public." *Critical Inquiry* 24, no. 2 (1998): 547–66.

Billington, Ray Allen. "Maria Monk and Her Influence." *Catholic Historical Review* 22 (1936): 283–95.

———. *The Protestant Crusade 1800–1860: The Origins of American Nativism*. New York: Macmillan, 1938.

Bloch, Ruth H. *Gender and Morality in Anglo-American Culture, 1650–1800*. Berkeley: University of California Press, 2003.

———. *Visionary Republic: Millennial Themes in American Thought, 1756–1800*. Cambridge: Cambridge University Press, 1985.

Boydston, Jeanne. "Gender as a Question of Historical Analysis." *Gender and History* 20, no. 3 (2008): 558–83.

Brewer, Priscilla. *Shaker Communities, Shaker Lives*. Hanover, NH: University Press of New England, 1986.

Brodie, Janet Farrell. *Conception and Abortion in 19th-Century America*. Ithaca, NY: Cornell University Press, 1997.

Brown, Candy Gunther. *The Word in the World: Evangelical Writing, Publishing, and Reading in America, 1789–1880*. Chapel Hill: University of North Carolina Press, 2004.

Butler, Jon. *Awash in a Sea of Faith: Christianizing the American People*. Cambridge, MA: Harvard University Press, 1990.

Butler, Judith *Gender Trouble: Feminism and the Subversion of Identity*. 2nd ed. New York: Routledge, 1999.

Campbell, D'Ann. "Women's Life in Utopia: The Shaker Experiment in Sexual Equality Reappraised—1810 to 1860." *New England Quarterly* 51, no. 1 (1978): 23–38.

Casper, Scott E. "Case Study: Harper & Brothers." In *A History of the Book in America*, edited by Robert Gross and Mary Kelley, 128–37. Vol. 2. Chapel Hill: University of North Carolina Press, 2010.

Cayleff, Susan E. *Wash and Be Healed: The Water-Cure Movement and Women's Health*. Philadelphia: Temple University Press, 1987.

Cayton, Mary. "Canonizing Harriet Newell: Women, the Evangelical Press, and the Foreign Mission Movement in New England, 1800–1840." In *Competing Kingdoms: Women, Mission, Nation, and the American Protestant Empire, 1812–1960*, edited by Barbara Reeves-Ellington et al., 69–93. Durham, NC: Duke University Press, 2010.

Cerankowski, Karli June, and Megan Milks. "New Orientations: Asexuality and Its Implications for Theory and Practice." *Feminist Studies* 36, no. 3 (2010): 650–64.

Chambers, Thomas. *Drinking the Waters: Creating an American Leisure Class at Nineteenth-Century Mineral Springs*. Washington, DC: Smithsonian Institution Press, 2002.

Chambers-Schiller, Lee Virginia. *Liberty, a Better Husband: Single Women in America: The Generations of 1780–1840*. New Haven, CT: Yale University Press, 1984.

Chauncey, George. *Gay New York: Gender, Urban Culture, and the Makings of the Gay Male World, 1890–1940*. New York: Basic Books, 1994.

Cheng, Patrick S. *Radical Love: An Introduction to Queer Theology*. New York: Seabury Books, 2011.

Clark, Anna. *Desire: A History of European Sexuality*, 2nd ed. New York: Routledge, 2019.

———. "Twilight Moments." *Journal of the History of Sexuality* 14, no. 1/2 (2005): 139–60.

Clark, Emily. *Masterless Mistresses: The New Orleans Ursulines and the Development of a New World Society, 1727–1834*. Chapel Hill: University of North Carolina Press, 2007.

Cleves, Rachel Hope. *Charity and Sylvia: A Same Sex Marriage in Early America*. New York: Oxford University Press, 2014.

Cockrell, Dale. *Demons of Disorder: Early Blackface Minstrels and Their World*. New York: Cambridge University Press, 1997.

Cohen, Daniel A. "The Respectability of Rebecca Reed: Genteel Womanhood and Sectarian Conflict in Antebellum America." *Journal of the Early Republic* 16, no. 3 (1996): 419–61.

Cohen, Joanna. *Luxurious Citizens: The Politics of Consumption in Nineteenth-Century America*. Philadelphia: University of Pennsylvania Press, 2017.

Cohen, Patricia Cline. "The 'Anti-Marriage Theory' of Thomas and Mary Gove Nichols: A Radical Critique of Monogamy in the 1850s." *Journal of the Early Republic* 34, no. 1 (2014): 1–20.

———. *The Murder of Helen Jewett: The Life and Death of a Prostitute in Nineteenth-Century New York*. New York: Vintage, 1999.

Cohen, Patricia Cline, Timothy Gilfoyle, and Helen Lefokowitz Horowitz. *The Flash Press: Sporting Male Weeklies in 1840s New York*. Chicago: University of Chicago Press, 2008.

Colley, Linda. *Britons: Forging the Nation, 1707–1837*. New Haven, CT: Yale University Press, 1992.

Cook, James W. *The Arts of Deception: Playing with Fraud in the Age of Barnum*. Cambridge, MA: Harvard University Press, 2001.

———, ed. *The Colossal P. T. Barnum Reader: Nothing Else Like It in the Universe*. Chicago: University of Illinois Press, 2005.

Cooper, Wendy. *Hair: Sex, Society, Symbolism*. New York: Stein, 1971.

Cott, Nancy. "Passionlessness: An Interpretation of Victorian Sexual Ideology, 1790–1850." *Signs* 4, no. 2 (1978): 219–36.

Cronon, William. *Nature's Metropolis: Chicago and the Great West*. New York: W. W. Norton, 2009.

Davis, David Brion. "Some Themes of Counter-Subversion: An Analysis of Anti-Masonic, Anti-Catholic, and Anti-Mormon Literature." *Mississippi Valley Historical Review* 47, no. 2 (1960): 205–24.

D'Emilio, John, and Estelle B. Freedman. *Intimate Matters: A History of Sexuality in America*. 2nd ed. Chicago: University of Chicago Press, 1998.

de Courtais, Georgine. *Women's Hats, Headdresses and Hairstyles, Medieval to Modern*. Mineola, NY: Dover, 1973.

Deloria, Philip J. *Playing Indian*. New Haven, CT: Yale University Press, 1998.

Desmond, Jane C. *Staging Tourism: Bodies on Display from Waikiki to Sea World*. Chicago: University of Chicago Press, 1999.

De Wolfe, Elizabeth A. *Shaking the Faith: Women, Family, and Mary Marshall Dyer's Anti-Shaker campaign, 1815–1867*. New York: Palgrave, 2003.

Dolan, Jay P. *The Irish Americans: A History*. New York: Bloomsbury, 2008.

Dorsey, Bruce. "'Making Men What They Should Be': Male Same-Sex Intimacy and Evangelical Religion in Early Nineteenth-Century New England." *Journal of the History of Sexuality* 24, no. 3 (2015): 345–77.

———. *Reforming Men and Women: Gender in the Antebellum City*. Ithaca, NY: Cornell University Press, 2006.

Dowd, Gregory Evans. *A Spirited Resistance: The North American Indian Struggle for Unity, 1745–1815*. Baltimore: Johns Hopkins University Press, 1992.

Dunbar, Erica Armstrong. *A Fragile Freedom: African American Women and Emancipation in the Antebellum City*. New Haven, CT: Yale University Press, 2011.

Duncan, Jason K. *Citizens Or Papists?: The Politics of Anti-Catholicism in New York, 1685–1821*. New York: Fordham University Press, 2005.

Durkheim, Émile. "The Elementary Forms of the Religious Life." *Readings from Emile Durkheim*. Rev. ed. Edited by Kenneth Thompson, 107–25. New York: Routledge, 2004.

Eckhart, Celia Morris. *Fanny Wright: Rebel in America*. Cambridge, MA: Harvard University Press, 1984.

Eggleston, Larry G. *Women in the Civil War: Extraordinary Stories of Soldiers, Spies, Nurses, Doctors, Crusaders, and Others*. Jefferson, NC: McFarland, 2009.

Elliott, Emory, ed. *The Columbia History of the American Novel*. New York: Columbia University Press, 1991.

Emlen, Robert. "Shaker Dance Prints." *Imprint* 17, no. 2 (1992): 14–26.

Engs, Ruth C. *Clean Living Movements: American Cycles of Health Reform*. Westport, CT: Greenwood, 2000.

Enstad, Nan. *Ladies of Labor, Girls of Adventure: Working Women, Popular Culture, and Labor Politics at the Turn of the Twentieth Century*. New York: Columbia University Press, 1999.

Exman, Eugene. *The House of Harper; One Hundred and Fifty Years of Publishing*. New York: Harper & Row, 1967.

Fabian, Ann. *The Unvarnished Truth: Personal Narratives in Nineteenth-Century America*. Berkeley: University of California Press, 2002.

Feller, Daniel. "The Market Revolution Ate My Homework." *Reviews in American History* 25, no. 3 (1997): 408–15.

F. E. T. "Sketch of the Life of Mother Cornelia Connelly Foundress of the Sisters of the Holy Child Jesus 1809–1879." *Records of the American Catholic Historical Society of Philadelphia* 31, no. 1 (1920): 1–42.

Fitzgerald, Maureen. *Habits of Compassion: Irish Catholic Nuns and the Origins of New York's Welfare System, 1830–1920*. Urbana: University of Illinois Press, 2006.

Flaxman, Radegunde. *A Woman Styled Bold: The Life of Cornelia Connelly 1809–1879*. London: Dartman Longman and Todd, 1991.

Fogleman, Aaron Spencer. *Jesus Is Female: Moravians and Radical Religion in Early America*. Philadelphia: University of Pennsylvania Press, 2008.

Foster, Lawrence. *Religion and Sexuality: The Shakers, the Mormons, and the Oneida Community*. Chicago: University of Illinois Press, 1984.

———. *Women, Family, and Utopia: Communal Experiments of the Shakers, the Oneida Community, and the Mormons*. Syracuse, NY: Syracuse University Press, 1992.

Foster, Thomas A., ed. *Long before Stonewall: Histories of Same-sex Sexuality in Early America*. New York: New York University Press, 2007.

Foucault, Michel. *Discipline and Punish: The Birth of the Prison*. New York: Vintage, 1979.

———. *The History of Sexuality*. Vol. 1. New York: Vintage, 1978.

Francis, Richard. *Ann the Word: The Story of Ann Lee, Female Messiah, Mother of the Shakers*. New York: Arcade, 2001.

Freccero, Carla. *Queer/Early/Modern*. Durham, NC: Duke University Press, 2006.

Freeman, Elizabeth. *Beside You in Time: Sense Methods and Queer Sociabilities in the American Nineteenth Century*. Durham, NC: Duke University Press, 2019.

Fuentes, Marisa J. *Dispossessed Lives: Enslaved Women, Violence, and the Archive*. Philadelphia: University of Pennsylvania Press, 2016.

Fuhlman, J. Spencer. *"A Peculiar People": Anti-Mormonism and the Making of Religion in Nineteenth-Century America*. Chapel Hill: University of North Carolina Press, 2014.

Gac, Scott. *Singing for Freedom: The Hutchinson Family Singers and the Nineteenth-Century Culture of Reform*. New Haven, CT: Yale University Press, 2007.

Gamber, Wendy. *The Boardinghouse in Nineteenth-Century America*. Baltimore: Johns Hopkins University Press, 2007.

Garrett, Clarke. *Spirit Possession and Popular Religion: From the Camisards to the Shakers*. Baltimore: Johns Hopkins University Press, 1987.

Gedge, Karin E. *Without Benefit of Clergy: Women and the Pastoral Relationship in Nineteenth-Century American Culture*. New York: Oxford University Press, 2003.

Geertz, Clifford. *The Interpretation of Cultures: Selected Essays*. New York: Basic Books, 1973.

Gerber, Lynne. "'Queerish' Celibacy: Reorienting Marriage in the Ex-Gay Movement." In *Queer Christianities: Lived Religion in Transgressive Forms*, edited by Kathleen Talvacchia and Michael F. Pettinger, 25–36. New York: New York University Press, 2015.

Gilje, Paul. *Rioting in America*. Bloomington: Indiana University Press, 1999.

Gilsky, Joan, I. H. M. "The Official IHM Stance on Friendship 1845–1960." In *Building Sisterhood: A Feminist History of the Sisters, Servants of the Immaculate Heart of Mary*, comp. Sisters, Servants of the Immaculate Heart of Mary, 153–72. Syracuse, NY: Syracuse University Press, 1997.

Ginzburg, Lori. *Women and the Work of Benevolence: Morality, Politics, and Class in the Nineteenth-Century United States*. New Haven, CT: Yale University Press, 1992.

Gitter, Elisabeth G. "The Power of Women's Hair in the Victorian Imagination." *PMLA* 99, no. 5 (1984): 936–54.

Givens, Terry L. *The Viper on the Hearth: Mormons, Myths, and the Construction of Heresy*. New York: Oxford University Press, 1997.

Godbeer, Richard. *The Overflowing of Friendship: Love between Men and the Creation of the American Republic*. Baltimore: Johns Hopkins University Press, 2009.

———. *Sexual Revolution in Early America*. Baltimore: Johns Hopkins University Press, 2002.

Goffman, Erving. *The Presentation of Self in Everyday Life*. New York: Doubleday, 1959.

Gordon, Linda. *The Moral Property of Women: A History of Birth Control Politics in America*. 3rd ed. Champaign: University of Illinois Press, 2002.

Gordon, Sarah Barringer. "The Liberty of Self-Degradation: Polygamy, Woman Suffrage, and Consent in Nineteenth-Century America." *Journal of American History* 83, no. 3 (1996): 815–47.

Graburn, Nelson. "Tourism: The Sacred Journey." In *Hosts and Guests: The Anthropology of Tourism*, edited by Valene Smith, 21–36. Philadelphia: University of Pennsylvania Press, 1989.

Graham, Judith A. "The New Lebanon Shaker Children's Order." *Winterthur Portfolio* 26 (Winter 1991): 215–29.

Greenberg, Amy S. *Manifest Manhood and the Antebellum American Empire*. New York: Cambridge University Press, 2005.

Griffin, Susan M. "Awful Disclosures: Women's Evidence in the Escaped Nun's Tale." *PMLA/Publications of the Modern Language Association of America* 111, no. 1 (1996): 93–107.

Grimsted, David. *Melodrama Unveiled: American Theater and Culture, 1800–1850*. Berkeley: University of California Press, 1968.

Gross, Robert. "Introduction: An Extensive Republic." In *A History of the Book in America*, edited by Robert Gross and Mary Kelley. Vol. 2, 1–52. Chapel Hill: University of North Carolina Press, 2010.

Gross, Robert, and Mary Kelley, eds. *A History of the Book in America*. Vol. 2. Chapel Hill: University of North Carolina Press, 2010.

Guilfoyle, Timothy. *City of Eros: New York City, Prostitution, and the Commercialization of Sex, 1790–1920*. New York: W. W. Norton, 1994.

Gura, Philip. *American Transcendentalism: A History*. New York: Hill and Wang, 2007.

Guralink, David Bernard, ed. *Webster's New World Dictionary of the American Language*. New York: Prentice Hall, 1970.

Gustafson, Jane. "Celibate Passion." In *Sexuality and the Sacred: Sources for Theological Reflection*, edited by James B. Nelson and Sandra P. Longfellow, 277–81. Louisville, KY: John Knox, 1994.

Halperin, David M. "Forgetting Foucault: Acts, Identities, and the History of Sexuality." *Representations* (1998): 93–120.

Halttunen, Karen. *Confidence Men and Painted Women: A Study of Middle-class Culture in America, 1830–1870*. New Haven, CT: Yale University Press, 1986.

———. "The Pornography of Pain in Anglo-American Culture." *American Historical Review* 100, no. 2 (1995): 303–34.

Hasday, Jill Elaine. "Contest and Consent: A Legal History of Marital Rape." *California Law Review* 88, no. 5 (2000): 1373–505.

Hatch, Nathan O. *The Democratization of American Christianity*. New Haven, CT: Yale University Press, 1989.

Haynes, April. "Radical Hospitality and Political Intimacy in Grahamite Boarding Houses, 1830–1850." *Journal of the Early Republic* 29, no. 3 (2019): 397–436.

———. "Riotous Flesh: Gender, Physiology, and the Solitary Vice." PhD diss., University of California, Santa Barbara, 2009.

———. *Riotous Flesh: Women, Physiology, and the Solitary Vice in Nineteenth-Century America*. Chicago: Chicago University Press, 2015.

Hemphill, Katie M. "Selling Sex and Intimacy in the City: The Changing Business of Prostitution in Nineteenth-Century Baltimore." In *Capitalism by Gaslight: Illuminating the Economy of Nineteenth-Century America*, edited by Brian P. Luskey and Wendy A. Woloson, 168–89. Philadelphia: University of Pennsylvania Press, 2015.

Hessinger, Rodney. *Seduced, Abandoned, and Reborn: Visions of Youth in Middle-Class America, 1780–1850*. Philadelphia: University of Pennsylvania Press, 2004.

Heyrman, Christine. *Southern Cross: The Beginnings of the Bible Belt*. New York: Alfred A. Knopf, 1997.

Hill, Marilyn Wood. *Their Sisters' Keepers: Prostitution in New York City, 1830–1870*. Berkeley: University of California Press, 1993.

Howe, Daniel Walker. *What Hath God Wrought: The Transformation of America, 1815–1848*. New York: Oxford University Press, 2007.

Hudson, Graham. *The Design and Printing of Ephemera in Britain and America 1720–1920*. London: British Library, 2008.

Humez, Jean, ed. *Gifts of Power: The Writings of Rebecca Jackson, Black Visionary, Shaker Elderess*. Amherst: University of Massachusetts Press, 1981.

Johnson, Paul. *A Shopkeeper's Millennium: Society and Revivals in Rochester, New York, 1815–1837*. 25th anniversary ed. New York: Hill and Wang, 2004.

Johnson, Paul, and Sean Wilentz. *The Kingdom of Matthias: A Story of Sex and Salvation in 19th-Century America*. New York: Oxford University Press, 1994.

Jones, Martha. *All Bound Up Together: The Woman Question in African American Public Culture*. Chapel Hill: University of North Carolina Press, 2007.

Juster, Susan. *Disorderly Women: Sexual Politics and Evangelicalism in Revolutionary New England*. Ithaca, NY: Cornell University Press, 1994.

———. *Doomsayers: Anglo-American Prophecy in the Age of Revolution*. Philadelphia: University of Pennsylvania Press, 2003.

Kanter, Rosabeth Moss. *Commitment and Community: Communes and Utopias in Sociological Perspective*. Cambridge, MA: Harvard University Press, 1972.

———. "Commitment and Social Organization: A Study of Commitment Mechanisms in Utopian Communities." *American Sociological Review* 33, no. 4 (1968): 499–517.

Karras, Ruth Mazo. "Prostitution and the Question of Sexual Identity in Medieval Europe." *Journal of Women's History* 11, no. 2 (1999): 159–77.

Katz, Jonathan Ned. *The Invention of Heterosexuality*. Chicago: University of Chicago Press, 2007.

———. *Love Stories: Sex between Men before Homosexuality*. Chicago: University of Chicago Press, 2003.

Kelley, Mary. *Learning to Stand and Speak: Women, Education, and Public Life in America's Republic*. Chapel Hill: University of North Carolina Press, 2006.

———. "Pen and Ink Communion: Evangelical Reading and Writing in Antebellum America." *New England Quarterly* 84, no. 4 (2011): 555–87.

Kendrick, Walter. *The Secret Museum: Pornography in Modern Culture*. New York: Viking, 1987.

Kern, Lewis, *An Ordered Love: Sex Roles and Sexuality in Victorian Utopias — The Shakers, the Mormons, and the Oneida Community* (Chapel Hill: University of North Carolina Press, 1981.

Kitch, Sally L. *Chaste Liberation: Celibacy and Female Cultural Status*. Urbana: University of Illinois Press, 1989.

Klepp, Susan. *Revolutionary Conceptions: Women, Fertility, and Family Limitation in America, 1760–1820*. Chapel Hill: University of North Carolina Press, 2009.

Kreiser, Larry, and Philip N. Dare. "Shaker Accounting Records at Pleasant Hill: 1830–1860." *Accounting Historians Journal* 13, no. 2 (1986): 19–36.

LaFleur, Greta. *The Natural History of Sexuality in Early America*. Baltimore: Johns Hopkins University Press, 2018.

Laird, Paul R. *The Cambridge Companion to the Musical*. Cambridge: Cambridge University Press, 2002.

Lampert, Sara. "'Thy First Temple in the Far, Far West!': Re/shaping Theatre in St. Louis, MO 1837–1839." *Ohio Valley History* 18, no. 2 (2018): 25–47.

Lawrence, Anna M. *One Family under God: Love, Belonging, and Authority in Early Transatlantic Methodism*. Philadelphia: University of Pennsylvania Press, 2011.

Lears, Jackson. *Fables of Abundance: A Cultural History of Advertising in America*. New York: Basic Books, 1994.

Lhamon, W. T. *Raising Cain: Blackface Performance from Jim Crow to Hip Hop*. Cambridge, MA: Harvard University Press, 2000.

Linsley, Susanna. "The American Reformation: The Politics of Religious Liberty, Charleston and New York 1770–1830." PhD diss., University of Michigan, 2012.

Lofton, Kathryn. "Everything Queer?" In *Queer Christianities: Lived Religion in Transgressive Forms*, edited by Kathleen T. Talvacchia, Michael F. Pettinger, and Mark Larrimore, 195–204. New York: New York University Press, 2015.

Lott, Eric. *Love and Theft: Blackface Minstrelsy and the American Working Class*. New York: Oxford University Press, 1995.

Loughran, Trish. *The Republic in Print: Print Culture in the Age of U.S. Nation Building, 1770–1870*. New York: Columbia University Press, 2007.

Love, Heather. *Feeling Backward: Loss and the Politics of Queer History*. Cambridge, MA: Harvard University Press, 2007.

Lyons, Clare. *Sex among the Rabble: An Intimate History of Gender and Power in the Age of Revolution, Philadelphia, 1730–1830*. Chapel Hill: University of North Carolina Press, 2006.

MacCannell, Dean. *The Tourist: A New Theory of the Leisure Class*. New York: Shocken Books, 1976.

Mackintosh, Will B. *Selling the Sights: The Invention of the Tourist in American Culture*. New York: New York University Press, 2019.

———. "'Ticketed Through': The Commodification of Travel in the Nineteenth Century." *Journal of the Early Republic* 32, no. 1 (2012): 61–89.

Manion, Jen. "Language, Acts, and Identity in LGBTQ Histories." In *The Routledge History of Queer America*, edited by Don Romesburg, 213–23. New York: Routledge, 2018.

Mannard, Joseph G. "Maternity . . . of the Spirit: Nuns and Domesticity in Antebellum America." *U.S. Catholic Historian* 5, no. 3/4 (1986): 305–24.

———. "'What Has Become of Olivia Neal?': The Escaped Nun Phenomenon in Antebellum America." *Maryland Historical Magazine* 105, no. 4 (2010): 348–36.

Maria Thérèse, SHCJ. *Cornelia Connelly*. Westminster, UK: Newman Press, 1963.

Maupin, Armistead. *Logical Family: A Memoir*. New York: Harper, 2017.

McConville, Brendan. *The King's Three Faces: The Rise and Fall of Royal America, 1688–1776*. Chapel Hill: University of North Carolina Press, 2006.

McCurdy, John Gilbert. *Citizen Bachelors: Manhood and the Creation of the United States*. Ithaca, NY: Cornell University Press, 2009.

McGreevy, John T. *American Jesuits and the World: How an Embattled Religious Order Made Modern Catholicism Global*. Princeton, NJ: Princeton University Press, 2016.

McGuinness, Margaret. *Called to Serve: A History of Nuns in America*. New York: New York University Press, 2013.

McKenna, Kevin E. *The Battle for Rights in the United States Catholic Church*. Mahwah, NJ: Paulist Press, 2007.

McNeil, Betty Ann, and Martha Libster. *Enlightened Charity: The Holistic Nursing Care, Education, and Advices Concerning the Sick of Sister Matilda Coskery, 1799–1870*. United States: Golden Apple Publications, 2009.

Miller, Amy Bess. *Shaker Herbs: A History and Compendium*. New York: Clarkson N. Potter, 1976.

Miller, Stephen J. *From Shaker Lands and Shaker Hands: A Survey of the Industries*. Lebanon, NH: University Press of New England, 2007.

Moore, R. Laurence. *Selling God: American Religion in the Marketplace of Culture*. New York: Oxford University Press, 1994.

Mooney, Catherine M. *Clare of Assisi and the Thirteenth-Century Church: Religious Women, Rules, and Resistance*. Philadelphia: University of Pennsylvania Press, 2016.

Morgan, David, and Sally Promey, eds. *The Visual Culture of American Religions*. Berkeley: University of California Press, 2001.

Morrow, Diane Batts. *Persons of Color and Religious at the Same Time: The Oblate Sisters of Providence, 1828–1860*. Chapel Hill: University of North Carolina Press, 2002.

Myles, Anne G. "Border Crossings: The Queer Erotics of Quakerism in Seventeenth-Century New England." In *Long before Stonewall: Histories of Same-sex Sexuality in Early America*, edited by Thomas A. Foster, 114–43. New York: New York University Press, 2007.

Nissenbaum, Stephen. *Sex, Diet, and Debility in Jacksonian America: Sylvester Graham and Health Reform*. Westport, CT: Greenwood, 1980.

Noll, Mark A., Karl August Von Reisach, and Elizabeth Cramer. "A Jesuit Interpretation of Mid-Nineteenth-Century America: 'Mormonism in Connection with Modern Protestantism.'" *Brigham Young University Studies* 45, no. 3 (2006): 39–74.

Nord, David Paul. "Benevolent Books: Printing, Religion, and Reform 1790–1840." In *A History of the Book in America*, edited by Robert Gross and Mary Kelley, 221–46. Vol. 2. Chapel Hill: University of North Carolina Press, 2010.

———. *Faith in Reading: Religious Publishing and the Birth of Mass Media in America*. New York: Oxford University Press, 2007.

Odell, George C. D. *Annals of the New York Stage*. Vol. 6. New York: Columbia University Press, 1931.

O'Donnell, Catherine. *Elizabeth Seton: American Saint*. Ithaca, NY: Cornell University Press, 2018.

Opal, J. M. *Beyond the Farm: National Ambitions in Rural New England*. Philadelphia: University of Pennsylvania Press, 2011.

———. "Exciting Emulation: Academies and the Transformation of the Rural North, 1780s–1820s." *Journal of American History* 91, no. 2 (2004): 445–70.

Ordover, Nancy. *American Eugenics: Race, Queer Anatomy, and the Science of Nationalism*. Minneapolis: University of Minnesota Press, 2003.

Orelus, Pierre. *The Agony of Masculinity: Race, Gender, and Education in the Age of "New" Racism and Patriarchy*. New York: Peter Lang, 2010.

Orsi, Robert. *Between Heaven and Earth: The Religious Worlds People Make and the Scholars Who Study Them*. Princeton, NJ: Princeton University Press, 2005.

———. "Is the Study of Lived Religion Irrelevant to the World We Live in? Special Presidential Plenary Address, Society for the Scientific Study of Religion, Salt Lake City, November 2, 2002." *Journal of the Scientific Study of Religion* 42, no. 2 (2003): 169–74.

Paton, Diana. "Decency, Dependence, and the Lash: Gender and the British Debate over Slave Emancipation, 1830–34." *Slavery and Abolition* 17, no. 3 (1996): 163–84.

———. *No Bond but the Law: Punishment, Race, and Gender in Jamaican State Formation, 1780–1870*. Durham, NC: Duke University Press, 2004.

Paz, Denis G. *The Priesthoods and Apostasies of Pierce Connally: A Study of Victorian Conversion and Anticatholicism*. Lewiston, NY: Edwin Mellen, 1986.

Perry, Lewis. *Childhood, Marriage, and Reform: Henry Clarke Wright, 1797–1870*. Chicago: University of Chicago Press, 1980.

Petro, Anthony M. "Celibate Politics: Queering the Limits." In *Queer Christianities: Lived Religion in Transgressive Forms*, edited by Kathleen T. Talvacchia, Michael F. Pettinger, and Mark Larrimore, 37–47. New York: New York University Press, 2015.

Pettinati, Joseph, dir. *Hand of God*. DVD. Random Room Entertainment, 2012.

Phelan, Shane. *Sexual Strangers: Gays, Lesbians, and Dilemmas of Citizenship*. Philadelphia: Temple University Press, 2001.

Prause, Nicole, and Cynthia A. Graham. "Asexuality: Classification and Categorization." *Archives of Sexual Behavior* 36, no. 3 (2007): 341–56.

Price, Jacob M. "The Last Phase of the Virginia-London Consignment Trade: James Buchanan and Co., 1758–1768." *The William and Mary Quarterly* 43, no. 1 (1986): 64–98.

Procter-Smith, Marjorie. *Shakerism and Feminism: Reflections on Women's Religion and the Early Shakers*. Old Chatham, NY: Shaker Museum and Library, 1991.

Reynolds, David S. *Beneath the American Renaissance: The Subversive Imagination in the Age of Emerson and Melville*. Cambridge, MA: Harvard University Press, 1988.

Rich, Adrienne. "Compulsory Heterosexuality and Lesbian Existence." In *Powers of Desire: The Politics of Sexuality*, edited by Ann Snitow, Christine Stansell, and Sharon Thompson, 177–203. New York: Monthly Review Press, 1983.

Richards, Leonard L. *"Gentlemen of Property and Standing": Anti-Abolition Mobs in Jacksonian America*. New York: Oxford University Press, 1971.

Rickards, Maurice, ed. *The Encyclopedia of Ephemera: A Guide to the Fragmentary Documents of Everyday Life for the Collector, Curator, and Historian*. New York: Routledge, 2000.

Roediger, David. *The Wages of Whiteness: Race and the Making of the American Working Class*. New York: Verso, 1991.

Rosenberg, Charles. *The Cholera Years: The United States in 1832, 1849, and 1866*. Chicago: University of Chicago Press, 1987.

Roseneil, Sasha. "Living and Loving beyond the Boundaries of the Heteronorm." In *Families in Society: Boundaries and Relationships*, edited by Linda Mckie and Sarah Cunningham-Burley, 241–60. Bristol, UK: Bristol University Press, 2005.

Rubin, Gayle S. "Thinking Sex: Notes for a Radical Theory of the Politics of Sexuality." In *Culture, Society and Sexuality: A Reader*, edited by Richard Parker and Peter Aggleton, 143–68. New York: Routledge, 1999.

———. "The Traffic in Women: Notes on the 'Political Economy' of Sex." In *Toward an Anthropology of Women*, edited by Rayna Reiter, 157–210. New York: Monthly Review Press, 1975.

Ryan, Kelly A. *Regulating Passion: Sexuality and Patriarchal Rule in Massachusetts, 1700–1830*. New York: Oxford University Press, 2014.

Ryan, Mary. *Cradle of the Middle Class: The Family in Oneida County, New York, 1790–1865*. New York: Cambridge University Press, 1981.

————. *Mysteries of Sex: Tracing Women and Men through American History*. Chapel Hill: University of North Carolina Press, 2006.

————. "Narratives of Democracy, or History without Subjects." *American Literary History* 8, no. 2 (1996): 311–27.

Sanchez, Anita. *Mr. Lincoln's Chair: The Shakers and Their Quest for Peace*. Granville, OH: McDonald & Woodward, 2009.

Sanchez-Eppler, Karen. *Touching Liberty: Abolition, Feminism, and the Politics of the Body*. Berkeley: University Press of California, 1993.

Schroth, Raymond. *The American Jesuits: A History*. New York: New York University Press, 2007.

Schultz, Nancy Lusignan. *Fire & Roses: The Burning of the Charlestown Convent, 1834*. New York: Free Press, 2000.

————. "Introduction." In *Veil of Fear: Nineteenth Century Convent Tales*, vii–xxx. West Lafayette, IN: Purdue University Books, 1999.

Schwarz, Richard W. *John Harvey Kellogg, M.D.: Pioneering Health Reformer*. Hagerstown, MD: Review and Herald Publishing Association, 2006.

Scott, Joan Wallach. "Gender: A Useful Category of Historical Analysis." In *Gender and the Politics of History*, 28–52. New York: Columbia University Press, 1999.

————. "The Evidence of Experience." *Critical Inquiry* 17, no. 4 (1991): 773–97.

Scully, Pamela. "Masculinity, Citizenship, and the Production of Knowledge in the Postemancipation Cape Colony, 1834–1844." In *Gender and Slave Emancipation in the Atlantic World*, edited by Pamela Scully et al., 37–55. Durham, NC: Duke University Press, 2005.

Sears, Hal D. *The Sex Radicals: Free Love in High Victorian America*. Lawrence, KS: Regents, 1977.

Sears, John. *Sacred Places: American Tourist Attractions in the Nineteenth Century*. New York: Oxford University Press, 1989.

Sedgwick, Eve Kosofsky. *Epistemology of the Closet*. Berkeley: University of California Press, 2008.

Sellers, Charles. *The Market Revolution: Jacksonian America 1815–1846*. New York: Oxford University Press, 1991.

Shea, Daniel B. *Spiritual Autobiography in Early America*. Madison: University of Wisconsin Press, 1988.

Shelley, Thomas J. *Greenwich Village Catholics: St. Joseph's Church and the Evolution of an Urban Faith Community, 1829–2002*. Washington, DC: Catholic University of America Press, 2003.

Sheumaker, Helen. *Love Entwined: The Curious History of Hairwork in America*. Philadelphia: University of Pennsylvania Press, 2007.

Sipe, A. W. Richard. "Frequently Asked Questions." Accessed December 5, 2020. http://www.awrsipe.com/Interviews/2012-11-05-FAQ.html.

Sklar, Kathryn Kish. "All Hail to Pure, Cold Water!" *American Heritage* 26 (December 1974): 64–69, 100–101.

Smith, Ryan K. *Gothic Arches, Latin Crosses: Anti-Catholicism and American Church Designs in the Nineteenth Century*. Chapel Hill: University of North Carolina Press, 2011.

Sokolow, Jayme. *Eros and Modernization: Sylvester Graham, Health Reform, and the Origins of Victorian Sexuality in America*. London: Associated University Presses, 1983.

Sprugg, June. *By Shaker Hands*. New York: Knopf, 1975.

Stacey, Judith. "The Families of Man: Gay Male Intimacy and Kinship in a Global Metropolis." *Signs* 30, no. 3 (2005): 1911–35.

Stansell, Christine. *City of Women: Sex and Class in New York, 1789–1860*. New York: Knopf, 1986.

Stein, Stephen J. *The Shaker Experience in America: A History of the United Society of Believers*. New Haven, CT: Yale University Press, 1992.

Stern, Madeline, ed. *Publishers for Mass Entertainment in Nineteenth Century America*. Boston: G. K. Hall, 1980.

Sterngass, John. *First Resorts: Pursuing Pleasure at Saratoga Springs, Newport, and Coney Island*. Baltimore: Johns Hopkins University Press, 2001.

Stevenson, Louise. "Homes, Books, and Reading." In *A History of the Book in America*, edited by Scott Casper et al., 319–30. Vol. 3. Chapel Hill: University of North Carolina, Press, 2007.

Stokes, Melvin, and Stephen Conway, eds. *The Market Revolution in America: Social, Political, and Religious Expressions, 1800–1880*. Charlottesville: University Press of Virginia, 1996.

Stott, Richard. *Jolly Fellows: Male Milieus in Nineteenth-Century America*. Baltimore: Johns Hopkins University Press, 2009.

Strong, George Templeton, and Vera Brodsky Lawrence. *Strong on Music: The New York Music Scene in the Days of George Templeton Strong*. Vol. 2, *Reverberations, 1850–1856*. Chicago: University of Chicago Press, 1995.

Stuart, Elizabeth. "Sacramental Flesh." In *Queer Theology: Rethinking the Western Body*, edited by Gerald Loughlin, 65–75. Oxford: Blackwell, 2007.

Sylvain, Phillipe. "Monk, Maria." In *Dictionary of Canadian Biography*. Vol. 7. University of Toronto, 2003, http://www.biographi.ca/en/bio/monk_maria_7E.html.

"Sylvester Graham." In *Food and Drink in American History: A "Full Course" Encyclopedia*, edited by Andrew F. Smith, 1142. Vol. 1. Santa Barbara, CA: ABC-CLIO.

Sylvester, Nancy, I. H. M. "PFs: Persistent Friendships." In *Building Sisterhood: A Feminist History of the Sisters, Servants of the Immaculate Heart of Mary*, comp. Sisters, Servants of the Immaculate Heart of Mary, 173–92. Syracuse, NY: Syracuse University Press, 1997.

Tager, Jack. *Boston Riots: Three Centuries of Social Violence*. Lebanon, NH: University Press of New England, 2001.

Talvacchia, Kathleen, Michael F. Pettinger, and Mark Larrimore. *Queer Christianities: Lived Religion in Transgressive Forms*. New York: New York University Press, 2015.

Talbot, Christine. *A Foreign Kingdom: Mormons and Polygamy in American Political Culture, 1852–1890*. Chicago: University of Illinois Press, 2013.

Taves, Anne. *Religious Experience Reconsidered: A Building-Block Approach to the Study of Religion and Other Special Things*. Princeton, NJ: Princeton University Press, 2009.

Taylor, George Rogers. *The Transportation Revolution, 1815–1860*. New York: Rheinhard, 1951.

Toll, Robert C. *Blacking Up: The Minstrel Show in Nineteenth-Century America*. New York: Oxford University Press, 1977.

Tucher, Andie. *Froth and Scum: Truth, Beauty, Goodness, and the Ax Murder in America's First Mass Medium*. Chapel Hill: University of North Carolina Press, 1994.

Tyrrell, Ian. *Sobering Up: From Temperance to Prohibition in Antebellum America, 1800–1860*. Westport, CT: Praeger, 1979.

Urry, John. *The Tourist Gaze*. London: Sage Publications, 2002.

Walters, Ronald G. "The Erotic South: Civilization and Sexuality in American Abolitionism." *American Quarterly* 25, no. 2 (1973): 177–201.

Warner, Michael. *Publics and Counterpublics*. New York: Zone Books, 2002.

Weeks, Jeffrey, ed. *Same Sex Intimacies: Families of Choice and Other Life Experiments*. London: Routledge, 2003.

Wergland, Glendyne R. *One Shaker Life: Isaac Newton Youngs, 1793–1865*. Amherst: University of Massachusetts Press, 2006.

———. *Sisters in the Faith: Shaker Women and Equality of the Sexes*. Amherst: University of Massachusetts Press, 2011.

Weston, Kath. *Families We Choose: Lesbians, Gay Men and Kinship*. New York: Columbia University Press, 1991.

Whisman, Vera. *Queer by Choice: Lesbians, Gay Men, and the Politics of Identity*. New York: Routledge, 1996.

White, Deborah Gray. *Ar'n't I a Woman?: Female Slaves in the Plantation South*. New York: W. W. Norton, 1999.

Williams, Richard. *Called and Chosen: The Story of Mother Rebecca Jackson and the Philadelphia Shakers*. London: Scarecrow, 1981.

Wilson, Arthur Herman. *A History of the Philadelphia Theater 1835–1855*. New York: Greenwood, 1968.

Winiarski, Douglas L. *Darkness Falls on the Land of Light: Experiencing Religious Awakenings in Eighteenth-Century New England*. Chapel Hill: University of North Carolina Press, 2017.

Winship, Michael. "Manufacturing and Book Production." In *A History of the Book in America: Volume 3: The Industrial Book, 1840–1880*, edited by Michael Winship et al., 40–69. Chapel Hill: University of North Carolina Press, 2007.

Wittberg, Patricia. *The Rise and Decline of Catholic Religious Orders: A Social Movement Perspective*. Albany: State University of New York Press, 1994.

Wittig, Monique. "One Is Not Born a Woman." In *The Straight Mind and Other Essays*, 9–20. Boston: Beacon, 1992.

Yacovazzi, Cassandra L. *Escaped Nuns: True Womanhood and the Campaign against Convents in Antebellum America*. New York: Oxford University Press, 2018.

Young, James Harvey. *The Toadstool Millionaires; A Social History of Patent Medicines in America before Federal Regulation*. Princeton, NJ: Princeton University Press, 1961.

Zimmerman, Jonathan. "Dethroning King Alcohol: The Washingtonians in Baltimore, 1840–1854." *Maryland Historical Magazine* 87, no. 4 (1992): 374–98.

Index

Note: Pages referencing material in illustrations are italicized

Barber, Mary, 26
Bardstown, Kentucky, 45
Barnum, P. T., 129–31, 142
Barnum's American Museum, 129–31,
    135, 139, 179n27
Bates, Issachar, 50, 51, 75–76, 87–88, 90
Bates, Lovina, 80
Battle Creek Sanitarium, 150–51
Battle of Gettysburg, 147–48
Believers in Christ's Second Appearing.
    See Shakerism
Bellevue Hospital, 150
Bennett, James Gordon, 32, 73, 161n22,
    162n44
Bethel African Methodist Episcopal
    (AME) Church, 67
Billington, Ray Allen, 11
"Black Shakers" (Fellows's Ethiopian
    Opera Troupe), 19, 123–29, 131, 142,
    146, 177n1, 178n19. *See also*
    minstrelsy
Black women, 15; as Grahamites, 70;
    Jackson, Rebecca Cox, 50, 67–71, 127,
    128; "Jezebel" stereotype, 69, 127;
    "Mammy" stereotype, 127; moral
    reformers, 11, 70; sexual abuse of,
    under slavery, 15, 70–71, 159n63;
    sexuality of, 178n11; "wench" role,
    126–27; women religious, 69–71.
    See also race; women
Bloomers, 35, 125, 126, 127
Borgia, St. F., 114
Boston, Massachusetts, 2–3; Amory
    Hall, 3, 31; Boston Charitable
    Mechanics Association, 43, 102;
    Boston Medical and Surgical Journal
    (journal), 34; *The Boston Quarterly
    Review* (journal), 162n41; *Boston
    Satirist and Blade* (newspaper),
    161n23; Boston Stereotype Foundry,
    175n36; *Life in Boston* (newspaper),
    100, 102; Mariner's Church, 106
Bowen, Clara, 85–86
Boydston, Jeanne, 17
Boyle, Elizabeth, 61, 84

branding. *See* marketplace, sexual
    restraint in the
Brinley Hall, 129
Brooks, Adeline, 60
Brophy, Bridget, 64, 168n54
Brown's Literary Omnibus (journal),
    34–35
Brownson, Orestes, 31, 162n41
Bruni, Frank, 152
Bunker Hill, 75
Bunkley, Josephine, 112, 176n63
Burlando, Francis, 147–48
Burtsell, Richard L., 61–64, 168n51
Butler, Judith, 22, 160n5, 160n14
Byrne, Mary, 64

Cabinet of Modern Art (anonymous),
    27–29, 161n29
California Gold Rush, 98
Calvinism, 52
Cambell, David, 7–8, 34, 46, 60, 116,
    141–42, 177n84
Cambell, Sylvia, 60
Canada: convents in, 113–15, 135, 138,
    140, 143, 144; Sulpician seminary in,
    61, 63
Cane Ridge Revival, 6, 156n20
Canterbury, New Hampshire, Shaker
    settlement in, 98, 102, 128–29, 135,
    141, 174n22, 174n32
capitalism. *See* marketplace, sexual
    restraint in the
Carmelite nuns, 69, 75
Cassey, Amy, 70
castration anxiety, 36–37
Catholicism: abolition of monasteries
    and convents, 9; anti-Catholic
    violence, 2–3, 113–14, 133, 156n10;
    Catholic envy, 107–8, 112–15; *Catholic
    Herald* (newspaper), 112, 176n58,
    181n76; Catholic tracts, 84–85, 112,
    114–15, 176n58, 181n76; Catholic
    University of America, 27; celibacy of
    Catholic male, 8, 11–12, 60–67, 86,
    106–7, 152; celibacy of women

religious, 8, 11–12, 60–67, 86, 106–7,
152; *Connelly vs. Connelly* (1840),
79–83; critiques of Shakers, 157n27;
cultural tourism, 140–41; family,
breaking of, 79–86; family, remaking
of, 86; history in America, 6–7;
identities of sexual restraint in,
60–67; obedience, vow of, 40, 45, 61,
168n61; "pornography of pain," in
anti-Catholic literature, 30, 70–71,
162n36, 169n83; poverty, vow of, 61.
See also chastity, vow of; confession;
male religious; women religious
celibacy, 152; of Catholic male, 8, 11–12,
60–67, 86, 106–7, 152; celibate
femininity, 17, 21; celibate masculinity, 17, 21, 33; definition of, 12–13, 48;
deviance of, 14–16; gay celibacy,
158n39; queerish celibacy, 157n38;
queerness of, 10; "unnaturalness," of
sexual restraint, 18, 20–22, 49, 51, 61,
71, 89, 152–53; of women religious, 8,
11–12, 60–67, 86, 106–7, 152. *See also*
Shakerism, celibacy in
censorship, 8
Chapman, Eunice, 37, 38
charism, 82–83, 152
Charlestown, Massachusetts. *See* Mount
Benedict convent
Charlotte Temple (Rowson), 12, 25
chastity, 61, 69, 80, 168n63; aura of, 105;
definition of, 12, 48; premarital, 110
chastity, vow of, 7, 40, 83–84; fragility
of, 66–67; perpetual, 80–81
children: in broken families, 80–82;
Grahamism's effects on, 91, 92;
indentured among Shakers, 43, 79,
120, 171n24; infanticide, 2
choice, 152–53; "born-this-way"
biological imperative, 49, 51–52,
166n7; families of, 72, 79
cholera outbreaks, 103, 111–12, 147,
176n61
Christ. *See* Jesus
Christian Mirror (newspaper), 116

Christians, early, 9, 52, 157n27
Church, Frederick, 108
circumcision, 36
citizenship, 39
civil deadness, 37, 158n55. *See also*
coverture
Civil War, 115, 147–50
Clarissa (Richardson), 12
Clark, Mary, 140–41
class. *See* middle class; working class
Cleveland, Frances, 105, 174n32
Clinton, George, 5
Cole, Thomas, 108
Collegio Urbano, 61, 62, 63
"coming out," role of, 12, 18, 73, 153,
158n48, 170n9
communitarian groups, 6, 12, 52–53, 94,
156n21. *See also* nuns; Shakerism;
utopian societies
compulsory heterosexuality, 55
confession, of sins, 75, 117, 144,
164n70; confessors, role of, 64–65,
81, 84, 86
Confessions of a French Catholic Priest
(Morse), 40, 164nn68–69
Congregation of the Mission (Vincentians), 42, 164n73
Connelly, Cornelia, 79–83, 171n35.
See also Society of the Holy Child
Jesus
Connelly, Pierce, 80–82
Connelly vs. Connelly (1840), 79–83
convent boarding schools, 7, 107–11,
121–22
Convent of the Sacred Heart, 107
Convent of the Visitation, 107
Convent's Doom (Frothingham), 24
conversion, 76–79, 80, 85–86; converts,
81, 84, 106, 116, 182n17; experiences
of, 75, 117–18, 177n78
Corbett, Thomas, 102, 105–6
coverture, legal practice of, 4, 14, 37,
76, 84, 91
Cox, Joseph, 67
cult of true manhood, 33

eugenicist ideology, 92, 172n73
evangelism: among Shakers, 105–6; missionary activity, 6, 76, 112, 144
Evans, F. W., 148–49
Evening Post (magazine), 130

family, breaking of, 18, 72–86, 160n9; Catholics, 79–86; logical family, 72; Shaker communities, 37–39, 74–79; Shaker men, 75–76; Shaker women, 76–79
family, remaking of, 17, 18, 72–74, 86–93, 151; Catholics, 86; choice, families of, 72, 79; familial language, use of, 72, 86, 170n3; Grahamism, 90–93; in loco parentis, 111; Shakers, 86–90. *See also* friendship
fashionable tour, 135, 136–37, 140; *The Fashionable Tour* (Davison), 136, 138, 180n51
Fay, Maria, 140, 143, 144
FDA (United States Food and Drug Administration), 100
Fellows, J. B., 123, 177n1. *See also* "Black Shakers"
Fellows' Ethiopian Opera Troupe ("Black Shakers"), 19, 123–29, 131, 142, 146, 177n1, 178n19. *See also* minstrelsy
Female Jesuit, The (Luke), 25–26
female masculinity, 25, 32, 41–42, 106–7, 111–12
Female Moral Reform movements, 11, 15, 41, 70, 161n22
femininities, 17, 151, 160n6; ability to transcend traditional roles of, 149–50; celibate femininity, 17, 21; feminine ailments, 142; feminine virtues, 107
feminism, 153; lesbian feminism, 22; second-wave, 10
Fenwick, Bishop, 2, 26
"Fi Hi Hi: The Black Shakers Song and Polka" (minstrel song), 123, 177n1. *See also* "Black Shakers"; minstrelsy
First Great Awakening, 6
Fitch, Bushnell, 54–55

Fitton, Octavia, 144–45, 146
flash press, 22, 66, 95, 100, 102, 161n23, 167n49
Foster, Thomas, 16
Foucault, Michel, 16, 143, 159n71, 166n5, 181n75
Fourierists, 35
fraud, 40
free love, 35, 181n68
Frémont, John C., 35
friendship: platonic, opposite-sex, 18, 71, 88–90. *See also* family, remaking of; same-sex bonds of affection
front region, 140, 180n59
Frothingham, Charles, 24

Gates, Benjamin, 148–50
"gathering in" (of Shakers), 54, 68, 76
gay, etymology of the word, 93, 174n20
gay and lesbian civil rights movement, 153
gay celibacy, 158n39
Geertz, Clifford, 9, 118
gender, 17, 20–47; definition of, 160n6; dichotomy, around sexual restraint, 41–42; equality of, 73, 91; gender identity and sexuality, relationship between, 22–23, 160n14; *Gender Trouble* (Butler), 160n5, 160n14; male monsters, 32–42; separate spheres, 17, 23, 42–47, 86–87, 164n76; "Union of the Sexes," 88; vinegar-faced sisters and feminine seducers, 23–32. *See also* drag; femininities; masculinities; men; passion, gendered ideas of; sexual abuse; women
gender deviance: as caused by sexual restraint, 21–23, 39, 41–42, 47, 111, 151; race and, 69–71; veiling ceremony as, 26–29
Georgetown Academy of the Visitation, 108
Gettysburg College, 147–48
Godey's Lady's Book (magazine), 30, 105
Goffman, Erving, 140, 180n59

gospel of works, 52

Gove Nichols, Mary, 31–32, 42, 46–47, 73, 116, 142, 162n44, 181n68

Graham, Sylvester, 116, 118–19, 121, 157n32; charismatic leadership of, 94; death of, 150; demographic identity of, 14; "Lecture to Mothers," 3–4, 7–8, 31, 60; *A Lecture to Young Men on Chastity*, 55, 90, 172n64; portrayal of, 34; training as a minister, 11

Graham diet, 8, 34, 59–60, 116–22, 141–42, 157n25, 157n32, 160n10; Graham bread, 116, 119; Graham Crackers, 150–51, 182n15; Graham Restorator, 116–17; labor involved in cooking, 46, 121; at Oberlin College, 60; Shakers on, 118–22, 177nn83–84, 177n89

Grahamism, 94, 156n24; anti-Graham violence, 3; children, effects on, 91, 92; cultural tourism, 141–42; division of labor in, 46–47; family, remaking of, 90–93; Graham boarding houses, 34, 46, 117, 141, 157n25, 177n84, 180n64; identities of sexual restraint in, 56–60; labor, gendered division of, 46–47; married couples, rules for, 12–14, 73, 90–91, 172n64; race in, 70–71; as a religious system, 9–10, 116–22, 177n78, 177nn83–84, 177n89; water-cure resorts, 141–42, 181n68

Grahamites, 9–10, 18, 117–18, 150–51, 177n78; Alcott, William Andrus, 8, 31, 57, 116–17, 119, 121, 172n64; Black followers, 70; Cambell, David, 7–8, 34, 46, 60, 116, 141–42, 177n84; female followers, 3, 31–32, 59–60, 70, 121; Gove Nichols, Mary, 31–32, 42, 46–47, 73, 116, 142, 162n44, 181n68; "The Grahamite and the Irish Pilot" (*Brown's Literary Omnibus*), 34–35; male followers, 33, 34–36, 41, 57–59, 121; "pure livers," 116

Graham Journal of Health and Longevity (journal), 46–47, 56–57, 90, 118–19, 120–21, 156n25, 157n26, 177nn83–84; David Cambell, as editor of, 7–8, 34, 46, 60, 116, 141–42, 177n84

The Great Republican Reform Party (Maurer), 35–36

Greene, Mary Ignatia, 112

Greylock, Godfrey, 20–21, 138, 160n1

guidebooks, travel, 135–38, 142

hair, symbolism of, 29–30, 162nn30–31

Hale, Sarah Josepha, 107, 111

Hancock, Massachusetts, Shaker settlement in, 20–21, 79, 89, 138, 143, 145–46, 163n54

Harmonists, 12

Harper's Magazine, 102, 173n8, 181n72

Harrison, Mary St. John, 2–3

Harvard, Massachusetts, Shaker settlement in, 98, 102, 119

Haskins, Enoch, 79

Haskins, Jane, 79

Hawthorne, Nathaniel, 138–39

Haynes, April, 11, 158n44

Hazel, Henry, 30

health, 57–59, 90; feminine ailments, 142; *Health Journal & Advocate of Physiological Reform* (journal), 60, 117–18; *Library of Health* (journal), 8; Shaker medicines and herbs, 95–103, 104, 105–6, 121–22, 173n7, 174n17, 174n20–31. *See also* Graham

heteronormativity, challenges to, 10, 15, 158n39, 170n5. *See also* family, remaking of; lesbian, gay, bisexual, and transgender (LGBTQ) politics; queer; same-sex bonds of affection

heterosexuality: as compulsory, 55; definition of, 159n64; heterosexual matrix, 160n14

hoaxes, 130–31

holiday time, 135–36

Holy Child schools, 83, 171n47

"holy living," 67

homosexuality, 16, 166n5, 168n65, 182n20. *See also* lesbian, gay, bisexual,

and transgender (LGBTQ) politics; queerness
homosocial bonds of affection. *See* same-sex bonds of affection
Horn, Eph, 123, 127–28, 129. *See also* "Black Shakers"
Hotel Dieu convent, 26, 39–40, 140, 144, 146, 164n66; *Awful Disclosures of the Hotel Dieu* (Monk), 23, 108, 133–34, 142
Hughes, John, 61, 165n82
Hugo, Victor, 40, 164n69
The Hunchback of Notre Dame (Hugo), 40, 164n69
Hunt, Harriot K., 31
hydropathy, 141–42, 181n68
hymn lyrics, Shaker, 51–52

identities, of sexual restraint, 17–18, 48–71; acts, *versus* identities, 16, 166n5; Catholic religious life, celibacy and, 60–67; Graham system, living the, 56–60; Jackson, Rebecca Cox, 67–71; Shaker celibacy, learning, 50–56
immoral didacticism, 160n12
immoral reform, 22, 73
Inaugural Ball, 105
industrial innovation, of Shaker communities, 143, 181n72
industrial revolution, 175n38
infanticide, 2
Inman, Louisa, 58–59
intersectionality, 11, 158n44
Irving, Elizabeth, 79
Irving, Elmira, 79
Irving, Jestiner, 79
Irving, John, 79

Jackson, Charles, 100
Jackson, Rebecca Cox, 50, 67–71, 127, 128
Jackson, Samuel S., 67
Jacques, George, 57–59, 167nn33–34, 167n36

Jay, David, 152–53
Jefferson County, Arkansas, 86
The Jeffersonian (newspaper), 99
Jenks, Reverend, 31
Jesuits, 80, 81, 82, 138, 161n20, 161n24; female, 24, 25–26, 29–30
Jesus, 43–44, 52, 85, 106; brides of, nuns as, 83–85
Jewett, Helen, 25, 161n22
"Jezebel" stereotype, 69, 127
Johnson, Paul, 14
jolly fellows, 33

Kelley, Abby, 32, 162n44
Kellogg, John Harvey, 150–51
Kelly, Eulalia, 86
Kendall, George, 119
Know-Nothing movement, 13, 30–31, 62, 149, 158n55, 161n24

labor, 90; ability to remain unmarried, relation to, 73–74; of cooking Graham diet, 46, 121; nursing professions, 7, 115, 147–48, 149–50; white collar managerial work, 17n64, 94; work and leisure, modern concepts of, 135–36. *See also* marketplace, sexual restraint in the
labor, gendered division of, 43–47; Catholic men, 45–46; Catholic women, 44–45; Grahamites, 46–47; Shakers, 43–44, 88–90, 164n78
Ladies' Physiological Institute (LPI), 31, 46, 162n42
Ladies Physiological Society (LPS), 46, 59–60
Lebanon Springs, New York, 39, 76–77, 135–37, 142, 177n83. *See also* Mount Lebanon, Shaker settlement of; New Lebanon, New York
"Lecture to Mothers" (Graham), 3–4, 7–8, 31, 60
A Lecture to Young Men on Chastity (Graham), 55, 90, 172n64

Lee, Ann, 43–44, 50, 131, 156n14, 156n18, 163n61, 165n79; founding "Shaking Quakers" sect, 4–6, 106; imprisonment of, 150; revelation against sex, 8

legal battles, 13; *Connelly vs. Connelly* (1840), 79–83; against Shakers, 5–6, 131–33, 146, 149

leisure culture, 135–36. *See also* tourism

lesbian, gay, bisexual, and transgender (LGBTQ) politics: "born-this-way" biological imperative, 49, 51–52, 166n7; "coming out," role of, 12, 18, 73, 153, 158n48, 170n9; lesbian and gay rights movement, 166n7; lesbian feminism, 22; modern, 10. *See also* homosexuality; same-sex bonds of affection

Lewis, Dio, 55

Liberator, The (newspaper), 31, 91

libertine republicans, 33

libido, 15; male, 21–22, 33–34, 36, 58, 152; "unnaturalness," of sexual restraint, 18, 20–22, 49, 51, 61, 71, 89, 152–53

Library of Congress, *35*

Library of Health (journal), 8

Life in Boston (newspaper), 100, 102

liminal experience, 108, 177n78

Lincoln, Abraham, 148–50, 172n55, 182n8

lithography, 127–28, 139, 142, 174n17

lived experience, 18, 165n4; definition of, 48–49. *See also* identities, of sexual restraint

lived religion, 10, 157n35

living museum, 143

logical family, 72

Long before Stonewall (Foster), 16

Lyon, Catherine, 132

MacCannell, Dean, 138, 181n70

Maine, 113–15; Maine Law, 35; Shaker communities in, 115, 119, 144–45, 151, 182n17

male privilege, loss of, 14, 31

male religious, 7, 35–36, 39–40, 41, 61–64, 85; celibacy debates, among priests, 62–63, 152; decline in numbers of, 151; labor, gendered division of, 45–46; as "male monsters," 32–42; seminary requirements and rules, 65–67, 169n67; sexual abuse, allegations of, 2–3, 132–33, 152, 164n70. *See also* Catholicism; Jesuits

Mammoth Cave, 142

"Mammy" stereotype, 127

manliness, 33, 39

Mariner's Church, 106

marketplace, sexual restraint in the, 18, 94–122, 150–51, 173n6; Catholic nursing professionals, 111–12, 121–22, 176n58, 176n61; Convent boarding schools, for girls, 106–11, 112–15, 121–22, 175n40, 175n49, 176n52, 176n58; Graham system, as a religious system, 116–22, 177n78, 177nn83–84, 177n89; "made-in-America" marketing, 103; purity, marketing of, 99–100, 102, 103, 108; racialization of, 18, 97, 103, 106; Shaker fashion, 103, 105, 173n8, 174n32; Shaker medicines and herbs, 95–103, 104, 105–6, 121–22, 173n7, 174n17, 174nn20–31. *See also* tourism, to celibate communities

market revolution, 13–14, 17, 173n2

marriage, 133–34; to Christ, 83–85; coverture, legal practice of, 4, 14, 37, 76, 84, 91; Grahamism rules for, 12–14, 73, 90–91, 172n64; marital rape, 91–92, 93, 172n70; *Marriage and Parentage or the Reproductive Element of Man* (Wright), 90–92; marriage reform, 3–4, 7, 11–12, 151, 152; as middle-class norm, 14; never-married people, increase of, 73–74, 170n11; spiritual wifery, 172n61. *See also* divorce; Graham

Marsh, Bela, 90–91, 116
martial manhood, 33
Martineau, Harriet, 138–39
Mary Joseph, Sister (Ursulines), 114–15
masculinities, 17, 21, 33, 58, 151, 160n6; attacks on, 9; celibate masculinity, 17, 21, 33; female masculinity, 25, 32, 41–42, 106–7, 111–12; martial manhood, 33; mocking of, 127; nonmilitarist masculinity, 148–50; restrained manhood, 33. *See also* men
Massachusetts Charitable Mechanics Association, 100
masturbation, 34, 57–58, 141, 150, 157n32, 158n44, 167n33; Graham lectures against, 3, 7–8, 55, 70, 90, 172n64; nocturnal emissions, 55
Matthew, Gospel of, 52
Maupin, Armistead, 72
Maurer, Louis, 35–36
Maynard, Lovina, 75, 76
McGlynn, Doctor, 63
McNemar, Richard, 36, 50, 163n57
McSweeny, Doctor, 62, 168n51
Meacham, David, 88
mechanical reproduction, 142, 181n70
melancholy, 58, 63, 118, 177n78
men: castration anxiety, 36–37; circumcision, 36; cult of true manhood, 33; "designing men," 5–6; effeminization of, 34, 37, 39, 41; Grahamites, male, 33, 34–36, 41, 57–59, 121; jolly fellows, 33; male libido, 21–22, 33–34, 36, 58, 152; male privilege, loss of, 14, 31; martial manhood, 33; in middle class, 14, 31, 33, 56, 135; patriarchy, 21, 37, 39, 55, 76, 151; rake, figure of the, 22, 25, 41; restrained manhood, 33; in working class, 2, 17, 33, 127. *See also* bachelors; male religious; masculinities; same-sex bonds of affection; Shaker men
Methodists, 72; circuit riders, 13, 36–37

middle class, 73, 94, 130–31, 151, 172n64, 173n2; identity, emergence of, 13–14, 56, 109, 135–36; men, 14, 31, 33, 56, 135; "middling classes," 13–14; sexual values of, 10, 40–42; upper middle class, 107; women, 3, 70, 111, 166n8
military service: conscription, 148–50, 182n8; nursing, 7, 115, 147–48, 149–50
militia: duty of, 37–38, 39; in Ohio, 1–2, 36
Millenarianism, 117
Millennial Laws, Shaker, 66
minstrelsy, 19, 178n11; "Black Shakers" (Fellows' Ethiopian Opera Troupe), 19, 123–29, 131, 142, 146, 177n1, 178n19; olio routine, 125–26; "Shaking Quakers" troupe ("Shaker Sisters and Brothers"), 128–33, 139, 146, 179n27, 179n33
Minter, Jeremiah, 36–37
Miss D. T. Killbourn's Academy, 109
missionary activity, 6, 76, 112, 144
modernization, sexual reform as a metaphor for, 56–57
Moffat, Mary Edmond St. George, 3, 26, 46
Monk, Maria, 10–11, 24, 39–40, 114, 144, 163n66; *Awful Disclosures of the Hotel Dieu* (Monk), 23, 108, 133–34, 142
Montreal, Canada: convents in, 135, 138, 140, 143; Sulpician seminary in, 61, 63
"moral culture," 110–11
moral reform movements, female, 11, 15, 41, 70, 161n22
moral suasion, 47
Moranvillé, Father, 84
Moravians, 12–13
Mormonism, 11, 15, 24, 156n21, 170n3
Morning Herald (newspaper), 32
Morse, Samuel F. B., 40, 164nn68–69

"passionless" nature, 17, 50, 69, 70, 91, 105, 110–11, 166n8
patriarchy, 21, 37, 39, 55, 76, 151
Paul, Saint, 9
Pearson, John, 116
pennyroyal, 102, 174n23
people tourism, 180n48
performance, of sexual restraint, 18–19, 41, 123–46, 164n71, 179n32; "Black Shakers" (Fellows' Ethiopian Opera Troupe), 19, 123–29, 131, 142, 146, 177n1, 178n19; *The Pet of the Petticoats* (Catholic melodrama), 123, 133–34, 179nn39–40; "Shaking Quakers" troupe ("Shaker Sisters and Brothers"), 128–33, 139, 146, 179n27, 179n33. *See also* tourism, to celibate communities
Perot, Rebecca, 68
Perry, Lewis, 93
Perry, Nathaniel, 116
The Pet of the Petticoats (melodrama), 123, 133–34, 179nn39–40
petticoat lecturers, 32
Philadelphia, Pennsylvania: Quakers in, 140; Shaker community in, 67–71, 127, 128, 169n71
Pierce, Franklin, 133
platonic relationships between men and women, 18, 71, 88–90. *See also* friendship
Pleasant Hill, Kentucky, 143
pleasure culture, 15, 159n62, 163n48
"Poor Unfortunate" archetype, 25, 31–32, 161n22
pornography, 40; "pornography of pain," 30, 70–71, 162n36, 169n83
Porter, Elijah, 99
poverty, vow of, 61
predestination, 52
pregnancy, sex during, 91
Prentiss, Ephraim, 120, 177n89
priests. *See* male religious
Priest's Prisons for Women (pamphlet), 30

print publications, 18, 35–38, 50, 82, 91, 160n12, 160n15, 173n8; anti-Shaker romances, 41, 123; autobiography, 54; Catholic tracts, 84–85, 112, 114–15, 176n58, 181n76; "dark reform" literature, 160n12; diary entries, 53–56, 57–59, 63, 92, 167nn33–34, 167n36; engravings in, 27–29; flash press, 22, 66, 95, 100, 102, 161n23, 167n49; guidebooks, travel, 135–38, 142; *Health Journal & Advocate of Physiological Reform* (journal), 60, 117–18; *Library of Health* (journal), 8; pamphlets, 1–2, 22, 30; seduction narratives, 22, 25, 41–42, 108, 161n22; Shaker manuscripts, 105–6, 119–20, 174n22, 175n36; travelogues, 9, 138–42. *See also* escaped nun stories; *Graham Journal of Health and Longevity* (journal)
prisons and asylums, 5, 140, 143, 150–51, 167n33, 181nn75–76
private and public, dichotomies of, 18, 72–73, 170n5
privilege, loss of, 14, 31
Privy Council, 82
promiscuity, 36–37, 163n48
property: Shakers, relinquishment by, 3–4, 13, 37–39, 50; women as, 12, 30, 55, 79, 82
prostitution, 22, 41, 70, 93, 95, 159n69, 174n20. *See also* sex work
Protestantism, 25–26, 108; African Methodist Episcopal (AME) Church, 67, 69; Baptists, 75–76; Calvinism, 52; Methodists, 13, 36–37, 72; predestination, 52; Protestant Reformation, 8–9, 157n27; secret Catholics, fear of, 2, 39. *See also* convent boarding schools
public and private, dichotomies of, 18, 72–73, 170n5
"pure livers," 116. *See also* Grahamites
purity, marketing of, 99–100, 102, 103, 108. *See also* marketplace, sexual restraint in the

Quakerism, 8, 140, 159n71
queerness, 72, 153; "involuntary
    queerness," of Christianity, 10; queer
    identities, 16; queerish celibacy,
    157n38; "queerplatonic" relation-
    ships, 153; of Shaker dance, 178n19.
    See also lesbian, gay, bisexual, and
    transgender (LGBTQ) politics;
    same-sex bonds of affection
queer theory, 11, 22–23, 166n7

race, 39; "Black Shakers" (Fellows'
    Ethiopian Opera Troupe), 19, 123–29,
    131, 142, 146, 177n1, 178n19;
    eugenicist ideology, 92, 172n73;
    gender deviance and, 69–71; in
    Graham System, 70–71; "Jezebel"
    stereotype, 69, 127; "Mammy"
    stereotype, 127; marketplace,
    racialization in, 18, 97, 103, 106;
    Native Americans, 2, 39; St. Benedict
    the Moor Catholic Church, 168n51;
    whiteness, 33, 39, 126, 135, 166n8.
    See also antislavery movement; Black
    women; Jackson, Rebecca Cox;
    slavery
Raffinesque, Constantine Samuel, 98
rake, figure of the, 22, 25, 41
rape, marital, 91–92, 93, 172n70
Rathbone, Reuben, 156n19, 163n54;
    Reasons Offered for Leaving the Shakers
    (Rathbone), 36
Recollet convent, 140
Reed, Rebecca, 112, 133, 164n70; Six
    Months in a Convent (Reed), 2–3,
    23–24, 40, 110
religion: definition of, 9–10, 118;
    Graham system as type of, 116–22;
    religious tourism, 107–8; sacredness,
    157n33
reproductive freedom, 91–92, 174n23
Republican Coalition, 35–36
Restell, Madam, 32
restrained manhood, 33
Revelation, book of, 52

Revolution, American, 5, 75, 150
Rome, Italy, 80, 82
Rosamund (Culberston), 24
Rubin, Gayle, 15, 159n65, 160n14, 166n6
Ruth, Eldress, 56

Sabbathday Lake, Maine, Shaker
    settlement in, 151, 182n17
Sabbath worship, of Shakers, 130–31,
    138–39, 143, 145
"sacred theater," 52
sacrifice, 29, 51–54, 56, 61, 80–81, 83,
    86, 117, 119–20; "The Sacrifice"
    (Sartain), 27–29, 161n29
sadism, 30
St. Ann's Church, 61
St. Joseph's Academy, 107, 108, 109, 110,
    111
St. Joseph's House, 147–48
St. Mary's of the Barrens Seminary, 65,
    66–67, 168n59, 168n66
same-sex bonds of affection, 18, 73,
    86–88, 172n55; female friendship,
    85–86, 172n55; innuendo, 25;
    particular friendships, 18, 65–66, 87,
    168n63; relationships, 16, 66. See also
    friendship; homosexuality; queerness
Sanger, Margaret, 92, 172n73
Sargent, Lucius, 20–21
sarsaparilla syrup, 100, 102, 106, 174n22
"sawdust bread." See Graham diet
School of the Visitation, 109
"searching self," 51–52
Second Great Awakening, 11, 78–79,
    156n20
seduction, 15, 36, 39–40, 70, 110–11,
    112, 144; narratives of, 22, 25, 41–42,
    108, 161n22. See also escaped nun
    stories
seminaries, female, 109
separate spheres, 17, 23, 42–47, 86–87,
    164n76
Seton, Elizabeth, 7, 84, 165n83
"sex panics," 4
sex positivity, 153

sexual abuse: allegations in Catholic Church, 2–3, 132–33, 152, 164n70; of enslaved women, 15, 70–71, 159n63; marital rape, 91–92, 93, 172n70

sexual deviance, sites of, 136

sexual essentialism, 15

sexuality: gender identity and, relationship between, 22–23, 160n14; as modern invention, 16

sexual respectability, 166n6

sexual restraint: definition of, 11–12; "unnaturalness" of, 18, 20–22, 49, 51, 61, 71, 89, 152–53. *See also* abstinence; celibacy; chastity; identities, of sexual restraint; virginity

sexual revolution, first, 15

sex work, 95, 100, 102; prostitution, 22, 41, 70, 93, 95, 159n69, 174n20

Shakerism, 10, 56; Alfred, Maine, settlement in, 115, 119; anti-Shaker romances, 41, 123; anti-Shaker violence, 1–2, 6, 131, 150; apostates, 51, 53–56, 128–33, 142, 156nn18–19, 163n54, 164n71, 172n61; "Black Shakers" (Fellows' Ethiopian Opera Troupe), 19, 123–29, 131, 142, 146, 177n1, 178n19; Canterbury, New Hampshire, settlement in, 98, 102, 128–29, 135, 141, 174n22, 174n32; children, indentured, 43, 79, 120, 171n24; Church Family membership, 53–54; covenant, 38, 54–55, 132–33; cultural tourism, 136–40; decline of, 151, 175n38; Enfield, New Hampshire, settlement in, 79, 95–97, 98, 143; Era of Manifestations, 139, 169n70, 175n38, 177n89, 178n19; evangelism in, 105–6; family, breaking of, 37–39, 74–79; family, remaking of, 86–90; "gathering in," 54, 68, 76; on Graham diet, 118–22, 177nn83–84, 177n89; Hancock, Massachusetts, settlement in, 20–21, 79, 89, 138, 143, 145–46, 163n54; Harvard,

Massachusetts, settlement in, 98, 102, 119; history of, 4–6; hymn lyrics, 51–52; industrial innovation of, 143, 181n72; labor, gendered division of, 43–44, 88–90, 164n78; legal battles against, 5–6, 131–33, 146, 149; manuscripts, 105–6, 119–20, 174n22, 175n36; men's fashion, 105; military service in, 148–50, 182n8; New Hampshire, settlements in, 119, 131; pacifism in, 37–38, 75, 148–50; Philadelphia, Pennsylvania, community in, 67–71, 127, 128, 169n71; property, relinquishment of, 3–4, 13, 37–39, 50; Sabbathday Lake, Maine, settlement in, 151, 182n17; Sabbath worship, openness to public, 130–31, 138–39, 143, 145; *Shakerism Detected* (Smith), 38; "The Shaker Lovers" (melodrama), 41, 123; *The Shaker Manual* (booklet), 105–6, 174n22, 175n36; "Shakers, Their Mode of Worship" (lithograph), 127–28; "A Shaking Courtship" (comedic play), 129; Shirley, Massachusetts, settlement in, 148; slaveownership in, 169n69; Sodus Bay, New York, settlement in, 68; thoughts on Catholic celibacy, 8–9; union meetings, 88–90, 172n61. *See also* Mount Lebanon; Turtle Creek

Shakerism, celibacy in, 5–6, 8–9, 11–12, 139; architecture of gender segregation, 43; heterosocial relationships within, 88–90; identities of, 50–56; men, 36–39

Shakerism, craft work in, 89–90, 149–50; medicines and herbs, 95–103, 104, 105–6, 121–22, 173n7, 174n17, 174nn20–31; Shaker fashion, 103, 105, 173n8, 174n32. *See also* marketplace, sexual restraint in the

Shaker men: celibacy of, 36–39; family, breaking of, 75–76; fashion of, 105

gaze, 136, 140, 146; travelogues, 9, 138–42. *See also* cultural tourism

Townsend, Mira Sharpless, 140, 142, 144

transcendent truths, 117

transportation revolution, 98, 135–36, 160n15

travelogues, 9, 138–42

Tripure, Dr. and Mrs., 128–29

Trois-Rivières, Canada, convent in, 113–15, 138, 140

Turtle Creek, Shaker settlement in, 36, 38, 163n61; riot at, 1–2, 150

twilight moments, 17, 159n73

"ultraist" reformers, 118, 126

Uncle Tom's Cabin (Stowe), 30–31

Union army, 147–48

union meetings, Shaker, 88–90, 172n61

"Union of the Sexes," 88

Union Village, Ohio, Shaker settlement in, 98

United States Treasury, 148

"unnaturalness," of sexual restraint, 18, 20–22, 49, 51, 61, 71, 89, 152–53

Urban College of Propaganda, 61. *See also* Collegio Urbano

Ursuline nuns, 26, 40, 75, 108, 110, 138; in New Orleans, 43, 69–70, 107; Trois-Rivières, Canada, convent in, 113–15, 138, 140. *See also* Mount Benedict convent

Usher, Ellis, 113–14, 115

Usher, Martha, 113–14

Usher, Rebecca, 113–15, 122

utopian societies, 52–53, 151; celibacy in, 12–13. *See also* communitarian groups; Shakerism

valerian, extract of, 95–97, 100, 106

vanity, sin of, 26, 65, 168n61

Vatican, 80–81

vegetarianism, 8, 23, 46, 59, 121, 142, 150. *See also* Graham diet

veiling ceremony, sexualization of, 26–29

venereal diseases, treatments for, 100, 102

vice, commodification of, 95

Vincent de Paul, Saint, 65, 164n73, 165n83, 168n59, 169n67

vinegar-faced sisters, 23–32, 133–34. *See also* women religious

violence, 3–4, 13, 146, 149; anti-Catholic, 2–3, 113–14, 133, 156n10; anti-Graham, 3; anti-Shaker, 1–2, 6, 131, 150

virginity, 20, 106; definition of, 12

virtue: definition of, 70; feminine virtues, 107; sexual, women's, 12, 30, 33, 69, 95, 105, 110–11, 150

Wadsworth, John, 99

Wallace, Reverend, 1

War of 1812, 148

War of Independence, 15, 37, 148

Washingtonian Society, 57, 167n32

water-cure resorts, 141–42, 181n68

Watervliet, New York, Shaker settlement in, 5, 53, 67–71, 76, 89, 119–20, 135, 145, 177n89

Webster, Noah, 48

Weir, Robert, 26

Wells, Freegift, 120

Wells, Seth, 119, 120, 177n89

"wench" role, 126–27

West Point, 75

"What Shall We Have for Dinner" (*Graham Journal of Health and Longevity*), 46

Wheeler, Fanny, 129

whiteness, 33, 39, 126, 135, 166n8. *See also* race

White Sulfur, Kentucky, 45

Wickham, Mary Seraphina, 42, 45

Willard, Julia A., 129, 130

Williams, George, 118

Winterthur Museum and Library, 77, 95–96, 100, *101*, *104*

Wiseman, Bishop, 81

Wittig, Monique, 22

women: "accomplishments," female, 107, 109–10, 115, 176n52; Bloomers, 35, 125, 126, 127; female desire, 3; female masculinity, 25, 32, 41–42, 106–7, 111–12; Female Moral Reform movements, 11, 15, 41, 70, 161n22; Grahamites, female, 3, 31–32, 59–60, 70, 121; leadership, 42, 44–45; in middle class, 3, 70, 111, 166n8; "passionless" nature of, 17, 50, 69, 70, 91, 105, 110–11, 166n8; patriarchy, 21, 37, 39, 55, 76, 151; "Poor Unfortunate" archetype, 25, 31–32, 161n22; as property, 12, 30, 55, 79, 82; reproductive freedom, 91–92, 174n23; Republican motherhood, 69; satire of, 125, 127, 134; "Siren" archetype, 25, 41–42, 47, 161n22; who never married, 74, 115; women's rights, 35, 91–92, 162n36; in working class, 64, 110. *See also* autonomy; Black women; femininities; feminism; same-sex bonds of affection; sex work; Shaker women; virtue

women religious, 64–65; Black women, 69–71; celibacy of, 152; decline in numbers of, 151; labor, gendered division of, 44–45; in nursing professions, 111–12, 121–22, 176n58, 176n61; particular friendships among, 18, 65–66, 87, 168n63; running convent boarding schools for girls, 106–11, 112–15, 121–22, 175n40, 175n49, 176n52, 176n58; sisters, *versus* nuns, 7; as vinegar-faced sisters and feminine seducers, 23–32, 133–34. *See also* Catholicism; nuns; sisters; individual sects

Woodman, George, 114, 115

Woodward, Samuel B., 57, 167n33

working class, 4, 125–26; men, 2, 17, 33, 127; women, 64, 110

"world's people," 20, 43, 50, 68, 74, 97, 105, 118, 144–45

Wright, Fanny, 32

Wright, Henry Clarke, 73, 90–93

Wright, Lucy, 50, 55, 56

writ of replevin, 79

Young Ladies' High School of Boston, 109, 175n40

Young Ladies' Literary Institute and Boarding School, 108

Youngs, Benjamin, 87–88, 90

Youngs, Isaac Newton, 53–56, 69, 121

Zion Female Moral Reform Society, 70

Zion's Herald (reform publication), 31–32

Zoar communitarian group, 12